**BOCCONI
UNIVERSITY
PRESS**

Gimede Gigante

THE EVOLUTION OF FINTECH

Analysis of Valuation Metrics and Market Dynamics

Foreword by **Stefano Caselli**

Cover: Cristina Bernasconi, Milan
Typesetting: Corpo4 Team, Milan

Copyright © 2025 Bocconi University Press
EGEA S.p.A.

EGEA S.p.A.
Via Salasco, 5 - 20136 Milano
Tel. 02/5836.5751 – Fax 02/5836.5753
egea.edizioni@unibocconi.it – www.egeaeditore.it

Given the characteristics of the Internet, the publisher is not responsible for any changes of
address and contents of the websites mentioned.

First edition: August 2025

ISBN Domestic Edition 979-12-80623-75-1
ISBN Digital Domestic Edition 979-12-229-8073-7
ISBN International Edition 979-12-81627-69-7
ISBN Digital International Edition 979-12-81627-70-3

Table of Contents

Part 2 – Soft Indicators

Part 3 – The Relationship between Incumbents and Fintech

Foreword

by *Stefano Caselli*

At SDA Bocconi School of Management, each division is dedicated to cultivating excellence in specific areas of research and practice. The ICE—Innovation and Corporate Entrepreneurship division focuses on two deeply interconnected domains: innovation, which projects the future into the present, and corporate entrepreneurship, an indispensable driver of transformation in both established institutions and emerging ventures.

In line with this mission, the European FS Tech Hub was launched at the end of 2023 as a vertical initiative of the ICE division. The Hub aims to serve as a dynamic platform for analysing and exchanging ideas on financial innovation at the European level, engaging stakeholders across the ecosystem, including institutions, market operators, Fintech companies, and startups. More than a research centre, the Hub is designed to be a reference point for shaping the future of financial services through innovation, collaboration, and thought leadership.

This volume is one of the key outcomes of the European FS Tech Hub's inaugural research cycle. It addresses some of the most pressing and complex questions arising from the evolution of financial technology, particularly in the wake of the 2021–2022 speculative bubble. This period, marked by inflated valuations and over-optimistic projections, laid bare the inadequacies of traditional valuation models when applied to Fintech firms characterised by intangible assets, fast-changing business models, and uncertain regulatory landscapes. Against this backdrop, the research seeks to offer not only a comprehensive conceptual foundation for understanding Fintech, but also practical tools for navigating its multifaceted development.

The study develops along several analytical dimensions. First, it establishes a rigorous definition of Fintech, disentangling its various interpretations by integrating academic, regulatory, and business perspectives. This effort is not merely terminological: it forms the cornerstone for meaningful analysis in a field often clouded by hype and inconsistency. Second, the research conducts a wide-ranging empirical investigation of the global Fintech market, with particular attention to regional dynamics across the Americas, EMEA, and Asia-Pacific. This includes an in-depth analysis of market trends, investment flows, the rise of unicorns, and the comparative role of regulation and innovation capacity in driving Fintech development. Third, the study revisits the issue of valuation, highlighting the limits of models such as DCF and multiples, and proposing alternative methodologies better suited to early-stage and high-growth Fintechs. These include the Venture Capital Method, the Scorecard

Valuation, user-based models, and others, alongside a strong emphasis on soft indicators such as governance, regulatory readiness, management quality, and ecosystem engagement. Once considered marginal, these qualitative dimensions have emerged as essential for understanding the long-term sustainability and strategic viability of Fintechs, rather than a mere pursuit of growth at all costs. Building on this assumption, a multi-level study was conducted to gather empirical evidence on the relevance of soft indicators and to incorporate them into a revised valuation methodology by quantitatively assessing the impact of governance, management, regulation, and ecosystem factors on the value of Fintech companies.

Moreover, to bridge theory and practice, the research incorporates case studies that demonstrate how valuation approaches can be applied and tested in real-world scenarios. These insights are further enriched by an exploration of the growing convergence between traditional incumbents and Fintechs, highlighting collaboration models, M&A strategies, and post-integration challenges. The research methodology is grounded in academic rigour, combining literature reviews, workshops with the Hub's partners, and empirical analysis. This hybrid approach enables the Hub to capture both the theoretical foundations and the operational realities of the Fintech ecosystem. The result is a multidimensional analysis that not only maps what has happened but also equips policymakers, investors, and practitioners with tools to interpret what lies ahead.

Ultimately, this volume reaffirms the European FS Tech Hub's role as a catalyst for innovation and reflection. In a sector evolving rapidly under the combined pressures of technology, regulation, and consumer behaviour, the ambition is to foster a resilient, inclusive, and sustainable financial future. This book contributes to that effort: a call to think critically, act responsibly, and innovate together.

The European FS Tech Hub at a glance

Author's Note
This work has been conceived under my responsibility as Director of the ICE—Innovation and Corporate Entrepreneurship Division at SDA Bocconi School of Management. Any errors, omissions, or interpretations are solely mine and should not be attributed to the institutions, partners, or colleagues involved.
That said, the research presented in these pages could not have taken shape without the collective effort of the European FS Tech Hub. Researchers, fellows, and partners have contributed through analyses, discussions, and workshops that have greatly enriched the work. I am deeply grateful for their commitment, which has provided the foundation on which this narrative has been built.

The European Financial Services (FS) Tech Hub is a research initiative promoted by Professor Gimede Gigante within the ICE—Innovation and Corporate Entrepreneurship division of SDA Bocconi School of Management.

ICE—Innovation and Corporate Entrepreneurship is dedicated to companies that want to discover how to improve their innovation capacity. In particular, the ICE Innovation Journey is a path towards innovation, offering a variety of services and formats. While each company's innovation journey will be unique, it can follow a common framework, with each phase and format fully customisable to ensure the final path is tailored to the specific needs of the company.

ICE offers the following verticals, each defined by specialised expertise developed within its respective field:

- European FS Tech Hub, which is a European-level platform for the exchange of ideas that addresses topics of innovation, governance and evaluation.
- Digital Tech, which includes the most important technologies currently available and applies them to a wide range of sectors. For example: B2B + B2C software, SaaS solutions, marketplaces, Fintech, insuretech, marketing tech, adtech, HR tech, augmented and virtual reality, IoT, AI, blockchain, cybersecurity and much more.
- Made in Italy, which emphasises the importance of the skills emerging from the mapping of the most famous Italian brands, with a focus on excellence in the food, fashion and design sectors, and a 360-degree business perspective.

- Sustainability, which aims to explore the essential role played by climate change, social entrepreneurship, the circular economy, smart communities and smart cities, as well as clean technologies.

Launched at the end of 2023, the European FS Tech Hub stands as a reference point for innovation in the financial services sector, creating a collaborative ecosystem involving institutions, industry associations, companies, financial operators, startups and researchers at an international level.

Designed to explore key emerging trends in the Fintech sector, the European FS Tech Hub focuses on innovative technologies, business models and governance in the European and global financial environment. Its objectives include the development of advanced management skills, the dissemination of best practices and the promotion of an entrepreneurial and innovative culture. FS Tech Hub activities include:

- Academic and applied research: In-depth studies on the evolution of Fintech, from the digitisation of financial services to the growth of sectors such as Insurtech, Regtech, Cryptocurrency Exchange, etc.
- Events and workshops: Regular meetings with industry experts, professionals and academics to exchange ideas and keep up to date with the latest trends.
- Training and dissemination: Training programmes for managers and professionals to strengthen the skills needed to meet the challenges of the future.

Led by Professor Gimede Gigante with an innovative approach, this initiative addresses the challenges of the digital economy, encouraging synergy between academia and industry and positioning the Hub as a point of reference for practitioners. The team is composed of the following:

- Gimede Gigante—Hub Director SDA Bocconi
- Andrea Cerri—Deputy Coordinator Hub SDA Bocconi
- Silvia Rella—Hub Analyst SDA Bocconi
- Jessica Baro—Hub Researcher SDA Bocconi
- Raffaele Turazzo—Hub Researcher SDA Bocconi
- Francesca Scarlini—Hub Researcher SDA Bocconi
- Pierpaolo Cuglietta—Hub Researcher SDA Bocconi.

The European FS Tech Hub is organised into three working groups: the Advisory Council, the Advisory Board and the Committee of Executive Partners.

The Advisory Council, at the time of writing, was composed by the following:

- Stefano Caselli—Dean SDA Bocconi and Chairman Advisory Council European FS Tech Hub
- Silvia Attanasio—Head of Innovation ABI and President ABI Lab
- Maurizio Bernardo—President AssoFintech

- Giuseppe Donvito—President Italian Tech Alliance
- Gianluigi Greco—President AIxIA
- Chiara Mosca—Commissary Consob
- Simone Ranucci Brandimarte—Co-founder and President of Italian Insurtech Association
- Claudia Segre—President Global Thinking Foundation.

The Advisory Board, at the time of writing, was composed by the following:

- Matteo Arpe—President Tinaba
- Riccardo Corino—Chief Business Office ICCREA
- Gianmarco Gessi—Director of Innovation and Planning & Development Flowe Medionalum
- Paolo Gianturco—FSI Consulting & FS Tech Leader Deloitte
- Paolo Fiorentino—CEO Banca Progetto
- Natascia Noveri—Executive Director Innovation & Processes Intesa Sanpaolo.

The Committee of Executive Partners, at the time of writing, was represented by the following:

- Andrea Cilio—Chief Marketing Officer Tinaba
- Massimo Citoni—Italian Regional Manager eToro
- Andrea Coppini—Head of Digital Innovation & Multichannel Division ICCREA
- Stefano Curzi—Head of Innovation Strategy Intesa Sanpaolo
- Emanuele Di Palma—President BCC San Marzano
- Andrea Ferretti—Markets & Business Development Leader for FS EY
- Alessandro La Pergola—Chief Operating Officer Banca Progetto
- Giacomo Mazzanti—Partner Deloitte
- Demetrio Migliorati—Head of Innovation Mediolanum
- Nicola Occhinegro—CEO & Founder Finanza.tech
- Leonardo Patroni Griffi—President Banca Popolare di Puglia e Basilicata.

The European FS Tech Hub was born and developed, thanks to the collaboration of several strategic partners representing some of the most important financial and technological realities in Italy. These include the following:

- Institutional Partners: ABI Lab, Italian Association for AI, AssoFintech, Global Thinking Foundation, Italian Insurtech Association, Italian Tech Alliance
- Founding Partners and Sponsors: Banca Progetto, Deloitte, Gruppo BCC Iccrea, Intesa Sanpaolo, Banca Mediolanum, Tinaba
- Premium Partners: BCC San Marzano di San Giuseppe, Banca Popolare di Puglia e Basilicata, Esperia Investor, eToro, EY, Finanza.Tech
- Supporting & Startup Partners: Tiscali, ConosciESG, Expert Revolution.

These collaborations strengthen the role of the European FS Tech Hub as a platform for dialogue and innovation, contributing to the definition of innovative solutions for a rapidly evolving sector.

Through its activities, the European FS Tech Hub acts as a catalyst for innovation in Fintech, helping to create a future in which financial services are more accessible, efficient and sustainable. A special acknowledgement is extended to Alessandra Perrazzelli, Vice General Director of Bank of Italy, and Massimo Doria, Head of Milano Hub Innovation Center of Bank of Italy, in their respective roles at the time of drafting this work, for their continuous support and the valuable exchanges on key topics of interest, which have contributed to shaping this work.

The research developed was realised in collaboration with the Hub partners through plenary workshops, which aligned the objectives of the participants with those of the research itself, providing concrete answers to the needs of the innovative financial services sector.

The evolution of the Fintech ecosystem is strongly influenced by technological innovation and a changing regulatory framework. The sector is going through a consolidation phase, characterised by an increased focus on financial valuations, a growing interest in soft indicators and an increasingly close collaboration between startups and traditional financial players. Investors are also shifting their focus towards more sustainable metrics, reflecting the maturity of the market and increasing attention to governance, management quality and robustness of business models.

After a phase of strong expansion and exponential growth, Fintechs are redefining their role within the financial landscape, moving from being alternative players to the banking system to becoming strategic partners for traditional institutions. This shift is evident in the increase in M&A transactions, the spread of embedded finance and the integration of Fintech solutions into existing banking services.

In parallel, the Fintech ecosystem is experiencing an acceleration in the adoption of advanced technologies, from Artificial Intelligence (AI) to blockchain, with an increasing focus on the digitisation of banking processes, open banking and innovative payment solutions. The sector is increasingly influenced by regulatory and compliance factors, with regulators committed to balancing innovation with the need to ensure stability and security for the financial system.

The future challenge will be to build a resilient and sustainable Fintech ecosystem, capable of adapting to regulatory and technological changes without losing the innovative drive that has characterised its growth in recent years. Through this report and the activities of the European FS Tech, the aim is precisely to support the ongoing transformation of the financial landscape and provide the foundations for building an international ecosystem and a cutting-edge future.

Institutional Partners

ABI Lab AiA assoFintech Global Thinking IIA Italian Insurtech Association ITALIAN TECH ALLIANCE

Founding Partners & Sponsors

BANCA PROGETTO Deloitte GRUPPO BCC ICCREA INTESA SANPAOLO mediolanum BANCA tinaba

Premium Partners

BCC SAN MARZANO DI SAN GIUSEPPE BPPB European Investor eToro EY Building a better working world

Supporting & Startup Partners

TISCALI ConsciESG EXPERT REVOLUTION

Part 1
The Fintech Sector

A preliminary examination of the existing academic literature on Fintech reveals that a significant percentage of the studies analysed do not provide an unambiguous definition of the term and its areas of application. This observation lays the groundwork for the formulation of a research question centred on the need to clearly identify the disruptive technologies that have marked a turning point in financial services, as well as to understand how these innovations have also found application in related sectors, triggering the evolution of the business areas concerned.

To answer this question, the work uses a methodological approach that combines an analysis of existing literature with an exploration of definitions provided by recognised bodies in the field of Fintech. The aim is to build a solid theoretical framework that can serve as a reference point for future studies and practitioners.

In the next step, the study focuses on emerging trends in the Fintech landscape, with a particular focus on geographical differences between the Americas, EMEA (Europe, Middle East and Africa) and Asia-Pacific regions. The analysis aims to map the main challenges the industry is facing—from investment management to customer retention, from regulatory compliance to the integration of new technologies, from data security to risk control. This research allows the identification of critical areas on which to focus future innovation and development strategies.

A further dimension concerns the analysis of the valuation methods used to determine the value of Fintech companies. The research highlights how crucial it is to broaden the valuation horizon beyond traditional approaches, to include methodologies that consider qualitative and innovative aspects, which are often difficult to quantify, but crucial for understanding the real growth potential of companies in the sector. In this perspective, particular emphasis is given to the role of venture capital and other external factors that significantly influence the valuation of startups and Fintech companies, emphasising the need for a more complex and articulated valuation approach, capable of reflecting the dynamism and specificity of the sector.

Through meticulous analysis and critical reflection on the state of the art of Fintech, this part aims to make a significant contribution to literature, providing insights for further research and offering practitioners insights to successfully analyse the complexities of a constantly changing environment.

1   Fintech: Definition and Scope of Analysis

Definition of the term 'Fintech'

The main objective of this chapter is to outline the meaning attributed to the concept of 'Fintech' and define the scope of analysis of the research in question. In particular, the neologism 'Fintech', resulting from the fusion of the English terms financial and technology, designates the innovation in the financial sector facilitated by technological evolution. The Bank of Italy, in fact, defines the concept of Fintech as '*financial innovation made possible by technological innovation, which can manifest itself through new business models, processes or products, significantly affecting financial markets, institutions, or the range of services offered*' (Bank of Italy, 2017). This description echoes, as detailed below, the pioneering definition of Abraham Leon Bettinger, vice-president of the Manufacturers Hanover Trust, who, in 1972, provided the following description of the term: '*an acronym which stands for financial technology, combining bank expertise with modern management science techniques and the computer*' (Milian, Spinola, & Carvalho, 2019). It follows that the essence of Fintech manifests itself in the use of advanced technologies to increase the accessibility, efficiency and personalisation of financial services, ranging from the automation of banking transactions and payment systems, the development of participatory financing platforms, automated financial advice, to the adoption of cryptocurrencies and blockchain technology.

The incursion of Fintech into the fabric of the contemporary financial landscape has marked a significant turning point, introducing new players into the market, including technology startups and IT and social media giants. These new entrants have triggered direct competition with traditional financial institutions, forcing them to reconsider and reformulate their business strategies towards a renewed commitment to technological innovation. Fintech, while offering undoubted benefits such as increased convenience and speed in financial services, as well as improved access to them, also brings with it non-negligible challenges. Specifically, the most important issues are those related to customer loyalty, regulation, data security, privacy protection and assessing the impact of these new entities on the market. These issues require meticulous analysis and critical reflection by all the actors involved, who are called upon to establish a balance between supporting innovation and the fundamental need to guarantee financial stability and consumer protection (Bank of Italy, 2017).

Definition over time

The concept of Fintech, a term now familiar in the modern financial landscape, has its roots in the thinking of John Maynard Keynes. As early as 1920, Keynes realised the important connection between finance and technology, as expressed in his book *The Economic Consequences of Peace*.

It was, however, in 1972 that A. L. Bettinger first coined the term Fintech, describing it in an article entitled 'Fintech—A Series of 40 Time Shared Models Used at MHTC' as *'an acronym which stands for financial technology, combining bank expertise with modern management science techniques and the computer'*.

The adoption of the term acquired an official dimension when, in 2003, Fintech became the name of a stock market index, the Updata Financial Technology Index, representative of companies operating in the financial and technology fields. In 2015, the gradual evolution of the sector led to a new definition of Fintech offered by The Finanser, the Innovative Finance Blog, which defined it as an innovative financial industry aimed at applying technology to improve financial activities.

In 2017, the Treccani encyclopaedia described the concept of Fintech as the set of companies, mostly startups, which offer innovative services and products related to the banking, financial and asset sectors, managed mainly through technological solutions with minimal human involvement.

In 2018, the University of California, Los Angeles, provided an additional perspective by considering the concept of Fintech as a relatively new category of companies whose business model is based on digital products. This approach excludes traditional banks such as Citibank and Wells Fargo, which, although they now offer similar products, did not originally include a digital component. Finally, in 2021, Consob also offered a meaningful definition of Fintech, describing it as a transversal instrument of innovation that creates a complex web of relationships between traditional players and startups, as well as between regulated and unregulated entities (Consob, 2021).

In conclusion, the concept of Fintech has evolved from an initial definition that described it as the intersection of finance and technology to an established industry that today includes innovative, digitally driven companies that are redefining how they interact with the financial sector (Deloitte, 2024a).

The evolution of financial technology, known as Fintech, reflects the dynamic progress that has characterised financial services from the last century to the present. In 1950, the introduction of the first credit card in the United States was a milestone in the industry, allowing consumers to defer payments for goods and services. Later, in 1960, the advent of automated teller machines, or ATMs, changed the interactions between banks and their customers, offering unprecedented access to banking services.

The decade of the 1970s witnessed a significant transition with the start of electronic *trading* at NASDAQ, increasing the efficiency and accessibility of financial markets. This evolution found continuation in the 1980s, when banks, including Citibank and Manhattan Chase, introduced the concept of home banking, allowing personal finances to be managed remotely for the first time.

Figure 1   **The evolution of Fintech**

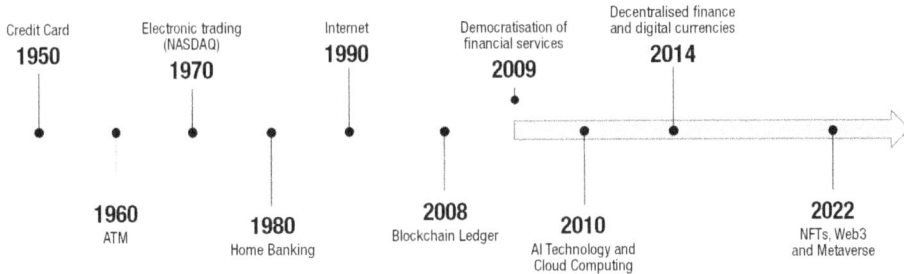

The timeline outlines key milestones in the evolution of Fintech from 1950 to 2022, highlighting innovations—from credit cards to the metaverse—that progressively enhanced the accessibility, efficiency and scope of financial services.

Source: Own elaboration based on data from Deloitte

With the advent of the Internet in 1990, there was a global expansion of financial services, further improving the accessibility and speed of transactions. This expansion was further catalysed in 2008 by the creation of the blockchain ledger, an innovation that introduced a new level of security and transparency to financial transactions.

2009 marked the beginning of the era of democratisation of financial services, emphasising the need to extend access to financial services to a wider audience. The technological evolution continued in 2010 with the improvement of AI and the introduction of cloud computing, which offered new tools for financial analysis and personalisation of services.

2014 saw the emergence of decentralised finance (DeFi) and the development of digital currencies issued by central banks, which offered innovative alternatives to the traditional financial system. Finally, 2022 was marked by the emergence of Non-Fungible Tokens (NFT), the evolution of Web3 and the debut of the Metaverse, pushing the boundaries of Fintech towards new models of digital asset ownership and exchange.

The described evolution testifies to the constant transformation of Fintech, not only in the area of individual financial management and investment but also in the broader context of the digital economy (Deloitte, 2024b).

The Fintech ecosystem

In order to deepen the understanding of the Fintech concept and its areas of application, a detailed analysis and definition of the intrinsic ecosystem that characterises it is essential. This ecosystem can be distinctly identified through the following key elements:

1. Fintech startups, such as emerging startups in areas such as payments, asset management, lending and crowdfunding.
2. Technology Developers, working in cutting-edge areas such as big data analytics, cloud computing, cryptocurrency and social media.
3. Governmental entities, represented by financial regulators and legislators.
4. Universities, Hubs and Accelerators, which foster the growth of Fintech startups and the dissemination of knowledge related to this sector.
5. Financial Customers which include both individuals and organisations.
6. Traditional Financial Institutions, such as banks, insurance companies, securities brokerage firms and Venture Capital.

Together, these elements act as catalysts for innovation, stimulating the economy and fostering both collaboration and competition within the financial sector. In this context, Fintech startups play a central role, standing out for their entrepreneurial spirit and for introducing significant innovations in various fields, from payments to insurance, via wealth management and crowdfunding. These initiatives have helped to reduce operating costs, focus on niche markets and offer personalised services that differ from the proposals of traditional financial institutions. Another key aspect of the Fintech sector is the ability to differentiate financial services, allowing consumers to select the most suitable offerings for their needs from a variety of providers, rather than relying on a single institution.

Governments have also played a significant role in providing a favourable regulatory environment for Fintech development, particularly in the aftermath of the 2008 financial crisis. This has seen traditional financial institutions subjected to tighter regulation, with the introduction of new capital requirements and reporting obligations imposed by government regulators. In this environment, financial customers emerge as the main source of revenue for Fintech companies, while traditional financial institutions are a key driver of innovation in the ecosystem (Lee & Shin, 2018). A key role is played by universities, hubs and accelerators that provide advanced research and specialised training, facilitate essential connections and resources, and promote the rapid growth of startups, contributing to the creation of a dynamic and innovative Fintech ecosystem.

Technologies, fields of application and business areas

Starting from the definition outlined and considering the current context, the concept of 'Fintech' represents a neologism that illustrates the integration of innovative technologies, such as those associated with the Internet (e.g., cloud computing and mobile internet), with the activities traditionally carried out in the financial services sector, including, by way of example, loans, payments, money transfers and various banking operations (Milian, Spinola & Carvalho, 2019). In light of these premises, the need to start the analysis from an examination of the main innovative technologies integrated into the traditional financial services sector emerges as imperative, in order to outline the main areas of application and related business areas.

Innovative technologies

We outline further the main technologies that have contributed to the innovation of the financial sector, commonly identified with the term 'Fintech' (Bank of Italy, 2021; Bank of Italy, 2023; Visconti, 2020a; McKinsey & Company, 2021a). This analysis aims to describe the various disruptive technological solutions, which, through implementation and integration into traditional financial management processes, have defined a new phase of development in the sector. The latter considers a wide range of applications, extending from the digitisation of banking processes to cryptocurrency, from the use of AI for the customisation of services to blockchain, which is set to be a revolutionary factor for the security and integrity of financial transactions. The importance of these technological innovations manifests itself not only in their effectiveness in improving and increasing the efficiency of existing services but also in their intrinsic ability to revolutionise the business areas concerned.

a. Artificial Intelligence (AI): Technology that enables computers, robots and other devices to simulate forms of human intelligence (European Parliament). This includes the ability to learn from experience, adapt to new situations, understand and respond to language commands, solve problems and, in some cases, demonstrate creativity. In the field of financial services, AI is particularly useful in automatically identifying factors that influence performance, thereby improving the accuracy of models used in the sector.
The latter finds application across the operational spectrum of the financial industry, improving both the customer interface, through customised products and tailored user experiences, and internal operations, such as intelligent processes and fraud detection through natural language processing (NLP). Such applications not only elevate the operational efficiency and security of financial transactions but also pave the way for new business models and continuous innovation in the analytics industry (McKinsey & Company, 2021b).
b. Big Data: A set of data of considerable size, held in repositories of a heterogeneous nature, i.e., with no direct mutual correlation. Unlike conventional systems, which are dedicated to the processing of structured data or data that can be structured by means of interconnected tables, the scope of big data extends to include also semi-structured data or data that are completely unrelated to any form of traditional structuring (e.g., information deriving from the web such as comments on social media, textual documents, audio recordings and video sequences). This variety of data, therefore, requires innovative methodologies for its management, analysis and interpretation, in order to derive value and meaning from it in a wide range of application contexts, ranging from predictive analysis to the personalisation of user experiences. The integration of big data in the financial services

sector manifests itself through the advanced processing and predictive analysis of large volumes of data, enabling financial institutions to optimise strategic decisions, personalise services for customers and improve operational efficiency and risk management (Bank of Italy, 2021).

c. Cloud Technologies: Technologies that facilitate access to a set of configurable and shared resources for data processing, including networks, servers, storage space, applications and services. These resources are provided readily, requiring minimal user intervention in their direct provisioning from the supplier. The distinctive feature of such technologies is the provision of a flexible and scalable platform, which allows users to take advantage of computing capabilities without having to deal with the physical management of the underlying infrastructure (hardware) (Bank of Italy, 2021).

Depending on the mode of access and infrastructure management, these technologies can be classified into different categories:

– Public Cloud technologies, which ensure that the infrastructure is accessible to the public, offer a high degree of efficiency in terms of resource sharing.

– Private Cloud technologies, which are characterised by the exclusive use of the infrastructure by a single entity or institution.

– Hybrid Cloud technologies, consisting of an architecture that integrates elements of both public cloud and private cloud, combining their advantages. Hybrid cloud technologies offer flexibility and scalability while providing additional control and security capabilities (Bank of Italy, 2021).

d. Distributed ledger technology (DLT), Smart Contract: A distributed ledger technology (DLT) based on an architecture in which all participants (nodes) in a network share access to a unified database, actively collaborating in its maintenance and updating through a decentralised process. This technology employs advanced cryptographic methods to guarantee the authenticity and security of the transactions carried out within the system, eliminating the need for centralised intermediaries (such as banks or government agencies) in the verification of transactions.

This technology also includes the concept of *'smart contracts'*, which are computer programmes designed to automatically execute predefined terms and conditions when specific events or conditions occur. These contracts are written in high-level programming languages and are autonomously activated to execute the stipulated transactions when the conditions are met, without the need for human intervention. Smart contracts find their main application in DLT networks and transactions involving virtual currencies, but their use is expanding into numerous other areas, offering an effective means to automate and make more efficient the execution of contractual agreements, while reducing the risks of default and disputes (Bank of Italy, 2021).

e. Open banking platform, API: Banking services using application programming interfaces (called *'open standard APIs'*). This approach enables the development of advanced applications and services that make use of the data and functionalities provided by the technological infrastructure of a third-party financial institution. *Open standard APIs* act as a communication bridge, allowing developers to securely and efficiently access a vast set of banking resources, such as account information, payment transactions and transfer data.

The adoption of these standards facilitates interoperability between different banking systems and third-party applications, thus promoting innovation and the creation of customised and highly functional financial solutions. This paradigm accelerates the process of digitisation of the banking sector but also paves the way for greater competition and collaboration between financial institutions and technology companies, helping to raise service standards, data security and operational efficiency (Bank of Italy, 2021).

f. Robot process automation (RPA): Technologies and solutions dedicated to automating work processes, including those using AI, designed to automatically manage and perform repetitive tasks. In particular, robotic process automation (RPA) in the context of the financial sector is often implemented to optimise and automate back-office operations, as well as to represent the natural evolution of workflow management systems.

   This technology is a strategic tool for financial institutions, enabling the reduction of lead times and increased accuracy in day-to-day activities. RPA applications can range from simple transaction processing and customer data management to more complex financial analysis and reporting, facilitating a vast number of processes from compliance and anti-fraud verification to customer service.

   The integration of AI with RPA further raises the level of automation, enabling systems to understand and interpret data with a degree of intelligence and adaptability that goes beyond the simple execution of pre-programmed tasks (Bank of Italy, 2021).

g. Biometric Technologies: Technologies dedicated to digital identity authentication comprising a set of electronic procedures and tools used, in accordance with current regulations, for the online identification and verification of an individual's identity. These systems are designed to facilitate the attribution and confirmation of authentication credentials, making possible both the initial registration of the customer and the integral management of the contractual relationship, operating exclusively through digital channels.

   This technological approach is crucial in today's environment to ensure the security and reliability of online transactions and digital services, enabling companies and institutions to authenticate the identity of their customers in a secure manner. Digital authentication technologies make use of advanced security mechanisms, including encryption and biometric analysis, to ensure that only authorised users can access sensitive services and information. In addition to enhancing security, these technologies also improve the user experience by simplifying and speeding up the identity verification process and eliminating the need for manual procedures (Bank of Italy, 2021).

h. Blockchain and Cryptocurrencies: Technology that provides a distributed and decentralised ledger of transactions and enables the existence of cryptocurrencies such as Bitcoin. This not only provides a platform for cryptocurrencies but also extends to a wide range of applications in the financial sector (PwC, Bitcoin, cryptocurrency, blockchain ... So what does it all mean?).

Cryptocurrencies function as a digital media of exchange, using cryptographic techniques to verify transactions and control the creation of new monetary units. Unlike traditional currencies, cryptocurrencies operate without a central authority, promoting a more open and decentralised financial system (PwC).

Blockchain technology makes it possible to reduce transaction costs and times, increasing security and transparency and facilitating access to innovative financial services. Among the most promising applications are:

- Cross-border payments: simplification of international transactions with reduced costs and faster execution times.
- Smart contracts: automation of agreements and contracts, with potential applications in numerous sectors.
- DeFi (Decentralised Financing): offering financial services without traditional intermediaries, such as banks, through the use of smart contracts on blockchain.
- Tokenisation: representation of real assets in digital form on blockchain, facilitating their trading and management.

While the cryptocurrency market remains subject to significant fluctuations, the adoption of blockchain technology looks set to grow, driven by interest in its applications in financial and non-financial sectors (Vention).

i. Payment Systems: A set of instruments, banking procedures and electronic systems that enable the transfer of money between entities. These systems have evolved and diversified considerably thanks to digital technology, giving rise to new payment methods that go beyond traditional banking instruments. Below are some specific examples:
   - Mobile Payment: Refers to the use of mobile devices, such as smartphones and tablets, to make payments. This system uses technologies such as Near Field Communication (NFC) or QR codes to enable fast and secure transactions directly from the mobile device.
   - Virtual POS (Point of Sale): Virtual POS is a solution that allows merchants to accept credit or debit card payments without the need for a physical terminal. This system is based on the use of software or web applications that can process transactions via the Internet.
   - Mobile Wallet: A mobile wallet is an application that stores payment information digitally on a mobile device, enabling the user to make payments and money transfers via their smartphone (Visconti, 2020a).

j. Internet of Things (IoT): Sensors and actuators, interconnected through complex networks of data processing systems, that form the fundamental infrastructure for actively monitoring and managing a wide range of actions related to objects, machines and phenomena in the natural world, including humans and animals. Sensors, sophisticated devices capable of detecting changes and environmental parameters, are essential for acquiring real-time data on specific physical or environmental conditions, such as temperature, humidity, pressure or movement. This data is then transmitted to the computing systems for processing, allowing an in-depth understanding of the state of what is being monitored.

Actuators, on the other hand, act in response to command signals processed by computing systems, performing specific physical actions such as moving, switching on, adjusting or switching off objects and machinery. Their function is crucial to actively intervene in the environment or processes, based on the analysis of data collected by sensors (Bank of Italy, 2021).

k. Immersive Technologies (Metaverse): Immersive technologies, such as the metaverse, are revolutionising the Fintech industry, offering new opportunities to improve operational efficiency and customer experience. The metaverse, an interconnected virtual environment that leverages virtual and augmented reality, enables Fintech companies to create immersive and interactive digital experiences. The adoption of the metaverse in the Fintech sector offers numerous benefits: Banks and Fintechs can create virtual branches where customers can interact with avatars to access financial services, participate in virtual advice and manage their finances in a safe and immersive environment. This approach not only improves accessibility but also reduces operational costs and increases customer satisfaction.

Furthermore, the use of technologies such as big data within the metaverse allows companies to collect and analyse huge amounts of data in real time. This data can be used to create predictive models that help identify emerging trends in customer and market behaviour, enabling companies to make more informed and strategic decisions.

In conclusion, the metaverse and big data are transforming the Fintech sector, offering new opportunities to improve efficiency, security and customer experience (International Journal of Computer Science and Information Technology, 2023).

After providing a brief description of the main technologies that have characterised the technological transformation of the financial sector, it is relevant to analyse their incidence in Fintech projects. Specifically, drawing on the survey carried out by the Bank of Italy during 2021, which focused on the Italian banking landscape (Bank of Italy, 2021), a categorisation of Fintech projects according to predominant technology is presented.

Chart 1 provides a comprehensive and systematic overview of Fintech projects categorised according to predominant technology. It shows a clear inclination towards the use of innovative technologies to enhance and diversify offerings in the financial sector. APIs represent the most adopted technology, with a significant overall investment, underlining their importance in facilitating integration and interoperability between different platforms and services. Cloud computing, divided into private, public and hybrid clouds, follows in importance, highlighting a growing interest in data security and operational efficiency. Also underlined is the focus on emerging technologies such as AI, including Machine Learning (ML) and NLP, which find applications in various areas, from improving customer experience to optimising inter-

Chart 1   **Fintech projects by prevailing technology**

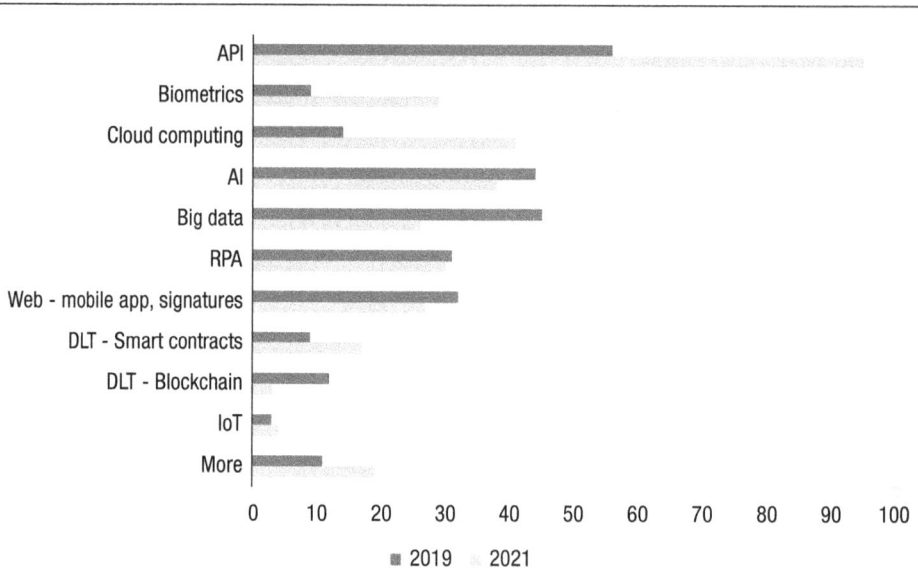

The bar chart classifies Fintech projects by core technology in 2019 and 2021. APIs dominate, followed by cloud computing and AI. The rise of DLT, biometrics and smart contracts reflects a shift towards secure, interoperable and data-driven solutions.

Source: Own elaboration based on data from Bank of Italy, 2021

nal processes. Considering business and governance processes, on the other hand, an increasing focus on innovation can be seen, with projects aiming at digitisation and automation to reduce costs and improve customer satisfaction. The analysis points to a varied distribution of investments, with some technologies, such as DLT and smart contracts, accounting for a smaller share of the total, but underlining the interest in the potential offered by blockchain and related technologies. This mapping of Fintech projects by prevailing technology reflects a rapidly evolving sector, where the adoption of advanced technological solutions is key to the development of more efficient, secure and personalised financial services, in response to the growing needs of an increasingly digitised and interconnected market.

Chart 2 shows that in the last analysis (Bank of Italy, 2023), there was a significant increase in the number of projects related to web-mobile platforms, AI, digital signatures, DLT and big data analysis. This represents a trend towards innovation and digitisation in various sectors. On the contrary, a reduction in the number of initiatives focused on the use of APIs and biometric technologies was observed, signalling a reorientation of priorities or technology development strategies.

Regarding cloud computing projects, although there has been a decrease in the total number, it is interesting to note an increase in terms of financial investments (Bank of Italy, 2023). This indicates that, although there have been fewer overall

Chart 2   **Variation of projects by type of technology**

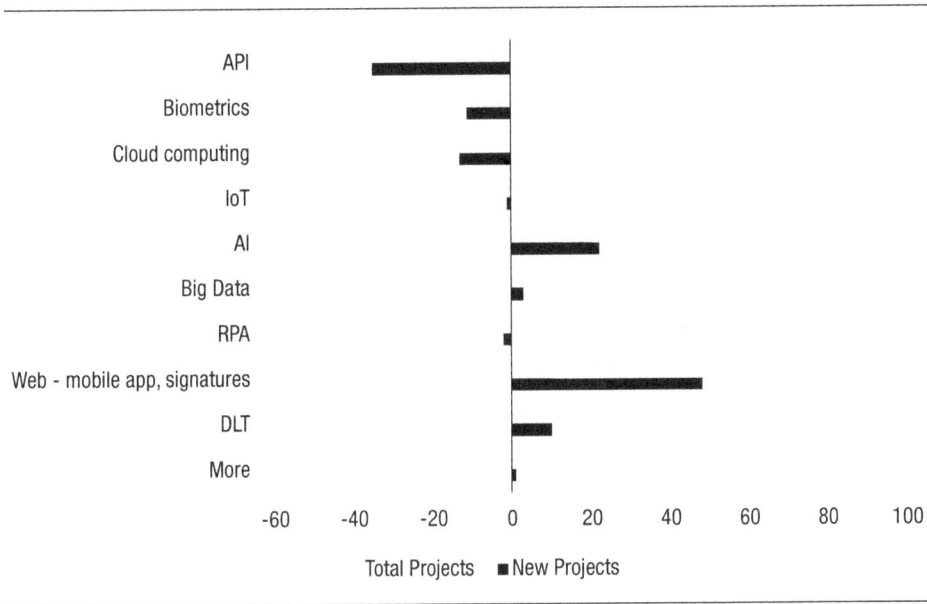

The bar chart illustrates shifts in Fintech project focus: web-mobile platforms, AI, DLT and big data saw increases, while APIs, biometrics and cloud declined. The trend highlights evolving priorities in innovation and digital transformation strategies.

Source: Own elaboration based on data from Bank of Italy, 2023

projects, those launched have required higher budgets, suggesting greater complexity or ambition in initiatives based on this technology. This shift in investment dynamics underlines the growing importance of cloud computing as a pillar for digital transformation and technological innovation.

Areas of application and business areas

The technologies outlined above find application in numerous contexts, which, in most circumstances, facilitate the evolution of the business areas concerned. In this regard, the main areas of application and the corresponding derived models are illustrated below, highlighting how these innovations can transform not only the financial services sector in the strict sense but also related sectors, offering new prospects for development and growth.

a. Open Finance
b. NeoBanks
c. Payment Systems (Paytech)
d. Digital Lending

e. TechFin
f. Financing Solutions, with a focus on Crowdfunding
g. Insurance (Insurtech)
h. Regulatory (Regtech)
i. Investments (Wealthtech)
j. Capital Markets
k. Microfinance (Micro-Fintech)
l. Real Estate (Proptech)

These areas of analysis represent emerging application areas that offer significant growth opportunities within the industry, highlighting the crucial role these technologies play in the development of financial services that can be described as innovative and secure.

Open Finance

Open banking represents a significant evolution in the financial services landscape, taking its place within the Fintech ecosystem, bringing innovation, increased competition and offering users a wide range of personalised services. The European Payment Services Directive (PSD2), which came into force in 2019 in Italy, has sanctioned the beginning of this change, requiring banks to open access to customers' current accounts to authorised third parties, subject to the consent of the users themselves. This paradigm, defined as open banking, allows these third parties to access bank data and information to create new services and applications, improving efficiency and transparency for account holders (Bank of Italy, 2023).

In the Fintech context, open banking acts as an accelerator for the development of new technological solutions in the field of payments and financial services, promoting innovation and personalisation of services offered to consumers. The ability to aggregate information from different bank accounts and initiate payments directly from the customer's account gives Fintech companies the opportunity to develop applications that can provide a comprehensive view of personal finances, improve savings management, facilitate more efficient and secure payments, and offer personalised financial advice.

The implementation of open banking in Italy, as in other EU countries, has required the creation of sophisticated technological infrastructures, such as APIs, which enable secure and controlled interoperability between banking systems and third-party applications. This has led to the emergence of so-called 'system platforms' or PSD2 *gateways*, which function as intermediaries between banks and Fintech service providers, simplifying access to data and ensuring the security and protection of sensitive customer information (Bank of Italy, 2023).

The introduction of Open Finance marks a crucial turning point for the financial sector, encouraging competition and innovation not only between traditional banks and Fintech companies but also enriching consumers with greater autonomy and flexibility in the use of their financial data. This evolution paves the way for a new banking model, strongly anchored in blockchain technology and software solutions that facilitate the creation of services through an integrated network of financial institutions and third-party service providers (Figure 2).

In this context, Open Finance represents a significant evolution from open banking, extending the sharing of financial data beyond current accounts to include an approach that provides a comprehensive financial view of the user, enabling institutions to create innovative and personalised services. Supported by the European Commission's FIDA framework, Open Finance promotes the secure sharing of data with authorised third parties, enhancing the customer experience through greater transparency, efficiency and offers tailored to individual needs.

The inclusion of data on mortgages, investments and insurance allows financial institutions to have a complete overview of users' finances. This facilitates the offering of more targeted and innovative products, such as personalised financial advice, wealth management and optimised investment plans. The European Commission's FIDA framework sets strict guidelines to ensure that data sharing is done in a secure and privacy-compliant manner, increasing users' trust in digital financial services.

In this context, authorised third parties, such as Fintech and other technology companies, can develop new applications and solutions that leverage aggregated financial data to offer improved and more integrated user experiences. This structural change in the financial sector promotes greater competition, pushing traditional institutions to innovate and adapt quickly to new market dynamics (Deloitte).

Figure 2   **From traditional banking to open banking and open finance**

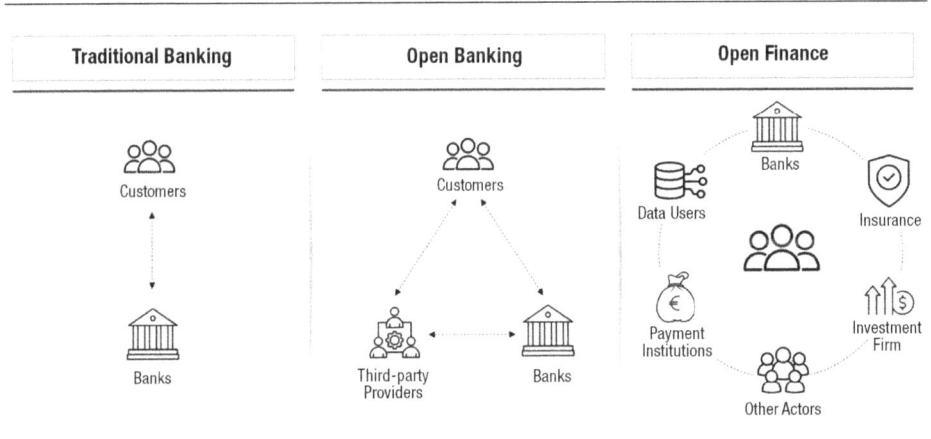

The diagram illustrates the evolution from traditional to open banking and open finance, showing the progressive expansion of data access and interaction among banks, customers, third-party providers and other financial actors in a connected ecosystem.

Source: Adapted from Deloitte

NeoBanks

Neobanks represent a significant aspect of the Fintech phenomenon, which has revolutionised the financial sector by introducing innovative approaches to the management and use of banking services. Characterised by complete digitalisation, these financial institutions operate without physical branches, offering services exclusively through online platforms and smartphone applications. Their rise is facilitated by the adoption of advanced technologies such as AI and ML, which make it possible to personalise the offer and optimise the user experience, promoting greater operational efficiency and reducing operating costs compared to traditional banks.

Neobanks are distinguished by their ability to respond quickly to the needs of modern consumers, who prefer fast, accessible and customisable banking solutions. Through the use of intuitive user interfaces and simplified processes, these digital banks appeal above all to a young, technologically savvy clientele, which seeks agile alternatives to conventional banking structures.

The absence of traditional physical infrastructure and the massive investment in technology translate into significantly lower operating costs, allowing *neobanks* to offer competitive rates and access market segments otherwise not effectively served by traditional banks. In addition, the operational agility and scalability of the solutions offered allow these entities to quickly adapt to a constantly changing environment, taking advantage of growth opportunities in an increasingly interconnected global market.

Despite numerous opportunities, *neobanks* face significant challenges, such as the need to build and maintain customer trust in a domain characterised by non-existent physical interactions. In addition, they must navigate a complex regulatory landscape while ensuring the security of user data in an era of growing privacy concerns. These challenges require a delicate balance between technological innovation and regulatory compliance, key elements for long-term success in the digital financial sector (Visconti, 2020a).

Payment systems

The payments sector within the Fintech sphere is one of the most transformative areas, capable of significantly influencing the way financial transactions are carried out (PwC, 2020). This sector encompasses a vast array of innovative solutions, ranging from mobile payment systems and digital wallets, which take advantage of the ubiquity of smartphones to enable secure and contactless purchases, to the use of blockchain technology and cryptocurrencies such as Bitcoin and Ethereum, which offer the promise of faster, safer and cheaper money transfers across borders. The integration of payment solutions directly into online platforms, known as embedded payments, is improving the digital shopping experience, reducing checkout steps and increasing sales conversions (BCG, 2023a). A crucial pillar in this area is security, with the implementation of Strong Customer Authentication (SCA) mandated by regulations such as PSD2 in the European Union, aimed at enhancing the security of online payments through the use of systems such as biometrics and 2FA (PwC, 2020). Two main market areas can be distinguished for the Fintech payments segment: retail and consumer payments and wholesale payments. Among the solutions offered are mobile wallets, P2P mobile payments, foreign currencies, real-time payments and digital currencies, which aim to simplify the process for speed, convenience and accessibility. Furthermore, the importance of mobile payment services is highlighted, which can be easily and surely implemented on devices through various methods such as NFC, QR codes and direct cardless payments (Giglio, 2021). Data protection and user privacy occupy a central position in the concerns of Fintech companies, which invest in advanced encryption technologies to preserve financial and personal information. Also distinctive of this sector is its commitment to the development of intuitive and usable user experiences, with the aim of making financial services accessible also to traditionally excluded segments of the population. This includes the provision of financial services to individuals without a bank account or living in isolated areas. Finally, the role of digital payments in supporting e-commerce and innovating the retail sector through technologies such as NFC for contactless payments highlights the cross-sectoral impact of this sector on the global economy. The relentless growth and innovation in Fintech payments continue to change the future of financial transactions, emphasising the relevance of advanced technologies, data protection and financial accessibility.

Digital lending

Peer-to-Peer (P2P) lending in the consumer and commercial sectors is one of the most relevant currents in the Fintech environment. These P2P lending models enable individuals and companies to engage in mutual lending and financing without going through traditional financial intermediaries such as banks. Such systems are distinguished by their ability to offer advantageous lending conditions, including competitive interest rates and streamlined and fast lending procedures. A distinguishing feature from traditional banking institutions is that these platforms do not act directly as a party to the loan agreement, but operate as digital intermediaries, connecting those in need of finance with potential lenders, and earning money through the collection of fees. This mode of operation exempts them from having to meet stringent capital requirements such as those imposed on banks, allowing such systems to handle potentially unlimited loan volumes. Innovation in Fintech lending is mainly manifested in the adoption of alternative credit assessment models, the use of online data sources for creditworthiness assessment, advanced data analysis for price risk management, the acceleration of lending processes and the reduction of operational costs. However, it is important to emphasise that the success of such platforms also depends on interest rate developments, an external factor over which companies have no direct control. Finally, the distinction between P2P lending and crowdfunding is crucial. Although both facilitate access to capital, crowdfunding focuses on financing specific projects, whereas P2P lending is typically geared towards debt consolidation or refinancing of credit cards (Giglio, 2021; Lee & Shin, 2018).

TechFin

TechFin designates those companies that, operating primarily in the technology sector, also extend their innovations to the financial sector and other business areas. Unlike Fintechs, which were founded with the specific aim of innovating the financial sector, TechFin are primarily technology companies that apply their advanced solutions to transform other sectors as well.

These companies employ cutting-edge technologies such as AI, ML, *blockchain* and big data analysis to develop solutions that not only increase operational efficiency but also improve security, personalisation and accessibility of services.

For instance, companies such as Google and Amazon, although primarily technology-driven, have integrated advanced financial services into their ecosystems, thus expanding their impact far beyond the original domain of technology (PwC, 2016).

The impact of TechFin is considerable and diverse, influencing how payments are handled, the security of transactions and even the creation of new business models that integrate financial services directly through technology platforms. These companies are not only bringing about significant changes in financial services but are also setting new standards for technological integration in traditional industries.

The TechFin concept thus represents an emerging trend in which technology does not simply act as a support to traditional operations but has an impact on the evolution of new solutions and operating models that extend across various sectors, with a particularly significant influence in the financial sector (EY).

TechFin, however, pose a significant challenge to the current regulatory framework. These companies often operate without being subject to specific regulations until they require authorisation for financial activities. This creates a situation of regulatory arbitrage, where TechFin can exploit their position to compete with traditional financial intermediaries, which incur significant compliance costs (Consob, 2018). The current regulatory framework is based on *an entity-based* approach, which is insufficient to address the specific operational peculiarities and risks associated with TechFin. Such activities, being unsupervised, may entail risks of fraud, conflicts of interest and privacy and data security issues. Moreover, the possibility of regulatory arbitrage, where companies may choose to operate in jurisdictions with lighter regulations, further amplifies these risks. Consequently, there is a need to develop new regulatory paradigms and implement internationally coordinated actions to ensure more effective and uniform supervision of these new entrants in the financial sector. These realities tend to develop in three stages: (1) in the first stage, a technology company uses the data it collects to improve its services and may send this data to traditional financial institutions or Fintech startups; (2) in the second stage, TechFin use this data to make informed business decisions, e.g., by improving risk management in lending; (3) in the third stage, some TechFin start offering financial services directly, competing directly with banks and other regulated entities. During this process, many TechFin reach advanced stages of their operations without being subject to regulation, raising significant concerns about financial stability and consumer protection (Social Science Research Network, 2017)

The rapid evolution of TechFins and their ability to operate outside traditional financial regulations pose a number of complex challenges for regulators. It is crucial to develop and implement new regulatory strategies that can balance technological innovation with the need to protect consumers and ensure the stability of the global financial system.

Financing solutions

The financing solutions segment in the Fintech context offers a set of innovative options for financing companies and startups, exploiting digital technologies to expand access to capital. These models are distinguished by their ability to adapt to the needs of different types of investors and companies, considering methodologies ranging from crowdfunding, club deals and the involvement of institutional investors (Visconti, 2020a).

- Crowdfunding: Fintech platforms dedicated to crowdfunding allow networks of individuals to evaluate and support the development of new products, media content and innovative ideas, with the aim of raising funds. The crowdfunding process is articulated through the interaction of three main actors: the project initiator, i.e., the entrepreneur seeking funding, the contributors, who may be motivated by interest in the cause or project in question, and the intermediary organisation, which facilitates dialogue and cooperation between the contributors and the project initiator. The latter plays a crucial role, as it gives contributors access to detailed information about different initiatives and funding opportunities for the development of products or services. There are several business models in the crowdfunding industry, among which reward-based, donation-based and equity-based models stand out (Giglio, 2021; Lee & Shin, 2018).
- The reward-based model has established itself as a particularly attractive option for fundraising, appealing to thousands of small businesses and projects. If interest is charged on the amount raised through this method, the borrower has the option of determining the interest rate he or she deems most appropriate, while at the same time undertaking to guarantee repayment within a predetermined time frame. In return for the financing received, the company normally offers a reward to the supporters of the project.
- Donation-based crowdfunding, on the other hand, represents a mechanism through which funds can be raised for charitable projects by inviting donors to contribute financially. In this case, the donor does not receive any material compensation, but rather a form of non-monetary recognition.
- The equity-based model proves to be particularly advantageous for small- and medium-sized enterprises (SMEs), as the rigidity of the requirements imposed by traditional banks in terms of capital ratios makes bank financing less accessible to them than in the past. This mode of crowdfunding allows entrepreneurs to attract investors interested in acquiring shares in their startups or other small private companies (Giglio, 2021; Lee & Shin, 2018).

Through the use of digital platforms and flexible business models, these solutions not only facilitate access to financing but also promote a more open and participative investment culture, characterised by diversification of opportunities and the breaking down of traditional barriers in the world of venture capital (Visconti, 2020a).

Insurtech

The insurtech sector is showing a significant evolution driven by the blending of cutting-edge technologies and the traditional world of insurance. With the emergence of technology trends such as AI, blockchain, ML and the increasing adoption of cloud-based solutions, insurance companies are harnessing these innovations to revolutionise operations, from underwriting to claims management, and to deliver an enhanced customer experience (Deloitte, 2023).

In particular, 2023 sees Insurtech focusing on enriching the customer experience, with companies seeking to differentiate themselves in a saturated market where price competition is increasingly fierce. Consequently, there is an emerging need to establish competitiveness through improved services that emphasise the user experience (Insurtech Insights, 2023). Indeed, in insurance Fintech business models, companies work to enable a more direct relationship between the insurer and the customer. They employ data analysis to calculate and match risk and, as the pool of potential customers grows, products are offered to meet their needs (Giglio, 2021).

The use of APIs is becoming a key pillar for making connections in the insurance ecosystem, promoting the integration of micro-insurance products in various markets and driving product simplification and customer- and service-focused engagement. This trend highlights the growing role of the insurance industry within the broader technology ecosystem, with an emphasis on value creation through technological innovation and the formation of strategic partnerships (Insurtech Insights, 2023).

Furthermore, innovative integration of cryptocurrency payments and insurance solutions for DeFi assets is occurring, marking an expansion of technologies that enable alternative payment methods. This shift towards unconventional payment solutions reflects continued innovation and the exploration of new opportunities in the insurance industry (Insurtech Insights, 2023).

The insurtech sector is therefore undergoing a digitisation-driven transformation, with insurance companies adopting emerging technologies to improve their operations and offer better customer experiences. This evolution could ensure not only increased efficiency and personalisation of insurance services, but also the evolution of new business models in the context of a rapidly changing market.

Regtech

The Regtech segment shows a remarkable growth phase while experiencing significant challenges stemming from the evolving regulatory and technological landscape. There is evidence of a wide range of applications for Regtech technologies, from credit risk analysis to security IT, underlining the growing importance of such solutions for banks and the financial sector in general (Thomson Reuters, 2023).

Regtech could ensure a significant improvement in risk management and customer experience for financial institutions by automating the monitoring and analysis of compliance data in real time. However, the risks associated with over-reliance on technology, potential data security hazards and regulatory divergences between jurisdictions are also highlighted (Finance Magnate, 2023).

The use of advanced technologies such as AI and ML is expected to see significant growth in the Regtech sector. These technologies have the potential to revolutionise *compliance* by automating manual processes and improving data analysis to identify regulatory violations. In addition, blockchain emerges as a promising technology to create secure and transparent transaction records, useful for demonstrating regulatory compliance (Finance Magnate, 2023).

Overall, the Regtech sector is at an evolutionary stage, with the potential to transform compliance and risk management in the financial sector.

Wealthtech

The Wealthtech segment within Fintech focuses on innovating wealth management through technology, offering services ranging from automated advice to personal financial planning tools and wealth management solutions. This field uses advanced technologies such as AI, big data and predictive analytics to offer personalised services to a wide range of clients, including those previously excluded from traditional wealth management services. One of the best-known Fintech business models for wealth management is automated wealth managers (*robo-advisors*) that provide advice. These *robo-advisors* employ algorithms to suggest a mix of assets to invest in based on client preferences and investment characteristics. The model described benefits from changing demographics and consumer behaviour that favour automated, passive investment strategies and a simple pricing structure (Giglio, 2021). The evolution of Wealthtech is driven by the demand for accessibility, efficiency and personalisation in financial services, with an increasing focus on cross-access to investment instruments. However, the industry faces challenges such as complex regulation and data security concerns. Despite these considerations, the digital transformation in *wealth management* is expected to make financial services more inclusive and tailored to individual needs, marking a significant step forward in wealth management and financial planning (Capgemini, 2023).

Capital markets

New business paradigms in financial technology are inspired by a broad set of capital market sectors, considering areas such as investment, currency exchange, trading, risk management and market analysis. One of the most promising segments within the capital market, as far as Fintech innovation is concerned, is the trading sector. Fintech platforms dedicated to trading provide investors with a digital platform through which mutual connections can be established, aimed at discussing and sharing insights and knowledge. These platforms also make it possible to set orders to buy and sell commodities and equities, as well as provide advanced tools for monitoring financial risks in real time. Another significant area within capital market-related Fintech business models concerns foreign exchange transactions. Traditionally, this type of service has been the monopoly of large financial institutions. However, innovations in the financial sector are greatly reducing the barriers to entry and costs associated with foreign exchange transactions for individuals and SMEs globally. Through the use of mobile applications, users have the ability to view currency quotes in real time and send and receive funds in different currencies, providing security and immediacy in transactions (Giglio, 2021; Lee & Shin, 2018).

Micro-Fintech

The Micro-Fintech concept considers the use of advanced digital technologies to deliver a range of *tailor-made* financial services including micro-credits, small deposits, micro-insurance and financial advice. This approach is crucial not only to open doors to previously inaccessible financial opportunities but also to promote broader financial inclusion. Tangible examples of Micro-Fintech range from the implementation of *mobile banking* in developing countries—where access to financial services via mobile devices transforms the management of personal and business finances—to the adoption of digital platforms that simplify obtaining credit or taking out insurance policies (Visconti, 2020a).

Proptech

The term Proptech, or Property Technology, is delineated as the integration of technological advancements and innovations derived from the Fintech sector within the real estate sphere. This definition considers a wide variety of technological solutions aimed at renewing and optimising the processes intrinsic to the real estate sector, considering aspects ranging from buying, selling and renting real estate, to managing real estate assets, through valuation, financing and investment in the sector. Solutions include online platforms dedicated to real estate transactions, specialised real estate management software, tools for in-depth analysis of market data, the use of virtual reality to facilitate remote real estate visits, automated property valuation systems and real estate-specific crowdfunding platforms. The ultimate aim is to instil greater efficiency, transparency and ease of access to real estate-related processes through the application of digital technologies aimed at significantly improving the user experience. The aim is therefore to reduce operating costs, speed up real estate transactions and increase the availability and accessibility of market-relevant information (Visconti, 2020a).

2 Empirical Analysis of the Fintech Sector

As mentioned above, the first definition of Fintech can be traced back to 1972. Since then, the number of technologies and the level of innovation has seen an exponential improvement, making Fintech an increasingly topical subject. In order to understand the dynamics, drivers and trends defining and influencing Fintech, an empirical analysis at both global and regional levels is proposed in the following paragraphs.

Global scenario

Over the past decade, the financial technology (Fintech) sector has undergone a profound transformation, influenced by technological advances, innovation and changes in consumer behaviour. This period of change has led to the rise of several Fintech companies in major geographies. As shown in **Chart 3** (Statista, 2024a), from the end of 2018 to January 2024, the number of companies increased by 147%, growing from 12,131 to 29,955. The region that showed the largest increase was EMEA (Europe, Middle East and Africa), with an increase of approximately 206% during the years of analysis. However, the Americas (North America, Central America, South America and the Caribbean) stands out as the region with the highest number of companies in each of the years analysed, showing a number of 13,100 Fintech companies in January 2024, an increase of almost 1,500 companies compared to the figure for May 2023.

Estimates regarding the evolution of the sector suggest a growth of the market globally, with a CAGR 2022–2028 of +15%, and a change in the weights of the geographical macro-areas within the global context (McKinsey & Company, 2023b). America, particularly North America, is expected to maintain its relevance in the Fintech sphere in the coming years, showing a share of global revenues of more than 40% until 2028 (McKinsey & Company, 2023b). Other geographical areas are expected to account for a smaller, but growing share of global revenues. In particular, Europe and Emerging Countries (Latin America, Africa, Middle East and Asia excluding China) are expected to increase their market share in the period 2022–2028 (**Charts 4 and 5**; McKinsey & Company, 2023b).

Chart 3   Number of global Fintechs by region 2018–2024

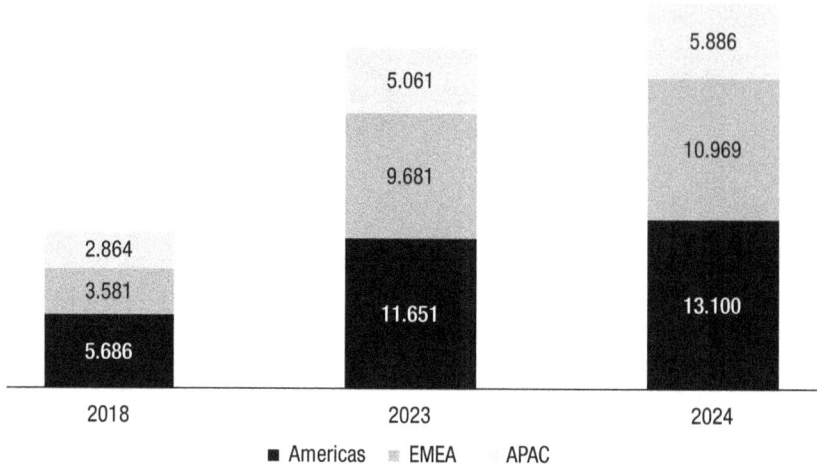

The 2023 data refer to May 2023, the 2024 data to January 2024.
The stacked bar chart shows the global rise in Fintech firms from 2018 to 2024, with totals growing from 12,131 to 29,955. The Americas lead in number, while EMEA records the highest growth rate, reflecting global expansion and regional acceleration.

Source: Own elaboration based on data from Statista, 2024a

Chart 4   Percentage of global Fintech revenues by region 2022–2028

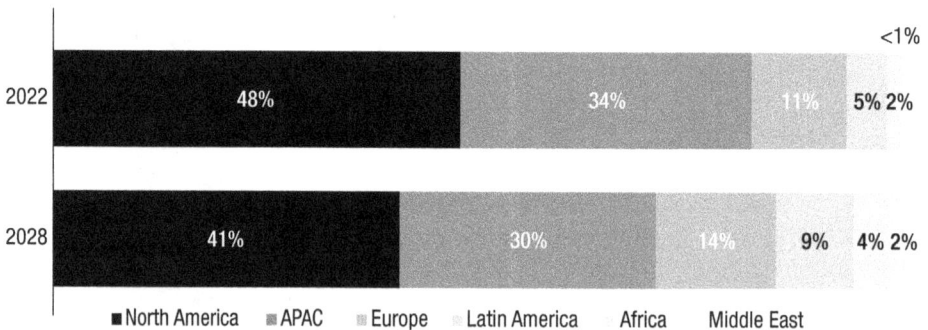

The stacked bar chart shows projected changes in global Fintech revenues from 2022 to 2028. While North America and Europe see declining shares, Latin America, Africa and the Middle East show growth, indicating a gradual shift towards emerging markets.

Source: Own elaboration based on data from McKinsey & Company, 2023b

Chart 5   Percentage of revenues Developed Countries vs Emerging Countries 2022–2028

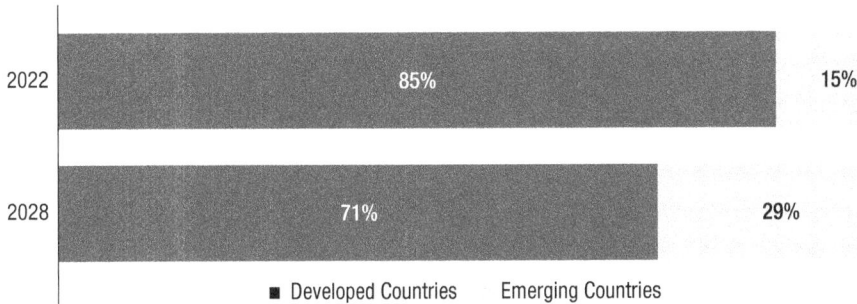

The stacked bar chart highlights the projected shift in Fintech revenue distribution from 2022 to 2028, with emerging countries increasing their share from 15% to 29%, signalling a growing contribution of these markets to global Fintech growth.

Source: Own elaboration based on data from McKinsey & Company, 2023

Investments

According to CB Insights estimates (CB Insights, 2023), global equity financing in the Fintech sector contracted to $39 billion in 2023 from $79 billion in 2022 and a peak of $141 billion in 2021 (Chart 6). Despite this slowdown, 2022 is still the second-best year in terms of both deal value and deal volume (6,108 compared to 6,172 in 2021). Factors such as geopolitical uncertainty, rising interest rates, inflation, downward pressure on valuations and the slowdown in the IPO market were found to be the main determinants of this regression (Statista, 2023a).

As shown in Chart 7, in recent years, America (particularly the United States) has led investments in the Fintech sector, accounting for about 69% of all investments (VC, PE and M&A) made globally in 2023 (KPMG, 2024). Europe emerged as the second largest geographic region for investments in Fintech, with the exception of 2022, when Asia-Pacific recorded a year-over-year increase of about $21 billion, in contrast to the other regions, for a total of about $51 billion invested in the sector.

Unicorns

The growth in the number of Fintech companies, investments from multiple sources and rapid technological development in recent years have led to the formation of unicorns, i.e., startups that have reached a valuation of $1 billion or more. In particular, the United States dominates the 2023 ranking (Chart 8), with a total of around 134 companies (Statista, 2023b), reflecting the country's predominant position in financial-technological innovation in terms of number of companies (Chart 3), share of total

Chart 6   **Global annual equity funding and deal count**

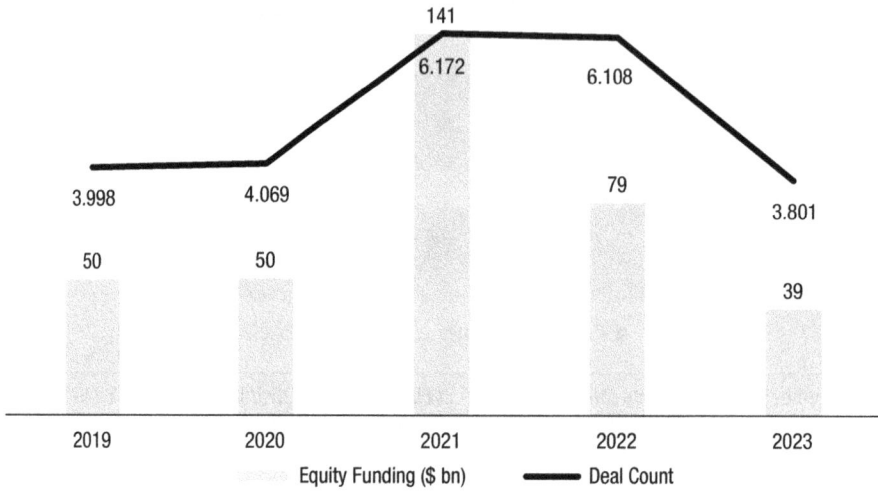

The combo chart shows a decline in global Fintech equity funding and deal count from the 2021 peak. Despite a strong 2022, 2023 marks a contraction driven by macroeconomic factors, including inflation, rate hikes and reduced IPO activity.

Source: Own elaboration based on data from CB Insights, 2023

Chart 7   **Fintech investments by region 2019–2023 ($ billion)**

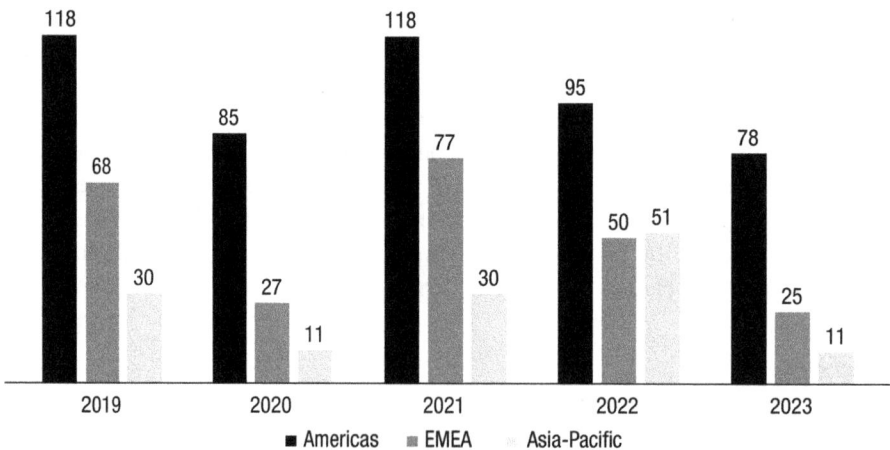

The bar chart shows regional Fintech investments from 2019 to 2023. The Americas consistently lead, with Europe in the second position, except in 2022 when Asia-Pacific surpassed EMEA with a notable increase, reflecting shifting investment dynamics.

Source: Own elaboration based on data from KPMG, 2024

Chart 8   **Top 10 countries with the most Fintech unicorns 2023**

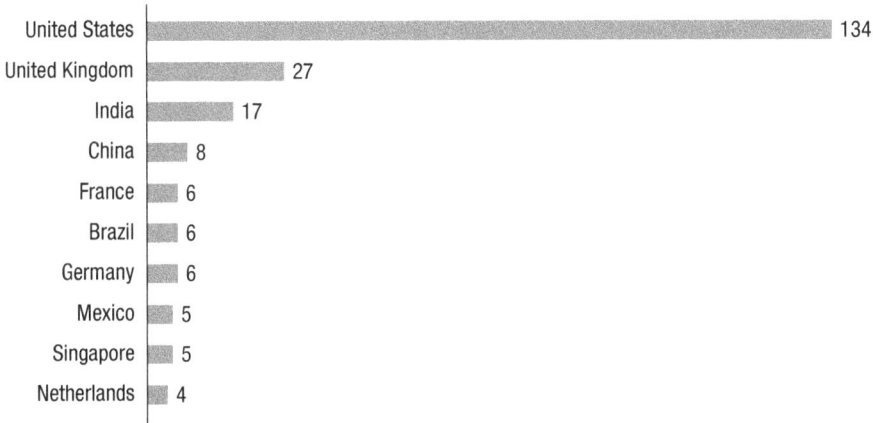

The bar chart ranks the top 10 countries by number of Fintech unicorns in 2023. The United States leads with 134 firms, followed by the United Kingdom and India. The data reflect regional disparities in Fintech maturity and innovation ecosystems.

Source: Own elaboration based on data from Statista

revenues (Chart 4) and investments in the sector (Chart 7). The UK follows the ranking with 27 unicorns, also indicating a strong presence in the sector and a clear lead over other European countries. India, on the other hand, ranks third with 17 companies, suggesting a growing financial technology innovation ecosystem (Statista, 2023b).

Drivers

The differences found across countries and geographic areas in terms of the number of Fintech companies, capital attraction and number of unicorns, raises the need to investigate the drivers that have enabled the sector to develop more. To investigate the potential explanations for these differences between countries, the structural characteristics of national economies were investigated with reference to the regulatory quality of countries, the level of development of financial markets and the innovation capacity of the same (Cornelli et al., 2021).

As the Fintech sector is relatively young and lacks established best practices, the presence of a structured regulatory environment could be particularly relevant. Moreover, the size of financial markets and access to finance in general go hand in hand with increased capital raising and business creation and may favour Fintech activities as they facilitate effective *matching* between investors and firms, being particularly relevant for fast-growing sectors. Finally, a more innovative environment is generally conducive to financing startups, as the positive knowledge externalities increase the returns on business formation and innovation. Since many Fintech firms

Chart 9   Key structural factors behind Fintech funding differences across countries

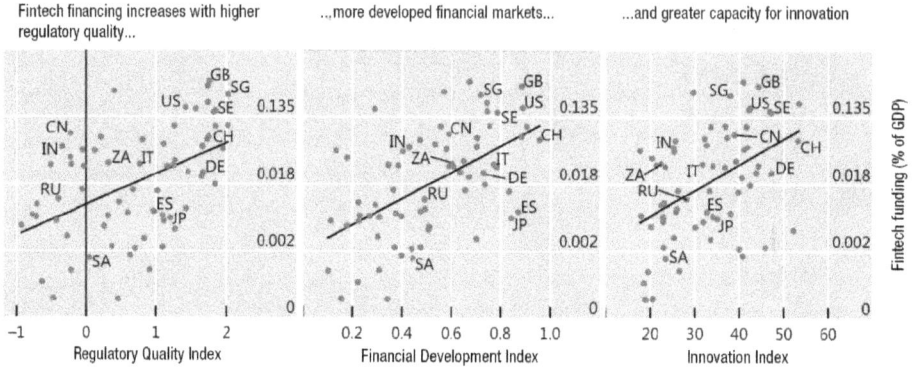

Each point corresponds to the national average for the period 2010–2019 of 68 countries. Fintech financing relative to GDP is subject to a winsorisation technique that considers percentiles 1 and 99. Fintech financing relative to GDP is shown on a logarithmic scale.

The scatter plots show that Fintech funding (% of GDP) is positively correlated with regulatory quality, financial market development and innovation capacity—key structural factors explaining cross-country differences in Fintech growth.

Source: Cornelli et al., 2021 (available at www.bis.org)

base their business models on new technologies, such as AI and *mobile technologies*, a national research capacity in these fields may be a key factor for the development of the sector (Cornelli et al., 2021).

As shown in **Chart 9**, when taken individually, these variables (development of the regulatory environment, size of national financial markets and innovation capacity of a country) are positively correlated with investments in Fintech (Cornelli et al., 2021).

Among the major markets, the United States and the United Kingdom rank high in the quality of financial market regulation and development, while they, as well as several European countries and China, score relatively high in innovation capacity (Cornelli et al., 2021).

From a comparative perspective, it can be seen that this result suggests an explanation of what emerged from previous analyses, with particular reference to **Chart 8** about the countries with the highest number of unicorns.

Prospective trends

The prevailing trends in the Fintech sector can be categorised into three main areas:

1. Market trends: concerning the evolution of the sector and its various components, examining the determinants of performance;

2. Trends related to technological developments: concerning emerging technologies that significantly influence and will influence the growth of Fintech;
3. Regulatory trends: a summary of developments, particularly at EU level, concerning new regulations and directives that could impact the Fintech industry.

Market trends

As far as market trends and the performance of the Fintech industry are concerned, there is particularly significant growth in three areas: neobanking, embedded finance and digital payments. These areas have shown, and are expected to continue to show, significant growth in the coming years.

An analysis of Statista's data (Chart 10) shows that the European neo-banking sector is expected to grow at a compound annual growth rate (CAGR) of 45% with reference to transaction value in the period between 2017 and 2028 (Statista, 2024c).

This segment is also configured as a driving force in the Fintech sector, as it is capable of driving the growth of *digital banking*. The market under analysis, in fact, is characterised by growing competitiveness, corroborated by the presence of consolidated entities and new emerging companies, among which Revolut and N26 stand out. In support of these considerations, we highlight data on the increase in the penetration rate of *online banking* in Europe, which rose by almost 20 percentage points between 2017 and the current period. Moreover, this rate is expected to grow steadily, reaching a share of 70% of the population (Chart 11).

Chart 10   **Expected development of the Neobanking sector 2024–2028 ($ billion)**

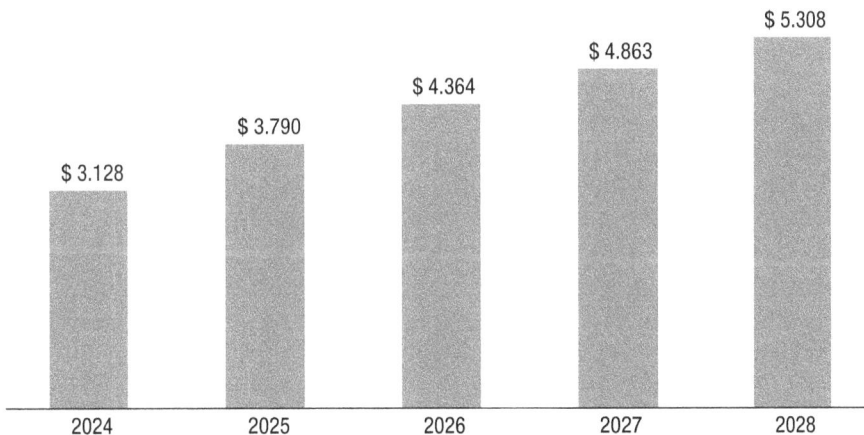

The bar chart illustrates the projected growth of the neobanking sector in Europe from 2024 to 2028, with transaction value expected to rise steadily from $3.1 to over $5.3 billion, reflecting strong market expansion and digital adoption trends.

Source: Own elaboration based on data from Statista, 2024c

Chart 11   Online banking penetration rate 2017–2028

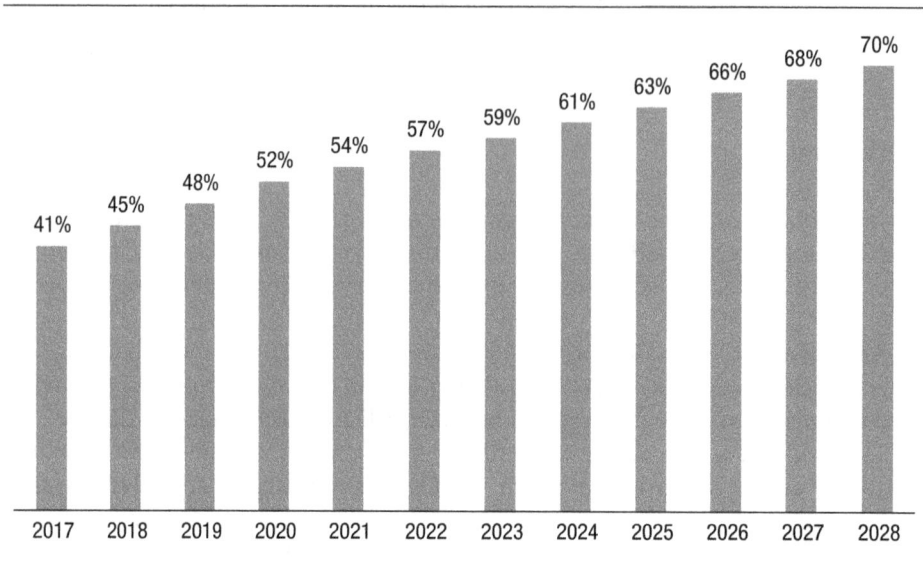

The bar chart shows the steady rise in online banking penetration in Europe, increasing from 41% in 2017 to a projected 70% by 2028. This trend reflects growing digital adoption, driving competition and innovation in the Fintech and digital banking sectors.

Source: Own elaboration based on data from Statista, 2024c

A further area of significant expansion is integrated finance, or *embedded finance*, which represents the integration of financial services and products or services of a non-financial nature. An example is an *e-commerce* company that offers its customers the possibility of opening a *branded* current account through a banking partner, directly on the company's platform. This is part of the broader context of open banking, which promotes the simplification of financial processes through the integration of heterogeneous financial services, facilitated by the sharing of consumers' banking and credit data. In the area of integrated finance, significant impetus comes from the widespread development of APIs, technologies that allow developers to incorporate banking services into *software* applications. Despite this, there remain concerns about the security of these practices, an issue that European authorities are carefully addressing, as will be discussed in more detail in the regulatory section below (7 Regulation).

Finally, closely related to the above, the digital payments sector is also growing rapidly, with a significant increase in the number of users year on year. The latter, in fact, is expected to grow steadily until 2028. According to Statista's current estimates, a 32% increase in the number of users is expected between 2023 and 2028, reaching 675 million users of these services. This figure stands out particularly when compared to the number of users in the *neo-banking* sector, which is expected to attract around 127 million users by the end of the forecast period analysed (Chart 12).

Chart 12   Expected number of users of digital payments and neobanking services 2023–2028 (million people)

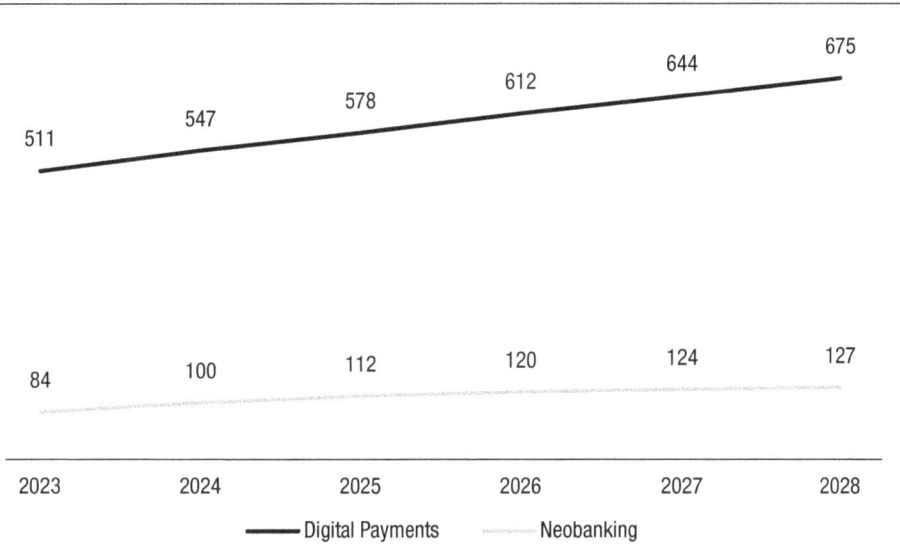

The line chart shows the projected growth in users of digital payments and neobanking services from 2023 to 2028. Digital payments are expected to reach 675 million users, while neobanking will grow more moderately, reaching 127 million by 2028.

Source: Own elaboration based on data from Statista, 2024c

Among the driving factors behind the popularity of digital payments is the rise of the Buy Now Pay Later (BNPL) segment, characterised by the presence of major players such as Klarna, Scalapay, Alma, Afterpay, Divido and Clearpay.

Although each segment among those analysed presents its own performance, the growth trends observed in the European Fintech industry share some common elements.

The first element characterising this growth is the growing interest of consumers in Fintech. A survey conducted by McKinsey in 2021 identified convenience in terms of both cost (32%) and ease of access to services (32%), as well as the speed with which the Fintech sector able to provide financial services compared to traditional players (30%) as the main reasons behind this *trend*.

In addition, increasing *smartphone* penetration rates and wide access to the Internet are improving the accessibility of Fintech solutions, stimulating demand for these services.

Finally, a key role was played by the Covid-19 pandemic, which accelerated the digitisation of services such as payments and investments, as consumers were forced to use these services remotely. The acceleration of digitisation that occurred during the pandemic has persisted thereafter, signalling a change in consumer preferences (McKinsey & Company, 2022).

Trends in technological developments

The technological innovations that are driving the evolution of the Fintech industry include AI, biometric technologies and APIs.

Artificial Intelligence

Given the vast amount of data that characterises most Fintech solutions and the technological basis on which many services are based, AI is particularly useful for providing support to the industry. In particular, in the Fintech sphere, AI sees applications in areas such as risk management, fraud prevention and document processing. Among the main benefits of using AI are the reduction of operational costs by streamlining processes and the personalisation of the banking experience for customers, which can improve the quality of service offered. The most recent disruptive innovation in this field is generative Artificial Intelligence (Gen AI), with well-known examples such as ChatGPT, Gemini and Microsoft Copilot. The introduction of these technologies has led to the evolution of various industries that are analysing how to deploy them most effectively. In the banking sector, according to an analysis by Deloitte, the implementation of Gen AI could lead to productivity gains of 27%–35% for *front-office* employees, including *marketing*, sales and customer service departments. Some banks, such as ABN Amro, are conducting pilot projects to understand how best to apply Gen AI, using it to summarise and analyse customer conversations. At the same time, Swedish startup Klarna has provided every employee with access to Gen AI language templates, encouraging experimentation with the technology to receive *feedback* on which functions could benefit most from its use.

In general, the opportunities arising from AI for the Fintech world are manifold. AI can be used to integrate *deepfake* detection techniques into anti-fraud systems to improve, for instance, the level of security in the area of digital payments. Furthermore, AI can be useful to improve employee *training* programmes on *phishing* and other data compromise techniques. However, the introduction of this technology presents various risks such as problems with authentication, which grow together with developments in *deepfake* technologies. *Chatbots* also give rise to privacy and data leakage problems.

Biometric technologies

Biometric technologies, also based on AI, represent another area of likely disruptive impact in the Fintech sector. These technologies have made significant progress in the fight against bank fraud. In the Nordic countries, many banking intermediaries have gained the trust of customers through the use of systems such as BankID and Interac Verified Systems. A direct application of these technologies manifests itself in the streamlining of credit-granting procedures through a faster and more automated *underwriting* process.

Application Programming Interfaces (APIs)

As far as APIs are concerned, they constitute a fundamental technology that is influencing the evolution of the Fintech industry. APIs are communication protocols that facilitate the interaction and sharing of information between different *software* components, such as a bank's internal *server* and mobile devices. Such technologies offer convenient and rapid access to financial services, and benefits from their use include reduced costs, data sharing between different entities, and the ability for banks to expand their services. APIs are experiencing robust and steady growth and, according to an October 2023 McKinsey survey, 88% of organisations believe APIs have become more relevant in the last two years, and over 81% consider them a strategic IT priority, with major banks devoting an average of 14% of their IT budgets to API-related initiatives (McKinsey, 2023).

Trends in regulation

In the regulatory arena, developments are crucial for the Fintech sector, as they affect the way consumers can interact with an industry that, while innovative, stems from the traditionally highly regulated financial services sector. The goal of regulators is to ensure that Fintech companies operate on an equal footing with traditional financial institutions, ensuring orderly access to these technologies to foster their development.

The Financial Data Access framework

One of the main regulatory trends in Europe is Open Finance, a more advanced concept than open banking. In recent years, significant efforts have been made to introduce open banking, a paradigm that, as seen above, involves the sharing of data between banks, consumers and companies offering financial services, in order to guarantee a more complete and faster service to the customer. Open Finance, however, extends this concept by promoting the creation of a collaborative system based on customer centricity and data sharing between various actors, such as banks, insurance companies, asset management companies, payment companies and other actors that use financial data to offer services.

The successful implementation of Open Finance is intrinsically linked to the presence of a regulatory regime that facilitates its support and regulation. Accordingly, EU lawmakers are currently drafting the Financial Data Access (FIDA) framework, a regulation designed to promote data sharing while simultaneously ensuring the security of this practice. This *framework* builds on the progress already made with the PSD2, which is currently being revised and included in a new iteration, PSD3, which will culminate in the Payment Services Regulation (PSR). Unlike previous European directives, such as PSD2 and PSD3, which set general objectives for member states, regulations such as the PSR are more detailed and binding. The PSR aims to provide greater clarity in the development of a common European interface for data access in the context of open banking. For example, under FIDA, data holders such as banks, insurance companies and investment funds will be obliged to share this information with users, i.e., companies that provide services based on this data, subject to the consent of the customers. Data subject to sharing will include deposits, loans, mortgages, investments and insurance policies.

The introduction of Open Finance poses several challenges for financial institutions. Firstly, the timeline for implementation will be tight, as the new data sharing scheme will have to be complied with within 18 months of the adoption of the regulation. Moreover, FIDA will require the sharing of a broad spectrum of financial data, necessitating the development of a wide range of APIs. Intermediaries will have to manage a large volume of data and will be responsible for its protection, security and privacy. Finally, intermediaries are likely to face an incremental level of competition, resulting from more players gaining access to strategic customer information.

In this context, the opportunities for intermediaries are considerable: The advent of Open Finance will enable banks and other financial institutions to monetise the data provided. These institutions will be able to offer new products and services and benefit from cross-selling by integrating services provided by third parties into their own offerings. Moreover, the benefits will also extend to customers, who will be able to enjoy a more personalised service tailored to their specific financial needs.

The Artificial Intelligence Act

AI has attracted wide debate at European level in recent years. In response to this growing interest, on 13 March 2024, the European Union adopted the Artificial Intelligence Act (AI Act), the first regulatory framework specifically dedicated to managing the risks associated with AI. This legislation aims to establish precise rules on the specific uses of AI, with the intention of easing the administrative and financial burdens on companies, with a particular focus on SMEs.

The regulation of AI is of paramount importance for the Fintech industry, as many of the services and technological innovations are based on various applications of AI. The regulatory clarity introduced by the AI Act is therefore crucial to ensure that Fintech entities can continue to develop and implement AI-based solutions in a responsible and safe manner, thus contributing to the sustainable growth of the entire industry.

The Digital Identity Framework

In the context of digital wallets and payments, the European Union is actively working on the development of the Digital Identity Framework, which builds on the former eIDAS framework. The primary objective of this regulatory initiative is to enhance trust in digital transactions by improving the effectiveness of online services and e-commerce platforms. The deployment of the Digital Identity Framework aims to remove the barriers that currently exist in relation to digital identity between different Member States. This will enable smoother cross-border interaction, facilitating access to and use of digital services in a more integrated and homogeneous European context, while ensuring a high level of security and protection of users' personal data.

The European Payments Initiative (EPI)

The European Union is currently developing an advanced solution for instant digital payments, known as the European Payments Initiative (EPI). This new payments scheme is designed to be used by consumers and merchants across Europe for a wide range of transactions. The initiative is expected to be implemented initially as a pilot project in the countries of Belgium, France and Germany, which together account for more than half of the *retail* cashless payments on the continent (McKinsey & Company, 2022).

Digital Euro

In the European context, especially at the political level, a debate is currently under way on the proposal to introduce an innovative digital single currency, called the Digital Euro. This proposal represents a crucial intersection between technological development, strategic autonomy and the protection of individual rights. However, despite the innovativeness of this initiative, in April 2024, the European Parliament decided to postpone further discussions regarding the Digital Euro to the next legislative term, so any concrete progress in this area is only expected in the coming years (Freshfields, 2024).

Challenges

The financial sector is currently facing a period of marked metamorphosis, marked by the emergence of innovations that are rewriting the paradigm of traditional financial services. Innovations in the Fintech sector emerging as potential catalysts for a structural renewal of the financial ecosystem, with their influence tending to intensify in parallel with the evolution of the sector itself. The current horizon identifies six cardinal challenges: investment management, customer administration, regulatory compliance, integration of new technologies, data security and privacy protection and risk control. Both rising Fintech firms and established financial institutions must navigate these challenges in an era of accelerating technological change and disruptive innovation (Lee & Shin, 2018).

The challenge of investment management

In today's increasingly competitive business landscape, the ability to accurately evaluate Fintech projects is particularly important. Without meticulous portfolio management, financial companies are exposed to the risk of being overwhelmed by the broad spectrum of Fintech technologies. Identifying profitable initiatives is a major challenge, and it is currently too early to envisage a portfolio of projects that can guarantee competitive and profitable outcomes. Financial institutions are faced with a dichotomous choice: They can either opt for investments in Fintech solutions, engaging in direct competition with startups in the sector, or they can pursue joint investments with such startups. The latter approach would allow institutions to stay on the cutting edge of technological innovation without the commitment of in-house development. As an example, a Fintech startup operating in the robo-advisory sector could benefit from the financial institution's expertise in modelling and analytics. At the same time, the financial institution could gain an in-depth understanding of customer preferences regarding Fintech services, as well as understand the underlying cost structures and potential revenue streams (Lee & Shin, 2018).

The challenge of customer management

In the competitive arena of customer attraction and retention, the crucial need for strategic customer relationship management emerges. The latter tend to use a plurality of services provided by different Fintech companies to meet diversified financial needs; for instance, they use Satispay for digital business transactions and Paypal for monetary transfers between individuals. Therefore, it is essential for Fintech companies to gain an in-depth understanding of their market segment and aspire to excel in providing quality services in that niche. In such a dynamic environment, word of mouth can play a decisive role in the success of a Fintech startup, timely and diligent resolution of customer issues is of paramount importance. Robo-advisors are designed to provide customised and continuous services to a broad spectrum of clients while minimising costs. Nevertheless, the human element retains a significant role in investment services. Providing a personalised experience without excessively impacting on operating costs proves to be a challenging, yet decisive objective for achieving and consolidating a stable customer base. Fintech firms are also called upon to respond effectively to the needs of generations X and Y, who are characterised by a higher technological propensity, thus requiring greater accessibility, convenience and customisation of products. Following the addition of Fintech channels, the presence of an integrated *client management* service (Lee & Shin, 2018) will therefore become even more important.

The regulatory challenge

Fintech financial institutions and startups face a number of regulatory challenges, including compliance with capital requirements, implementation of anti-money laundering (AML) protocols and implementation of data privacy and security measures. For traditional financial institutions, the financial burden to comply with these regulatory requirements and to compete with dynamic new entrants in the Fintech space is considerable. Existing regulations differ in their application depending on the nature of the financial services provided by the two types of entities. To exemplify, traditional banks are generally subject to a fractional reserve system with stringent criteria on how to provide credit based on the capital they hold, criteria that may not correspond in the context of Fintech startups, such as P2P lending platforms, which do not lend in the traditional form. In a scenario where regulatory evolutions tend not to keep pace with sectoral innovation, it is essential that Fintech firms maintain a high level of attention to possible regulatory evolutions that might affect their operations and identify effective strategies to manage and contain the potential risks arising from such changes (Lee & Shin, 2018).

The challenge of technology integration

Technology integration is a crucial element in ensuring continuity of customer service. Many Fintech initiatives make use of emerging technologies, which introduce significant challenges in integrating with existing systems. In addition to their own development initiatives, banks should establish partnerships and joint ventures with Fintech startups through corporate venture capital (CVC) and incubation programmes. Such synergies would allow traditional financial institutions to actively participate in external companies focused on the development of cutting-edge Fintech technologies. Nevertheless, the absence of a carefully outlined integration plan may make conventional banking processes incompatible with the emerging technologies and new business models that financial institutions aim to implement (Lee & Shin, 2018).

The challenge of security and privacy

The regulatory landscape's focus on data security and privacy is increasing. The risks are particularly acute for Fintech applications, where critical data stored on mobile devices are vulnerable to loss, theft or compromise. Fintech companies should therefore develop appropriate measures to protect sensitive customer data. Moreover, as trust plays an important role in the adoption of new technologies, it is in the interest of Fintechs to keep security and privacy a top priority. Ongoing collaboration between regulators, consumer protection organisations and Fintech companies aims to ensure the security services and value-added experiences for consumers (Lee & Shin, 2018).

The challenge of risk management

Fintech startups face varying financial and regulatory risks depending on their field of specialisation. For instance, smaller startups in the lending or mortgage sector expose themselves to higher counterparty risks than larger traditional competitors due to lower cash reserves. Startups active in robo-advisory asset management may expose their clients to significant financial risks and incur significant liability for losses caused by algorithmic malfunctions. Consequently, it becomes imperative for Fintech companies to place risk management at the core of their operational strategies, on a par with technological management. Moreover, considering that a considerable number of Fintechs were established in the wake of the 2008 financial crisis, it is imperative that these companies acquire a thorough understanding of their liquidity and interest risk (Lee & Shin, 2018).

Finally, it is particularly important to emphasise that the global economic scenario is characterised by different factors than in the past. Firstly, different interest rates than those known so far are expected, with a significant impact on market dynamics, access to credit and investment decisions. Secondly, *incumbent* companies, already established in the market, have shown considerable strength and responsiveness in recent years. Fintech startups seeking to revolutionise the financial sector are now competing with established institutions that have strengthened their positions and successfully innovated. Finally, venture capitalists are expected to adopt more selective approaches in the future. Investors will be more cautious and precise in assessing investment opportunities, seeking to minimise risks and maximise returns. This increased selectivity is likely to be due to the need to adapt to a more uncertain and complex economic scenario and a rapidly and constantly improving technological environment.

Regional scenario

America

Total Fintech investments in the Americas saw a contraction from $95.4 billion in 2022 to $78.3 billion in 2023, while the number of Fintech deals decreased in parallel from 3,467 to 2,136 (Chart 13). The United States attracted the most Fintech deals during the year, with $73.5 billion invested in 1,734 deals (KPMG, 2024).

The second half of 2023 was particularly soft for Fintech deals in the Americas, as investors further intensified their selection of potential deals. During the second half of 2023, the Americas attracted $38.4 billion of investment in 916 deals, of which the United States absorbed $34.8 billion in 627 deals (KPMG, 2024).

The United States has attracted the most investment, acting as the *main character* in the landscape of Fintech operations. Indeed, the United States is home to some of the most prominent Fintech companies of recent years. The following chart (Chart 14) shows the companies with the highest *enterprise value* in the United States in 2023 (Statista, 2023c).

Over the past year, within the US landscape, Brazil has been particularly prominent, attracting the second highest level of Fintech investment ever ($2.6 billion) (KPMG, 2024), including several large deals in the second half of 2023: Visa's $1 billion acquisition of payments company Pismo (Visa, 2024), and B2B Fintech enabler Qi Tech's raising of around $200m in a funding round led by General Atlantic (Reuters, 2023). Finally, we highlight the $560m acquisition of B2B Fintech software company Sinqia by Puerto Rico-based Evertec (Evertec, 2023).

Chart 13   **Total investment activity (VC, PE and M&A) in Fintech 2020–2023 |
Americas**

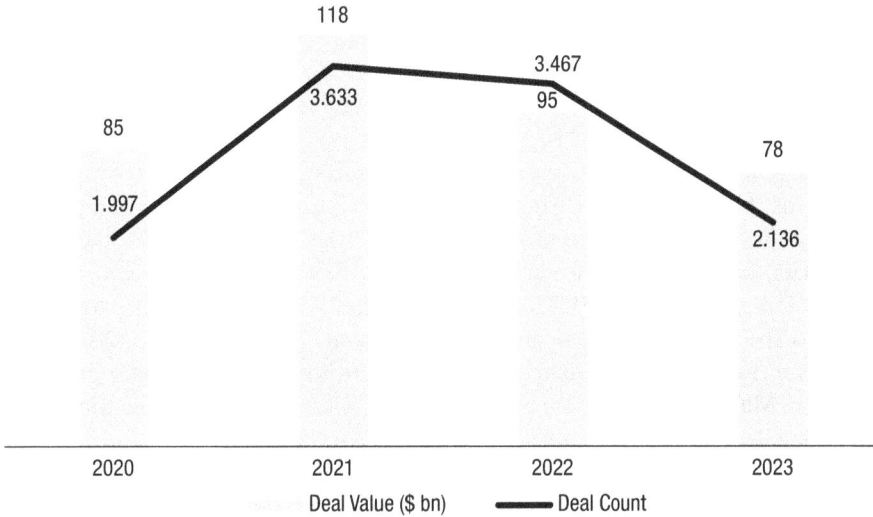

The combo chart illustrates Fintech investment activity in the Americas from 2020 to 2023. After peaking in 2021, both deal value and volume declined steadily, with 2023 marking a drop to $78 billion and 2,136 deals, reflecting broader market contraction.

Source: Own elaboration based on data from KPMG, 2024

Chart 14   **Top 10 US Fintech Companies in 2023 ($ billion)**

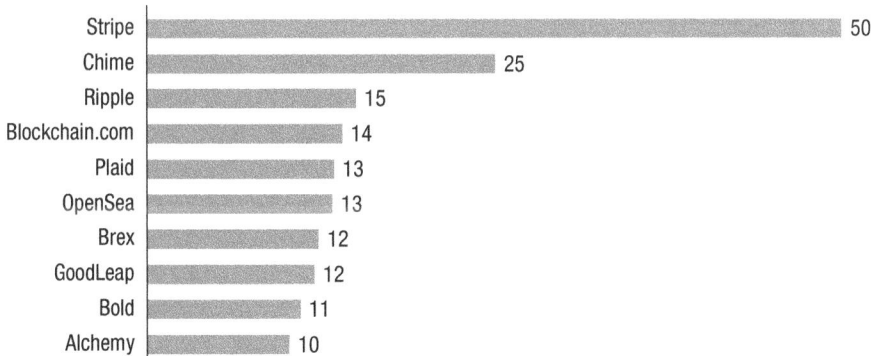

The bar chart presents the top 10 US Fintech companies by enterprise value in 2023. Stripe leads with $50 billion, followed by Chime and Ripple. The data highlight the dominant role of the US in hosting high-value firms within the global Fintech ecosystem.

Source: Own elaboration based on data from Statista, 2023c

EMEA

Fintech investments in the EMEA region grew significantly in the second half of 2023, with $16.3 billion in investments compared to $8.2 billion in the first half of that year. However, the annual total ($24.5 billion) represented the lowest level of Fintech funding in four years (**Chart 15**). Low *exit opportunities*, high interest rates, uncertainties and geopolitical conflicts pushed many investors in the region to hold back their capital (KPMG, 2024).

The largest transactions in the second half of 2023 took place in five different jurisdictions, highlighting the strength of the Fintech sector in EMEA, despite the current market weakness. The largest deals occurred in Sweden with the acquisition of Macrobond Financial for around $700m by US private equity firm Francisco Partners (Financial Times, 2023), in the Netherlands with the sale of part of PayU for around $610m to Israeli company Rapyd by Prosus NV (Bloomberg, 2023), in the United Arab Emirates with Tabby raising $200 million in a financing round led by Wellington Management (Tabby, 2023), and in Finland with the acquisition of Nomentia for a deal value of about $385 million (KPMG, 2024).

Analysing Europe in detail over the period 2019–2024 (**Chart 16**), the UK emerges as the leader with a total of 488 transactions. Despite the UK's strong presence, other countries showed considerable activity. Sweden, for instance, ranks second with 134

Chart 15   Total investment activity (VC, PE, M&A) in Fintech 2020–2023 | EMEA

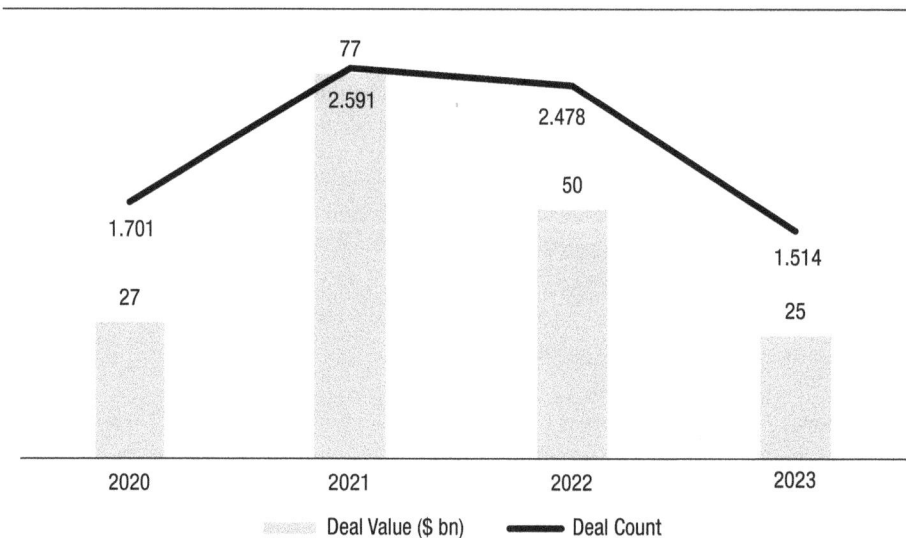

The combo chart shows Fintech investment activity in EMEA from 2020 to 2023. After peaking in 2021, both deal value and count declined, reaching their lowest in 2023. Geopolitical tensions and financial uncertainty contributed to investor caution.

Source: Own elaboration based on data from KPMG, 2024

Chart 16 Investments in Fintech startups by European country 2019–2024

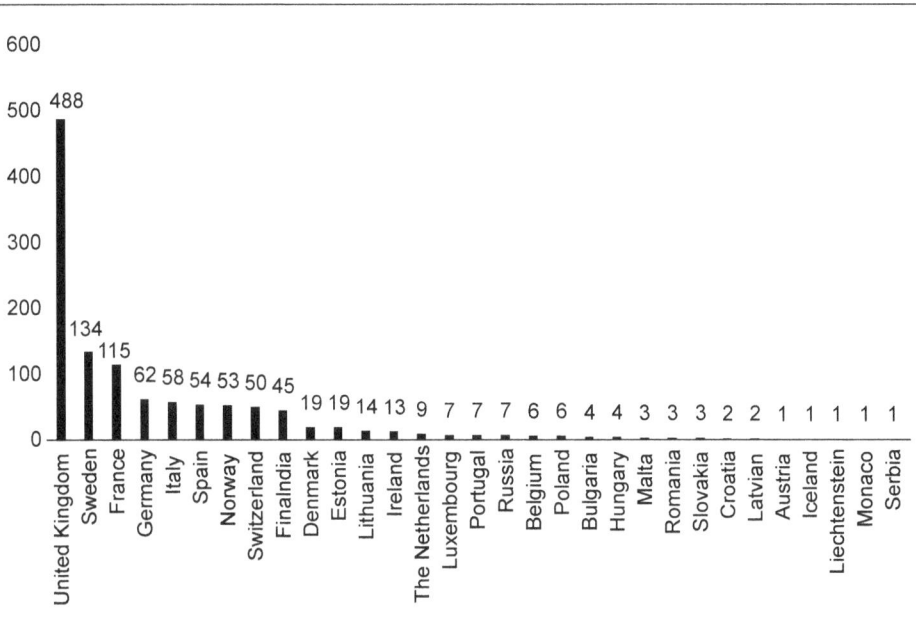

The bar chart presents Fintech startup investments by European countries from 2019 to 2024. The UK leads with 488 deals, followed by Sweden and France. Italy and Spain also show notable activity, reflecting regional diversity in Fintech engagement.

Source: Own elaboration based on data from Pitchbook

transactions, followed by France with 115. Italy and Spain, although having a smaller volume of transactions than the previous countries, still show a significant presence in the market with 58 and 54 transactions, respectively.

European trends

1. Variability in Fintech industry development among European countries
An analysis conducted by McKinsey categorised European countries according to three typical growth phases of a Fintech startup: founding, acquisition of funding and expansion. This classification uses specific key performance indicators (KPIs): The number of Fintech startups found per million inhabitants for the early stage, the volume of funding per capita and the number of transactions per million inhabitants for the middle stage, and for the last stage, the number of unicorns per million inhabitants and the percentage of workers in the Fintech industry in relation to the total workforce. From this assessment, it emerges that the UK and Sweden stand out as undisputed leaders in terms of Fintech development among the major European countries. Based on the scores obtained from these KPIs, it is relevant to note that Italy, together with Poland, ranks among the ten largest European economies by GDP

in the category of countries with the least development of the Fintech sector. This highlights how this industry is currently evolving at different rates across European countries.

2. The gap in Fintech development between the EU and the UK
Both the McKinsey report, mentioned above, and the reworking of the data represented in **Chart 16**, highlight how the UK plays the leading role in the European Fintech sector, particularly in terms of financial investment. The UK facilitates a significantly faster expansion of the Fintech market through substantial investments by funds and banking institutions, which are much more pervasive than those observed in EU countries. One of the main problems in the EU in this context lies in the restrictions imposed on institutional investors regarding investments in growth capital, which are vital for supporting startups in their pre-maturity stages of development. To illustrate, only 10% of insurance companies in Germany invest in alternative categories such as venture capital and private equity, compared to 30% in the UK. The easing of these restrictions could be an effective strategy to increase the competitiveness of the European Fintech market in the coming years.

In parallel, the European Union is implementing significant regulatory reforms in the Fintech sector, highlighting a commitment to closing the existing gap. These regulatory changes signal that the European Union and, more broadly, the European Economic Area, are progressively catching up. This phenomenon further underlines the critical importance of the regulatory environment in shaping the Fintech development landscape, confirming how the policies adopted are crucial for the future of the sector.

3. Increasing accessibility of financial services and evolving consumer expectations
The introduction of open banking and the future prospect of open finance are radically transforming the landscape of *financial* services, which will become progressively more interconnected. This interconnection will enable *providers* to offer an increasing number of services through a single integrated platform. This development is accompanied by a progressive rapprochement between the various financial services, which, together with increased accessibility for consumers, is substantially changing their expectations.

Asia-Pacific

2023 represented a challenging year for Fintech financing in the APAC region, with only $10.8 billion invested in 882 deals, down about 79% from the previous year. In fact, 2022 represented the best year since 2020 in terms of deal value, with a total investment of around $51.3 billion (**Chart 17**). Nevertheless, the number of deals completed (1,537) was down slightly from 2021, when a record 1,786 deals were recorded.

The second half of 2023 was less successful than the first half of the year, with Fintechs attracting $3.4 billion of investment, compared to $7.4 billion in the first

Chart 17   Total investment activity (VC, PE, M&A) in Fintech 2020–2023 | Asia-Pacific

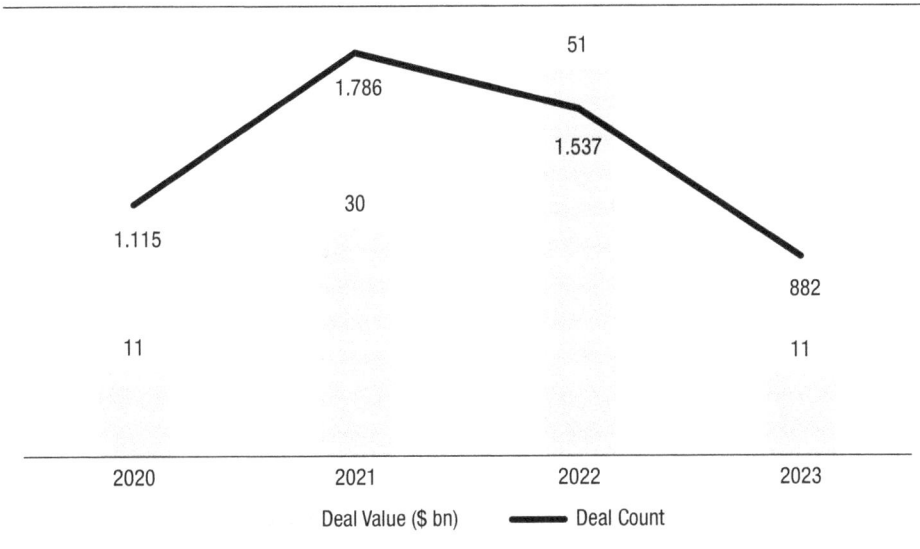

Deal Value ($ bn)   ——— Deal Count

The combo chart shows Fintech investment trends in Asia-Pacific from 2020 to 2023. After peaking in 2022, both deal value and count declined in 2023, with funding dropping to $11 billion and deals falling to 882, reflecting regional market headwinds.

Source: Own elaboration based on data from KPMG, 2024

half. VC deals led investment in the sector during 2023 with 775 deals totalling around $7.8 billion. PE and M&A, on the other hand, participated with a total of 107 deals totalling about $3 billion (KPMG, 2024).

Key facts occurring during the second half of 2023 include:

• The lack of exit opportunities contributed to the decline in investments by venture capitalists.
• AI-centred solutions have attracted increasing interest from investors.
• The Fintech sector in China is maturing, no longer as an innovative sector, but an established one, and changing the nature of investments.
• Singapore and Japan are prioritising the cryptocurrency segment in an attempt to establish themselves as market leaders.

3 Evaluation of Fintech Companies

How Venture Capitalists impact ratings

Among the main growth drivers of Fintech companies is their ability to attract capital. Venture capital, in particular, has emerged as particularly relevant in the investment activity of companies in the sector (**Chart 18**), able to support their innovation, influence their trends and, consequently, impact their valuations.

Venture capital is therefore one of the cornerstones of startup growth. VC entry not only provides companies with the necessary funds for innovation and growth but also brings management expertise, networking and legitimacy in the market. Furthermore, VC investments can lead to a revaluation of Fintech companies, often increasing their market value in view of future mergers, acquisitions or IPOs.

However, VC funding can also contribute to hype generation and inflated valuations, especially during periods of strong market growth. Investors compete for

Chart 18   Global investment activity (VC, M&A, PE) 2020–2023 ($ billion)

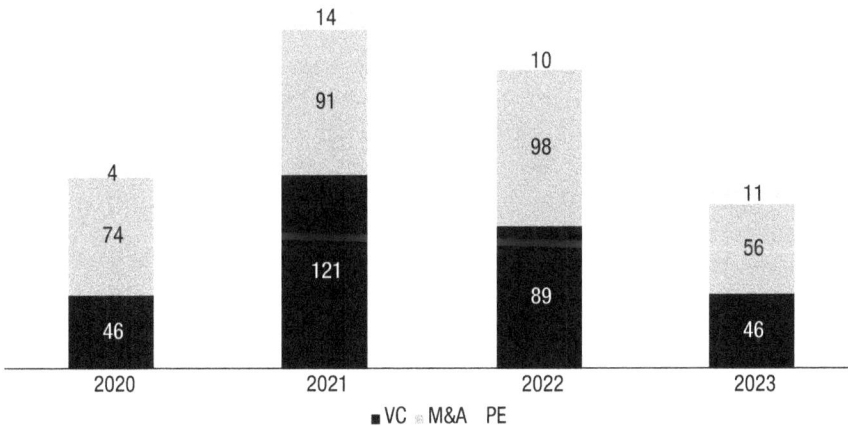

The stacked bar chart shows global Fintech investment activity from 2020 to 2023. While VC peaked in 2021, M&A became the leading component from 2022, indicating a shift in investment dynamics and growing consolidation trends within the Fintech sector.

Source: Own elaboration based on data from KPMG, 2024

promising Fintech companies, driving up valuations based on current potential rather than future profitability. Market corrections, fuelled by changes in investor sentiment, can lead to valuation corrections and industry downsizing.

Factors impacting the evaluation: Evolution of metrics considered in the evaluation

Since the collapse of the speculative bubble in 2022, the Venture Capitalist landscape has witnessed a fundamental shift in its investment strategies and prioritisation. Starting with traditional methods based on established metrics, the industry has subsequently turned towards innovative approaches that are better aligned with new market dynamics. This transformation has led to the emergence of four main trends, each representing a new element in the process of evaluating and selecting startups by venture capitalists. These emerging trends mark a strategic adaptation to change, highlighting a new period of defining investment decisions in the sector.

1. Adaptability: In an environment characterised by volatility, exacerbated by geopolitical conflicts, the ability of companies to quickly adapt to market changes has become paramount. In particular, 2021 showed record investments in the VC sector, driven by digital expansion and technological innovation. These factors have made it imperative for startups to demonstrate flexibility and resilience, shifting the focus of Venture Capitalist towards metrics that reflect these capabilities, in addition to traditional financial indicators such as Discounted Cash Flow (DCF) and EBITDA (KPMG, 2022b).
2. Technology: The valuation of technology emerges as a key criterion for Venture Capitalists during the evaluation and selection process of startups. Indeed, Venture Capitalists focus on the technological innovations proposed by startups, assessing not only their scalability and effectiveness but also their potential to revolutionise existing financial services. Technology becomes a critical point of differentiation, as it can offer significant competitive advantages, such as improved operational efficiency and access to new markets. In addition, Venture Capitalists examine a startup's ability to integrate new technologies with existing financial infrastructures and adhere to existing regulations. This approach makes it possible to identify those ventures that not only promise high financial returns but are also abreast of emerging technology trends and able to respond dynamically to market developments. Importantly, the valuation of intangibles, among which technology stands out, is becoming increasingly important in the modern economy, and this is particularly relevant for Fintech startups. These assets, being non-monetary and devoid of physical substance but capable of delivering economic benefits, present valuation difficulties due to the high information asymmetries that characterise them. The most common approaches to their valuation include the market approach, which is based on comparisons with similar assets; the cost approach, which considers the cost of reproduction or replacement; and the income approach,

which focuses on future economic benefits. The growing relevance of intangibles is linked to their ability to rapidly scale business operations, providing sustainable competitive advantages and supporting business strategies in generating cash flow. This is especially true for Fintech startups, where technology is a crucial component of the business model and overall company value (Visconti, 2020b).

3. Regulation: The impact of regulation on investment decisions in the financial technology (Fintech) sector is growing. Regulation is one of the crucial trends to consider as regulators around the world are still developing regulatory frameworks dedicated to the financial technology sphere. Currently, many startups operate in environments known as '*sandboxes*', which designate special regulatory conditions and allow Fintech companies to disregard many limitations typical of the financial sector, with the aim of fostering innovation. However, new regulations are emerging to mitigate or prevent the risks associated with this sector. It is crucial, however, to recognise that increased regulation does not necessarily imply a limitation of innovation but, on the contrary, could stimulate its development. Ciukaj and Folwarski noted a positive link between the Fintech Development Index and the Fintech Regulation Index (**Chart 19**). This suggests that a more articulated regulatory system could actually foster the evolution of the Fintech sector (Ciukaj & Folwarski, 2023).

Chart 19   Fintech Index vs. Regulation Index

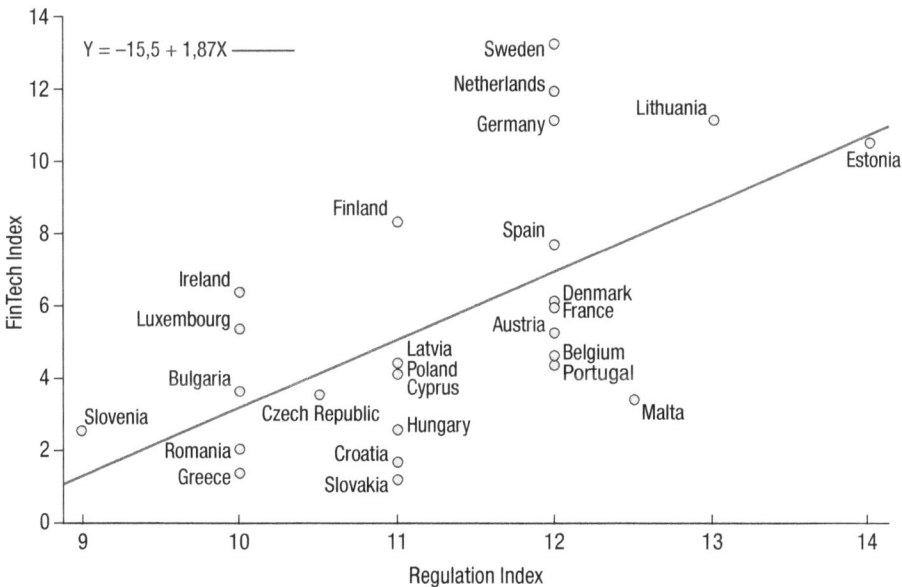

The scatter plot shows a positive correlation between the Fintech Index and the Regulation Index in European countries, suggesting that more structured regulatory frameworks may support Fintech.

Source: Ciukaj and Folwarski, 2023

4. Financial and business model sustainability: The focus on the sustainability of the business model and the current performance of startups is currently of considerable relevance. The previous emphasis on long-term growth prospects, which contributed to the speculative bubble, has consequently led to greater consideration of the financial health of the entities analysed. This shift in focus aims to ensure that valuations are rooted in solid data and reflect the real sustainability of the business model (KPMG, 2022b).

These considerations indicate the evolution and maturity achieved by the venture capital industry, which now considers investments with a greater focus on the resilience, technology and integrity of startups, without neglecting the importance of their financial return potential.

Furthermore, it is emphasised that sustainability is becoming a key factor for investors, driven both by market demand and increasingly stringent regulations. In particular, it is pointed out that this trend represents a key element, which is expected to be progressively integrated into the evaluation of startups by Venture Capitalists. In the future, Environmental, Social, and Governance (ESG) criteria are likely to become a central pillar in investment decision-making processes. These factors related to financial and environmental sustainability reflect an increased focus on risks and opportunities related to climate change and social responsibility. For these considerations, it is expected that Venture Capitalists will tend to select startups that not only promise solid financial returns but also operate in a responsible and sustainable manner, fostering fair and environmentally friendly economic growth (EY, 2024; Antler, 2021).

Investment strategies and external factors

Venture capital foundations adopt different investment strategies to navigate the dynamic Fintech landscape and capitalise on emerging trends:

1. *Stage-specific* investments: Venture Capitalists focus on financing startups at different stages, from seed rounds and Series-A rounds to later growth or pre-IPO stages. By providing seed and early-stage funding, venture capital firms nurture innovation and support the development of promising Fintech startups. In this respect, it can be seen from **Chart 20** that, as of 2020, Fintech deals have increasingly focused on companies in their early-stage phase (CB Insights, 2023).
2. Theme-based investments: Venture capital firms focus on specific topics in the Fintech sector, such as regtech, blockchain or AI-based products. This target strategy allows them to identify high-growth opportunities and support entrepreneurs operating in niche sectors.
3. Impact Investing: Some venture capitalists consider both financial returns and social impact when making investment decisions, prioritising investments in Fintech solutions that promote responsible lending, sustainability and financial inclusion, fostering positive change in the industry and society.

Chart 20   Annual percentage of internship deals

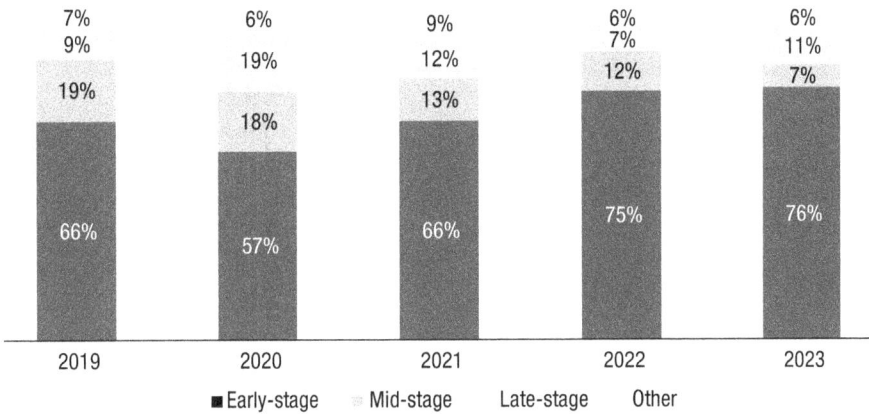

7%	6%	9%	6%	6%
9%			7%	11%
19%	19%	12%	12%	7%
	18%	13%		
66%	57%	66%	75%	76%
2019	2020	2021	2022	2023

■ Early-stage   ▨ Mid-stage   Late-stage   Other

The stacked bar chart illustrates the growing concentration of Fintech investment in early-stage deals from 2019 to 2023, rising from 66% to 76%. This trend reflects increased VC interest in supporting innovation at the foundational stages of development.

Source: Own elaboration based on data from CB Insights, 2023

4. Corporate Venture Capital (CVC): Established financial institutions increasingly collaborate and invest in Fintech startups through CVC arms. This collaboration gives startups access to valuable resources, markets and industry expertise, accelerating their growth and development.
5. Geographic targeting: A focused regional approach aims to prioritise Fintech companies in emerging markets that are poised for substantial growth. For example, China is a frontrunner in mobile payments and Fintech advancements, while India is a fast-growing Fintech sector with a strong emphasis on financial inclusion, and Africa represents an untapped market offering innovative solutions tailored to specific challenges.

Main challenges regarding the valuation of Fintechs

The Fintech sector, characterised by relentless innovation and rapid technological evolution, poses numerous challenges when evaluating entities operating in it, including: growth management, the impact of regulation, determining the cost of capital, the influence of future expectations and the complexity of business models. Growth management is a major focus of attention as Fintech companies find themselves in an extremely dynamic market environment, where the advent of emerging technologies and rapid changes make it difficult to forecast growth. The impact of regulation plays a decisive role, as the industry is subject to constant regulatory adjustments that can significantly influence business operations and market strategies. Determining the cost of capital also brings an additional element of challenge, related to the vola- tility and uncertainty characterising the Fintech sector, which can influence risk per- ception and, consequently, financial valuation models. Moreover, the impact of fu- ture expectations on the value of Fintech companies is considerable, as the prospects of technological innovation and the introduction of new services can change valua- tions substantially. Finally, the complexity of business models, often based on disrup- tive technologies such as *blockchain* and AI, introduces a further element of difficul- ty in analysing and understanding the real value of these entities.

In the face of these challenges, it is essential to adopt a flexible and adaptable val- uation approach, capable of integrating traditional methodologies with new metrics that accurately reflect the dynamic environment in which Fintech companies operate.

- Growth management: When evaluating Fintech companies, growth manage- ment represents a significant challenge, mainly stemming from the difficulty of predicting and quantifying future growth in a dynamic and innovative industry. These companies often introduce revolutionary business models and make use of cutting-edge technologies, resulting in a growth profile that cannot be compared to that of traditional companies. Consequently, conventional valuation methods, which are based on historical data and assume a certain market stability, are often inadequate (Damodaran, 2009).
- Market expectations greatly influence the perception and assessment of the growth potential of Fintechs. These realities are particularly sensitive to market fluctuations and speculation that can significantly change their valuation, some- times without a direct link to current financial performance. Moreover, evolving regulations and technologies can simultaneously open up new market opportuni- ties and impose operational restrictions. These external factors require the adop- tion of flexible forecasting models that can incorporate a wide range of dynamic variables and adapt quickly to changes.
- In order to effectively address these challenges, it is crucial to adopt an integrated approach in the valuation of Fintech companies, combining traditional indicators with new metrics capable of capturing the peculiarities of the sector. The imple- mentation of advanced methodologies is crucial to accurately reflect the com- plexity and volatility of the industry, balancing growth prospects with the risks associated with technological innovation and regulatory changes (McKinsey & Company, 2016a).
- Regulatory impact: The impact of regulation on the valuations of Fintech com- panies is significant, reflecting the highly regulated nature of the financial sec- tor and the rapidly evolving technologies employed by these entities. Regulations, which vary according to the geopolitical context, profoundly influence both the operations and growth strategies of Fintechs. Adapting to these regulations can entail considerable investment, in some cases limiting companies' ability to ex- pand and innovate. Regulatory uncertainty introduces a further element of com- plexity in estimating firm value, as policy fluctuations can directly impact the industry (Damodaran, 2009).

- The companies in question are forced to operate in a constantly changing regulatory environment, which can change not only their day-to-day activities but also investors' perceptions of risk.
- These elements underline the crucial and complex role of regulation in the valuation of Fintech companies. A thorough and specific analysis is therefore required, taking into account the ever-changing regulatory landscape and its direct impact on growth prospects and company value
- Determining the cost of capital: Determining the cost of capital for Fintech companies is a major challenge, given the particular nature of these companies operating in an environment of high uncertainty and rapid technological change. The cost of capital is a key element in evaluating any business investment, but for Fintechs, the estimation is complicated by the volatility and risk associated with continuous innovation in the financial sector.
- Traditional methodologies for estimating the cost of capital often fail to adequately capture the risk profile of such entities, as these techniques assume more stable and predictable market conditions (Damodaran, 2009). Fintech companies move rapidly and break existing paradigms, also allowing for significant variation in the market's perception of risk and directly influencing the cost of capital. In this context, it becomes essential to use flexible and modified valuation models that can take into account the dynamism of the sector and the impact of technological innovations on business risk. The determination of the cost of capital must therefore reflect not only general economic and market conditions, but also the specifics of the Fintech sector, which include factors such as evolving regulation, market acceptance of new technologies and the financial stability of the company in a changing environment.
- This complexity requires a sophisticated and customised analytical approach that can adequately assess the specific risk premium associated with Fintech transactions and provide a more accurate and representative estimate of their true cost of capital.
- Influence of future expectations: the influence of future expectations on the valuation of Fintech companies is a complex issue, given the speed with which technological innovations can transform the financial sector. These expectations can have a significant impact on the perceived value of these companies, especially when considering their potential to be disruptive to existing markets.
- Future expectations greatly influence how investors and the market value Fintech companies. Speculation about possible future successes or the adoption of emerging technologies can cause significant fluctuations in perceived value. Traditional valuation methodologies may have some critical elements when considering this type of speculative dynamics, as they tend to rely on historical data and may not adequately reflect potential growth trajectories (Damodaran, 2009).
- Moreover, the growth and innovation prospects of Fintechs are highly dependent on external factors, such as regulation or macroeconomic conditions, which can change rapidly and influence future expectations.
- Therefore, when evaluating Fintech companies, it is crucial to consider a model

that integrates not only current financial performance but also market expectations and possible future scenarios. This approach should help to formulate more
accurate and robust value estimates that reflect both growth potential and the
risks associated with operating in a dynamic and uncertain environment.
- Complexity of business models: The complexity of Fintech companies' business
  models represents a major challenge in their evaluation. These companies often
  incorporate innovative technologies and operating models that differ significantly
  from traditional business structures. This characteristic can make it particularly challenging for analysts and investors to understand the revenue sources and
  growth prospects of Fintech companies.
- The business models of such entities often rely on the use of advanced technologies such as *blockchain*, AI and ML, which can introduce new and complex variables into business valuation. These technologies not only transform internal processes but can also significantly alter customer interaction and market structure
  (Damodaran, 2009).

It can, therefore, be concluded that valuing a Fintech company requires a holistic approach that not only considers traditional financial indicators but also the company's
ability to adapt and thrive in a rapidly changing technological environment. This implies the integration of valuation models that can handle the high volatility and inherent complexity of Fintechs' business models, ensuring that the valuation accurately
reflects both the growth potential and unique risks associated with these innovative
entities. Addressing challenges related to growth management, the impact of regulation, determining the cost of capital, the influence of future expectations and the
complexity of business models therefore requires a diverse set of analytical skills.
Analysts must be able to interpret not only financial data but also the implications of
continuous technological innovations and changing regulations. In this context, the
evaluation of Fintechs transforms financial analysis from a standardised practice to a
dynamic process that must constantly evolve to remain relevant and effective.

Main evaluation methodologies

The Fintech revolution, characterised by the introduction of advanced technologies
in the financial services sector, represents a fundamental challenge for traditional
companies and banking institutions. This phenomenon, rooted in digital evolution
and the need to respond to an increasingly interconnected market, calls for a critical
reflection on the valuation methods of startups operating in this field. The distinction between traditional and alternative valuation methods emerges as crucial for understanding and correctly interpreting the potential and growth prospects of Fintech
firms. The former, based on established approaches such as discounted cash flows or
market comparables, need to be adapted to the innovative business models and evolutionary stages of companies. The latter, on the other hand, introduce new metrics
and considerations, emphasising the importance of variables such as scalability, tech-

nological innovation and the ability to intercept new consumer needs. In this context, the evaluation of Fintech startups is a complex process that requires a careful analysis of the sector's specificities and a deep understanding of emerging market dynamics (Visconti, 2020a).

Traditional methods

In the field of company valuation, particularly those of a more established nature, traditional methods occupy a role of primary importance, offering well-established and widely recognised tools for determining company value. These methods, which are the result of a long theoretical and practical evolution in the field of corporate finance, mainly fall into three distinct categories, each reflecting specific valuation logic and methodological approaches.

1. Discounted Cash Flow (DCF): This approach is based on projecting the future cash flows generated by the company, which are then discounted using an appropriate discount rate. This rate reflects the company's cost of capital, thus incorporating an estimate of the risk associated with the generation of the projected cash flows. The DCF method is particularly valued for its ability to provide an intrinsic valuation of the company, based on its actual economic and financial prospects.
2. Market Multiples: This method evaluates the company by comparing it with comparable companies, either already listed or recently traded. The most common multiples include the ratio of market price to earnings per share (P/E), enterprise value to EBITDA (EV/EBITDA) and other indicators that relate the market value of the company to specific balance sheet items or economic results. The use of these multiples allows for quick and easily interpreted evaluations, although their reliability depends heavily on the selection of an adequate sample of comparable companies and the correct interpretation of operational, financial and risk differences.
3. Book Value: This method is based on the valuation of the company's net assets as they appear on the balance sheet. Although this method may appear less sophisticated than the other two, it provides a solid basis for valuations that need to be anchored to the company's assets. In particular, the book value method is often used as a point of comparison or check for estimates obtained through more complex approaches, thus ensuring a holistic and balanced view of company value.

The Discounted Cash Flow (DCF) Method

The financial method identifies the value of a business according to the future benefits it is able to generate in terms of cash flows. The economic value is, therefore, equal to the sum of the present value of the cash flows that the aggregate of assets will be able to generate in the future, discounted at the rate of return on risk capital

or the weighted average cost of capital (WACC), depending on the cash flow configuration used.

According to the DCF method, the value of a company's economic capital is
equal to the algebraic sum of the discounted operating cash flows, also referred to as
Free Cash Flow from Operations ('operating cash flows' or FCFO) that can be generated over an explicit projection horizon and the so-called 'terminal value'; the latter
expresses the presumed value of the company after the last year of explicit projection
and is calculated on the basis of a normalised terminal FCFO, also discounted. The
rate used for the discounting process is the WACC.

The value thus obtained is the so-called 'Enterprise Value' or 'Company Value'.
From this measure, we arrive at the so-called 'Equity Value', or 'Capital Value', by
algebraically adding up the net financial position of the company on the same date.
In formula,

$$\text{Equity Value} = \sum_{t=1}^{N} \frac{FCFO_t}{(1+WACC)^t} + \frac{\frac{FCFO_N \times (1+g)}{(WACC-g)}}{(1+WACC)^N} - NFP$$

Formula 1—Equity Value by DCF Method

where
$FCFO_t$ = Operating flows (explicit projection period)
$FCFO_N \times (1+g)$ = Terminal value (synthetic projection period)
N = Explicit projection period
g = Long-term growth rate
NFP = Net financial position at valuation date
WACC = Weighted average cost of capital

In particular, operating flows represent the resources intended to satisfy all those
who contribute financial means to the company, i.e., shareholders and other financ-
ers. The terminal value represents the value of the company at the end of the explicit projection horizon, i.e., the time frame within which the estimates of the variables included in the calculation have greater reliability as to their actual occurrence.
The estimation of terminal value can be performed by discounting in perpetuity the
normalised operating cash flow, i.e., the sustainable cash flow that can be generated
for an indefinite time after the explicit projection horizon, against a given perpetual growth rate 'g' of the company and a given investment profile. The explicit projection period should be defined (while, at the same time, taking into account the difficulty in predicting with reasonable certainty events that will occur in the future) in
such a way that, at the end of this period, the company has reached a 'state of equi-
librium' in terms of growth prospects and sustainable profitability, given a certain
level of investments. As a rule, the explicit projection period should be able to extend over a 3–5-year time horizon, although this value depends substantially on the
characteristics of the company and its reference market in terms of stability, growth
and existing development opportunities. The financial structure used for the calcula-

tion of the WACC must reflect a normal or sustainable situation and may refer to the structure observed at the valuation reference date and expressed at market values, to a sector financial structure, derived from the analysis of a sample of comparable listed companies or to a prospective financial structure resulting from the financial dynamics of the company being valued during the explicit projection horizon.

The WACC is the average of the cost of debt capital and the cost of equity, weighted by their respective weights in a normal financial structure for the company being evaluated. The WACC represents the return expected by the company's lenders and shareholders for the use of their capital. In formula,

$$WACC = Ke \times We + Kd \times Wd \times (1 - tc),$$

Formula 2—WACC

where
WACC = Weighted average cost of capital
We = Weight attributed to equity
Wd = Weight attributed to third-party means (financial debt)
Ke = Cost of equity
Kd = Average cost of third-party assets
tc = Company's average tax rate

The cost of equity capital is commonly defined as the average return expected by the investor in the company's risk capital, i.e., the opportunity cost of equity capital. For the purpose of its determination, one of the most accepted methods in doctrine and professional practice is the Capital Asset Pricing Model ('CAPM'). According to the CAPM, the cost of equity capital is given by the sum of the rate of return on risk-free assets 'rf' and a Market Risk Premium multiplied by a β coefficient, which expresses the non-diversifiable risk borne by the company being valued. In formula:

$$Ke = rf + \beta \times \text{Market Risk Premium},$$

Formula 3—Ke

where
Ke = Cost of equity
rf = Rate of return on risk-free assets
Market Risk Premium = Average rate of return on venture capital investments
β = non-diversifiable risk 'beta' coefficient

Increasingly, recourse is made to the adjusted configuration of the CAPM, including an Alpha factor capable of approximating the company-specific risk in terms of *excess return* with respect to the CAPM in its basic configuration. Such a factor, in general, has the objective of introducing a further component of return on invested capital capable of offsetting the specific risks typically linked to the size of the company/asset under assessment, rather than to its characteristics in terms of corporate governance. For this reason, the coefficient is often referred to as the *size/execution premium*. In formula:

$$Ke = rf + \beta \times \text{Market Risk Premium.}$$

Formula 4—Ke Adjusted

Alternatively, the equity value can be calculated using the flows the free cash flow available to shareholders after all financing charges have been met, reflecting the value-generating capacity of the company for its owners (FCFE) and using the Cost of Equity (Ke) as the discount rate, which considers the rate of return required by shareholders by incorporating investors' expectations of risk and return.

The DCF method is widely recognised for its ability to reflect future financial projections and associated risks, providing a detailed, forward-looking picture of corporate value. Through the integration of business risk into the discount rate, the DCF succeeds in providing a valuation that reflects the return expected by investors with respect to the company's risk profile, providing flexibility and applicability to a wide range of business contexts, from established to emerging ones such as the Fintech sector. This methodology, which highlights a company's ability to generate value over time, is particularly relevant for analysing the value of technology start-ups, where innovation and market dynamics play crucial roles.

However, the DCF method is not without criticism, especially when applied in environments characterised by a high degree of uncertainty. Its sensitivity to under-lying assumptions, such as estimates of future cash flows and terminal value, introduces an element of speculation that can significantly affect the calculated value of the company. The problematic nature is accentuated in the case of startups, where the volatility of growth forecasts and the variability of business models make DCF a challenging methodology. The absence of an established financial history and rapid market developments increases the difficulties in defining an appropriate discount rate, making DCF valuation less reliable and more susceptible to valuation errors.

In conclusion, although DCF offers a comprehensive approach to analysing corporate value based on future economic performance, the accuracy of its assessments depends on the quality of the assumptions used and the ability to accurately interpret market trends and future developments. The methodology therefore requires an informed use, especially in contexts characterised by high uncertainty such as that of innovative companies and startups in the Fintech sector.

The Method of Multiples

Market criteria conceive the value of the company's capital as a function of the prices expressed on regulated markets or in private negotiations, for shares in the capital of the same or similar companies. This approach therefore disregards actual, historical and prospective asset and income values, and instead embraces the concept of the fair purchase price for assets with similar characteristics in a free market. Among the market criteria, we can distinguish the following methods:

- Stock market multiples method (*trading multiples*): This approach estimates the value of a company's economic capital on the basis of prices traded on organised markets for shares of comparable companies. The judgement of comparability is normally formulated on the basis of considerations regarding the weight of revenues generated in the core business by the company being evaluated, the product and market orientation, the size and prospective economic-financial fundamentals of the comparable companies being analysed. In detail, the relevant elements are generally: the business sector, size, reference markets, life cycle stage, financial structure, profitability prospects. The phase of determining multiples consists of calculating ratios between the valuation expressed by the market for comparable companies in terms of market capitalisation and their fundamental quantities (such as, e.g., turnover, EBITDA, EBIT, net income, book equity, cash flows). The multiples must be determined by ensuring homogeneity between the numerator and denominator in terms of fundamental relationships and accounting policies, and the stability of the multiples identified, by removing short-term abnormal factors from the analysis of the market capitalisations of the comparables. In general, it should be noted that stock market valuations, and thus the related multiples, refer to investments that are readily disposable. Consequently, it may be appropriate to apply corrective factors. For example, if the valuation object is an unlisted company, it is appropriate to consider a discount for the lower liquidity of the investment compared to the sample of comparables. The same reasoning can be applied when valuing a listed company in a segment characterised by lower trading volume levels than the *peers* from which the multiples are drawn.
- Comparable *transactions* method (*transactions multiples*): The comparable transactions method is based on the use of multiples recognised in acquisitions of companies comparable with the entity being valued. This methodology is based on multiples obtained by comparing the value recognised in the purchase and sale of such companies to significant economic or empirical quantities of the company considered. In particular, this methodology consists in identifying a *panel of* transactions deemed comparable with the entity being valued.

The multiples method is valued for its ability to integrate market-relevant information into valuation processes, which plays a decisive role in estimating the value of a wide range of companies. This methodology, similarly to DCF, bases its valuation on the financial data of the company under review, thus offering a comprehensive view that takes into account both the external environment and the internal performance of the entity being valued.

However, the multiples method manifests certain limitations, in particular its applicability is strongly conditioned by the availability of comparable companies and their listing on the stock exchange. This requirement translates into a particularly rel-

evant factor in the context of Fintech startups, which often present unique characteristics that hinder the identification of similar and adequately representative entities.
This aspect undermines the feasibility of the multiples method in such circumstances, limiting its effectiveness. In addition, the dependence on historical transactions
is a further disadvantage. Market conditions are subject to change over time, and the
adoption of data from transactions concluded in the past may entail the risk of obtaining valuations that no longer reflect current reality. This variability may therefore
generate estimates that are not accurately aligned with current market conditions,
thus compromising the reliability of the method.

The Book Value Method

The book value method, or book value, is a valuation technique that aims to establish the value of a company based on official financial information, such as balance
sheets and accounting documents. In particular, this approach focuses on the equity
of the company, calculated as the difference between the total value of assets and liabilities.

The essence of the book value method is based on the assumption that the items
reported in the company's financial documents adequately reflect the true value of
assets and liabilities. Therefore, calculating the value of equity by subtracting liabilities from total assets provides a tangible measure of the company's net worth.

One of the most appreciated aspects of this method is its simplicity and its direct correlation with reliable and verifiable financial data. As such, book value offers
a clear and immediate snapshot of the company's financial situation at the time of
valuation.

However, it is important to emphasise that this approach has limitations, particularly when it comes to evaluating fast-growing companies or startups. This methodology, in fact, does not take into account the future growth prospects of the company,
its potential increases in value from innovations, market developments or intangible
assets such as intellectual capital. For these considerations, focusing solely on book
value may not adequately reflect the true value-generating potential of a company.

In conclusion, while the book value method stands out for its practicality and immediacy in providing an estimate of corporate value based on concrete and verifiable
data, it is crucial to recognise its limitations, especially in dynamic and innovative
contexts, where the value of the company is significantly influenced by factors beyond the mere analysis of financial statements.

Alternative methods

In light of the reported areas of opportunity in traditional startup valuation methods,
primarily related to the lack of historical financial data, the absence of listed company comparables on the market and the crucial importance attached to future growth
prospects, there is a pressing need to identify alternative valuation methodologies. In

this context, there has been the development and adoption of alternative methodologies, characterised by a higher degree of flexibility and a more qualitative approach. These methodologies, emerging either as refined variations of traditional valuation processes or as radically innovative approaches, aim at integrating and enhancing qualitative parameters deemed of fundamental importance in the valuation of startups. This alternative methodological orientation turns out to be essential for correctly interpreting the complex and dynamic scenario in which startups operate, offering evaluation tools that transcend mere quantitative analysis and open up a deeper understanding of the growth potential and intrinsic innovation of these entrepreneurial entities.

In the following discussion, alternative approaches to evaluation will be examined, including:

1. Damodaran's Modified DCF, which adapts the traditional DCF model to the peculiarities of startups;
2. Adjusted Book Value, which revises the book value of the company by also considering intangible assets;
3. Adjusted Revenue Multiples, which uses revenue multiples adjusted for the specific sector of the reality analysed;
4. Berkus method, focusing on the evaluation of success potential based on specific key attributes;
5. Risk Factor Summation method (RFSM) for risk assessment;
6. Scorecard Valuation method, which compares the startup with others active in its sector;
7. Venture Capital, which estimates the return on investment;
8. First Chicago method, which considers different future scenarios;
9. Valuation by Stage method, which evaluates the startup according to its stage of development;
10. Duplication Cost method, which estimates how much it would cost to replicate the company from scratch;
11. User-Based Valuation method, which evaluates the company based on the value of its users;
12. Real Option Model, which considers the future options available to the company.

The Modified DCF Method of Damodaran

The early-stage company valuation method proposed by Aswath Damodaran, a professor at New York University's Stern School of Business, represents a significant evolution of the traditional DCF approach. Acknowledging the limitations of the application of the traditional DCF method to startups, mainly due to the difficulty in estimating predictable cash flows in these emerging realities, Damodaran introduces a Modified DCF Model that includes a number of *adjustments* aimed at taking into account the peculiar characteristics of the startups being valued (Jreisat et al., 2021)

This innovative model uses two main methodologies to estimate cash flows:

- The top-down approach starts with an analysis of the total market (Total Addressable Market – TAM) for the services or products offered by the startup, an estimate of the Served Available Market (SAM) and forecast of the Serviceable Obtainable Market (SOM) and an estimate of the time needed to reach it, assessing operating margins in relation to preliminary revenues and considering refinancing requirements (**Chart 21**).
- The bottom-up approach that focuses on drawing up a detailed budget that includes estimates of sales, operating expenses, taxes and any other investments, emphasising the importance of accuracy in financial forecasting.

One of the most critical aspects in evaluating startups via the DCF is also the calculation of the appropriate discount rate. Damodaran suggests the use of an average beta value derived from comparable companies in the sector, which is adequate to take into account the low diversification typical of entities investing in startups. Furthermore, given the absence of market quotations for equity and debt, he suggests using the average Debt/Equity ratio of the sector as a proxy for the entity under valuation.

Damodaran also introduces the concept of survival adjustment, evaluating the startup both on its commercial viability and on the risk of failure, based on average industry data and the use of the probit technique (a non-linear regression model, used when the dependent variable is dichotomous). For the terminal value calculation, he suggests considering perpetual cash flow growth, a period of time during

Chart 21   TAM, SAM, SOM

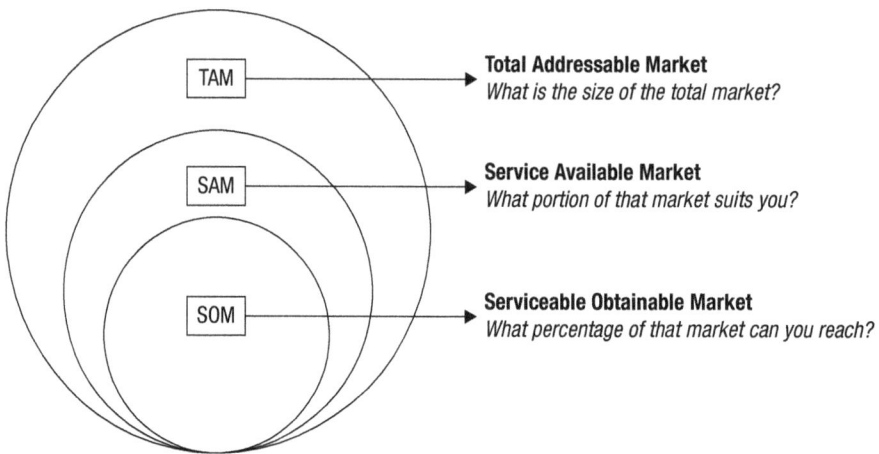

The diagram illustrates the TAM–SAM–SOM framework used in top-down valuation approaches. It distinguishes the total market size (TAM), the segment relevant to the firm (SAM) and the realistically reachable share (SOM) to guide early-stage projections.

which cash flows are maintained at a certain level or the assumption of liquidation of the company. It is also important to consider the risk associated with key people within the company, introducing a '*key person discount*' to reflect the possible loss of such persons.

In conclusion, Damodaran's Modified DCF Model overcomes many limitations of the traditional approach when applied to the startup context, demonstrating the flexibility and adaptability of the DCF in considering both financial and qualitative factors. However, it relies on a larger number of assumptions than the traditional DCF, entailing the risk of inaccurate valuations in the case of incorrect underlying assumptions. Nevertheless, this methodology offers a fundamental perspective for the evaluation of early-stage companies, emphasising the importance of a holistic approach adapted to the unique challenges that startups present (Jreisat et al., 2021).

The Adjusted Book Value method

The Adjusted Book Value method represents an advanced and detailed approach to the valuation of corporate assets and liabilities, aimed at more accurately reflecting their current market value (*fair market value*). This methodology is distinguished by its ability to update and adjust the net value of the company's assets, both tangible and intangible, and liabilities to express a financial picture that is as close as possible to market reality. In particular, the modified book value proves to be of paramount importance in the valuation of companies in financial distress or instability, as it allows for careful consideration of fluctuations in the value of tangible and current assets. These include, for example, inventories and receivables, as well as long-term assets such as land and tangible fixed assets. The methodology takes into account the market fluctuations of these assets, thus providing a more faithful estimate of company value.

One of the peculiarities of this approach is its ability to effectively adapt to the valuation needs of startups and growth-stage companies, which often have special characteristics and a high degree of uncertainty compared to established companies. Unlike the traditional book value method, the modified method includes additional valuation elements, such as goodwill, which represents the value of the company's brand, reputation and business relationships and the possibility of capitalising expected future profits.

The adoption of this methodology entails greater complexity in the analysis and calculation of company values but results in a more accurate valuation that is more in line with market reality. This is particularly important for the valuation of intangibles, whose values are notoriously difficult to quantify through more traditional methods. For such considerations, the modified book value method offers a more complete and realistic valuation framework, which is essential for investment, financing and strategic business decisions (Corporate Financial Institute).

The Adjusted Revenue Multiples Method

The valuation methodology defined as Adjusted Revenue Multiples focuses on the use of multiples based on the revenues of the entity being valued. This stems from the need to evaluate more advanced startups that are not yet profitable, but have a stable revenue stream. This technique is particularly effective for companies with a subscription-based business model, common among many startups in the Fintech sector. Indeed, the method emphasises the importance of recurring revenue, which is considered a key financial indicator for these companies, as it can provide a more solid basis for evaluation than other metrics that may be more volatile or less representative of the state of the art of the company analysed and its growth potential. However, one of the main difficulties remains the identification of an adequate panel of comparable companies. This requires finding other startups that not only operate in the same industry and have similar business models but are also at a comparable stage of development. Ideally, these comparable companies should be listed on the stock exchange or have participated in recent market transactions, so as to have public data available for comparison.

Moreover, this approach requires a detailed definition of the market and the company's positioning within it, as well as an in-depth analysis of the financial performance of comparable companies. Despite these challenges, the Adjusted Revenue Multiples methodology remains a key option for the valuation of Fintech startups due to its emphasis on recurring revenue and ability to provide valuations based on stable and predictable financial indicators.

The Berkus Method

The Berkus valuation model, conceived by Dave Berkus in 1996, represents a fundamental pillar for analysing and estimating the value of companies in their early stages of development. This methodology was originally presented in an academic study, symbolising its relevance and innovation in the field of startup investments. The premise on which the Berkus method is based is the following: Less than one in a thousand companies manages to meet or exceed turnover forecasts in their expected development stages. This finding emerges from extensive analyses and underlines the high uncertainty and risk associated with investments in the early stages of a startup (Jreisat et al., 2021)

The technique proposed by Berkus starts with an initial *pre-money* valuation, which is characterised by the absence of traditional financial considerations. The latter, in fact, is based solely on the assumption that the company will be worth more than USD 20 million five years after its inception. This approach assumes that the company can raise half a million dollars once five factors are met (Moro Visconti, 2020a).

- Sound Idea: The first factor relates to the mere presence of a concrete business idea, which decreases the investment risk.

Table 1   **Berkus Valuation Model: Qualitative Factors and Value Ranges**

Factors	Value ($)
Sound idea	0–500,000
Prototype	0–500,000
Quality of management team	0–500,000
Strategic relationships	0–500,000
Product rollout or sales	0–500,000

The table outlines the Berkus valuation model, which assigns monetary values to five qualitative factors—idea, team, prototype, strategic relationships and sales—to estimate early-stage startup value without relying on traditional financial metrics.

- Quality of Management Team: The second factor relates to the presence of a recognised Founding Team.
- Prototype: The third factor is related to the presence, or absence, of a prototype of the product to reduce technological risk.
- Strategic Relationships: The fourth factor relates to strategic alliances, understood as close agreements with possible suppliers and customers already interested in the product and able to reduce the risk of market entry and competition:
- Product Rollout or Sales: The fifth factor considers the startup's start of sales as an element that decreases the production risk.

Based on how the startup is positioned according to each of these factors, each is assigned a value between $0 and $500,000, with the latter subject to change depending on the market. The values are finally added together to arrive at a startup valuation (Kamal & Firmansyah, 2021).

In summary, the Berkus method provides a fundamental framework for evaluating startups in their most embryonic stages, highlighting critical factors that may influence their development and success. However, the evolution of the company towards more advanced stages, characterised by real revenue streams, requires an adjustment of the valuation model to take into account the new operational and financial dynamics.

The Risk Factor Summation Method (RFSM)

The RFSM of valuation is an advanced approach to analysing the value of companies in their early stages, going beyond what is offered by the Scorecard and Berkus methods by evaluating a larger number of variables. This method focuses on analysing a wide range of external risks that the company must manage in order to make a profit, emphasising the importance of an in-depth understanding of the context in which the company operates. Initially, the average *pre-money* value of new companies in the same industry and region is calculated, establishing a basis for valuation. Attention is then given to a number of risk factors that are given weight in the overall assessment. The high failure rate of new ventures, which varies between 70% and 90%, underlines the inherent difficulty in successfully running a business, both as a developer and as a shareholder (Kamal & Firmansyah, 2021). This statistic highlights the crucial importance of proactively identifying and managing potential risks to prevent failure. Among the various risk factors that can adversely affect business performance, the twelve main factors—risk management, stage of the business, regulatory/political risks, production risk, sales and marketing risk, fundraising/capital risk, competition risk, technology risk, legal risk, international risk, reputational risk and the potential for a profitable exit—are crucial in analysing the *pre-revenue* and *pre-money* value of a business. Each of these risk factors is evaluated with a *score* ranging from +2 (very positive) to −2 (extremely negative), and the resulting total is then adjusted by a coefficient of $250,000 for each positive or negative score within the evaluation system (Kamal & Firmansyah, 2021).

$$\text{Pre-money valuation} = \text{Average pre-money valuation}_{\text{sector}} +/- \text{Adjustments}$$

Formula 5—Pre-Money Valuation: RFSM

By integrating this information, it emerges that the RFSM not only offers a detailed methodology for risk assessment but also emphasises the importance of a balanced and judicious assessment of the various risk factors. Through this approach, the RFSM provides the tools for targeted and effective risk management that can support the company's long-term growth and stability.

The Scorecard Valuation Method

The Scorecard Valuation Method is an optimal technique for the valuation of companies in their early stages of development, allowing a direct comparison with other startups that have recently received investment in the same sector. This approach aims to adjust the estimated average value of similar companies to determine the *pre-money* valuation of the startup under consideration, taking into account only companies that are in the same stage of their life cycle.

The method is implemented in two distinct phases. In the first step, the average *pre-money* valuation of companies in the same geographical region and industry is calculated. The next step involves a comparison of the company under consideration with similar companies, based on a set of factors to which different weights are assigned (Jreisat et al., 2021). Generally, in order of importance, the factors considered are: quality of the management team, size of the opportunity (market size), quality of the product or technology, competition, sales channels and market partnerships, need for additional financing and other (e.g., geographical factors). Each of these factors is analysed individually and its previously assigned weight is multiplied by a comparison factor, based on how the analysed startup ranks against *peers*. If the company is below the peer companies in a class, it receives less than the total amount. Consequently, the sum of all variables is determined by the median value derived from the evaluation study (Kamal & Firmansyah, 2021).

This technique is based on a meticulous framework that considers several key factors in determining the value of a startup. The methodology emphasises the importance of a targeted, sector-specific comparison, making it particularly useful for investors and founders seeking to correctly position their startup in relation to the broader market and its dynamics. This approach not only provides an estimate of *pre-money* value based on robust comparative data but also offers a framework for the detailed analysis of a startup's potential relative to its direct competitors, emphasising the importance of a strong management team, a broad market opportunity and other factors critical to long-term success.

The Venture Capital Method

The Venture Capital Method (VCM) constitutes a rigorous and strategic approach used to evaluate companies in the startup phase or characterised by inherently uncertain business models and a limited ability to generate cash flow. The VCM methodology is articulated through several stages:

- Exit Value (Exit Value): The VCM starts with the determination of the possible value of the company upon exit from investment. This value is often associated with successful scenarios such as acquisitions by established companies or initial public offerings.
- Timing of the Exit: A crucial element is the estimation of the time period required to achieve the planned exit. This is intrinsically linked to the maturity of the business and market developments, directly influencing the return on investment.
- Discount Factor: The VCM applies a discount rate that reflects the risk associated with the investment. This rate takes into account variables such as the company's failure rate, market uncertainty and other industry-specific risk factors.
- Present Value Calculation: The present value of the company is calculated using the financial formula that considers the future exit value, the timing of the exit and the discount rate. This present value represents the maximum amount an investor would be willing to commit today, considering the expected future return and the associated risk.

The VCM is a valuation tool particularly suited to emerging entrepreneurial realities, offering a framework that tends to reflect investors' financial expectations. Through this method, an attempt is made to establish a business valuation that is as aligned as possible with the growth and success prospects of the entrepreneurial project, taking into consideration key variables such as the expected growth rate, the scalability of the business model and the potential return on investment. This alignment between the company's valuations and investors' expectations is one of the main advantages of the VCM method, making it possible to reduce uncertainty and negotiation during the capital-raising phase.

However, the practical implementation of the VCM method is not without its challenges. One of the main challenges concerns the assumptions related to the exit phase, i.e., the moment when the investor disengages from the investment, realising a potential gain. Forecasting this phase can be particularly difficult, given the need to anticipate future market conditions, the valuation of the company at that time and the existence of potential buyers. These variables, which by their nature are highly uncertain and speculative, introduce an element of complexity and potential inaccuracy into the valuations, which can affect investor confidence and the stability of the financing arrangement.

Another significant limitation of the VCM method is its applicability. Indeed, this evaluation approach is particularly suitable for startups and early-stage companies that are actively seeking funding and have already outlined a clear exit strategy.

Despite these limitations, the VCM method remains a key tool for investors and entrepreneurs operating in the startup ecosystem. It offers a meeting point based on shared assessments and a methodological approach that takes into account the specific peculiarities and challenges of the world of startups. Its effectiveness, however, will always depend on the ability to carefully manage basic assumptions and adapt to the rapid and often unpredictable dynamics of the market.

The First Chicago Method

The First Chicago method is an advanced approach to estimate the value of a startup by considering three different scenarios of future performance: base, upside and downside. This methodology assigns a specific weight to each scenario in relation to the probability of its occurrence, in order to obtain a weighted and representative company valuation (Jreisat et al., 2021).

- The base scenario represents the most probable development of the company, taking into account current conditions and realistic expectations. This scenario is given the highest probability of realisation, reflecting a balanced and moderate view of potential future performance.
- The upside scenario reflects a situation in which the startup exceeds expectations. This may occur due to factors such as favourable strategic positioning within the market, disruptive innovations or advantageous strategic partnerships. In essence, it represents the optimistic case in which the company achieves higher levels of success than initially expected.
- The downside scenario, on the other hand, illustrates the consequences of underperformance. This perspective takes into account adverse events, such as unfavourable market conditions, operational problems or the presence of high competition, which could adversely affect the value of the analysed entity.

For each of these scenarios, the valuation is usually calculated using recognised methods such as the DCF or the Venture Capital (VC) method, which provide a solid quantitative basis for determining the value of the company under different circumstances.

The First Chicago method is particularly appreciated for its ability to incorporate a variety of possible outcomes in the evaluation of startups, especially those that are still in a non-profitable stage. This approach provides a holistic and detailed view of the growth potential and risks associated with the investment (Visconti, 2020a).

However, applying this method requires in-depth analysis and the ability to accurately estimate the three scenarios, which makes this approach more complex than other valuation methods. Moreover, the determination of the probabilities associated with each scenario is inherently subjective and can vary significantly depending on the analysts' judgement, adding an additional layer of uncertainty to the final valuation. In conclusion, despite its challenges, the First Chicago method is recognised for its comprehensiveness and its ability to integrate risk assessment with opportunity assessment, relying on the robustness of established valuation methodologies such as the DCF and VC methods.

The Valuation by Stage Method

The Valuation by Stage method represents a pragmatic and flexible approach to the valuation of startups, focusing on the different stages of development that a nascent company goes through during its evolution. Based on five distinct stages, the method is based on the premise that as the startup progresses through these stages, the valuation increases proportionally due to the reduction of associated risks, its operation and growth in the market.

Each of these stages is characterised by specific milestones achieved by the company, which may include product development, the acquisition of the first customers, market expansion and other key indicators of progress. Each stage corresponds to a valuation range, which provides investors and founders with a rough guide to evaluate the company based on its current stage of development.

Despite its usefulness as a valuation tool, especially for startups in the seed stage, the Valuation By Stage method also has some limitations, mainly related to its qualitative nature. It is, therefore, advisable to use it as a complementary method, a sort of *rule-of-thumb* to obtain a preliminary valuation estimate, rather than as a definitive analysis. This approach provides an initial idea of the value of the company without requiring the development of complex calculations while bearing in mind the need for quantitative insights for more accurate and detailed valuations at later stages of development.

The Replacement Method

The 'Replacement Method' valuation method is based on an analysis of the expenditure required to replicate a given entity, calculating the capital required to create a similar entity with identical technology, intellectual property and physical resources. This valuation methodology takes into account various elements of expenditure, including tangible assets, which are valued according to their current market values and intangible assets, such as patents, trademarks and brand reputation, as well as costs incurred for research and product development. To these are added the company's liabilities.

$$\text{Net Asset Value} = \text{Tangible Fixed Assets} + \text{Intangible Fixed Assets} + \text{R\&D Costs} - \text{Liabilities}$$

Formula 6—Equity Valuation: Replacement Method

In the context of startups, this approach places particular emphasis on the costs associated with the formation and maintenance of a qualified technical team capable of developing comparable technologies. This methodology, focused on assets, proves to be objective and particularly suitable for startups with significant tangible assets. Moreover, it proves to be of great utility in exit cases involving the sale of assets.

However, it is important to point out some limitations of this method. Startups, especially in the Fintech sector, tend to be characterised by an *'asset-light'* business model, i.e., with few tangible assets. Moreover, the valuation of intangible assets can present considerable difficulties. Finally, one of the major critical aspects of this approach is the omission of the company's future growth prospects, an aspect of considerable relevance in the valuation of startups, whose potential for expansion and innovation is the key element in estimating the market value associated with them.

The User-Based Valuation Method

The User-Based Valuation method is particularly suited to emerging realities in the Fintech sector, an area characterised by the prevalence of startups that operate as intermediation platforms between different users. The peculiarity of these companies, which distinguishes them from traditional models, lies in their ability to generate value mainly through the increase in the number of users and the amplification of the volume of transactions managed. Precisely for this reason, the proposed evaluation approach places significant emphasis on indicators such as the number of active users, Gross Merchandise Value (GMV), i.e., the total value of goods sold through the platform, and the growth rate of users.

This methodology requires constant revision to adapt to fluctuations in critical metrics such as Customer acquisition cost (CAC) and retention rates, i.e., the ability to retain users over time. These metrics, in fact, have a decisive influence on the value attributable to platform-based businesses, indicating not only the ability to attract new users but also to retain existing ones, key elements for the long-term sustainability and growth of the company.

In implementing this approach, an in-depth understanding of market dynamics and user behaviour is therefore essential, as is constant attention to the evolution of costs directly related to customer acquisition and retention. The methodology, in this sense, is not limited to a mere application, but takes the form of a dynamic and flexible tool, capable of adapting to the specificities and needs of each individual Fintech startup.

Real Option Model

The real options valuation methodology offers an innovative framework for analysing the value of Fintech startups, incorporating management flexibility in the face of the uncertainty and high-risk characteristic of these projects. Unlike the traditional Net Present Value (NPV)-based approach, which may not fully reflect the challenges and opportunities of Fintech projects due to their experimental nature and the rapidly changing economic and regulatory environment, real options allow for strategic evaluation of decisions to postpone, expand, downsize or abandon such ventures (Lee & Shin, 2018).

This methodology uses advanced mathematical models, such as the Black-Scholes model and the binomial model, to quantify the value of strategic flexibility, thus offering a more accurate estimate of the value of a Fintech project.

Real options applicable to Fintech projects include (Lee & Shin, 2018):

1. The option to defer, i.e., to wait to see if a project will be profitable;
2. The option to expand, i.e., to invest more in a project that is profitable;
3. The option to abandon a project that is operating at a loss and sell or reallocate resources;
4. The option of downsizing a project that is operating at a loss.

The use of decision trees is recommended for the evaluation of real options as it facilitates the organisation of design perspectives based on management forecasts or simulated data. These tools, which are intuitive for decision-makers, allow flexible and realistic modelling of real options without the restrictions imposed by other evaluation models. Research by Smith and Nau (1995) has shown that decision trees and models based on binomial lattices can generate equivalent valuations, provided that risk is correctly specified (Lee & Shin, 2018).

The advantages of this approach include the ability to incorporate decision-making flexibility in uncertain future scenarios, making it particularly suitable for the ever-changing Fintech sector. However, the complexity of applying real options models requires a solid understanding of options theory and financial modelling techniques. Moreover, the methodology is highly dependent on the availability of accurate estimates of the value of the underlying *assets* and their variance, which can be difficult to acquire for unique and innovative projects. Model assumptions, including those related to interest rates and market forecasts, significantly influence the results, making the models sensitive to changes in external conditions.

In conclusion, although the real options approach has significant advantages in terms of flexibility and adaptability to uncertain conditions, its effectiveness is limited by the complexity of implementation and the need for reliable data. This makes the tool highly relevant, but at the same time challenging for the evaluation of Fintech startups, requiring a high level of *expertise* and understanding on the part of financial analysts.

Drivers of the value of a Fintech startup

The Fintech sector is distinguished by its intrinsic specificities, which emerge from business models uniquely belonging to this sphere. Therefore, in order to devise more accurate valuation methodologies, it is imperative to first gain an in-depth understanding of the metrics that influence the value of firms operating in the Fintech sector. By virtue of studies previously conducted by the SDA Bocconi's Innovation and Corporate Entrepreneurship (ICE) centre, it was possible to discern four main categories of metrics: financing, efficiency, size and customer base (**Figure 3**). Although these classifications can be extended to a vast number of startups active in sectors other than Fintech, the metrics identified to quantify each of the aforementioned dimensions are characterised by being peculiar to the sector in question.

1. Financing:
   - Loan default rate: Indicates the percentage of loans that are not repaid on time or are in default.
   - Time to Finance: A measure of the length of time required for a loan to be disbursed to the applicant.
2. Efficiency:
   - CAC: Represents the average cost incurred to acquire a new customer.
   - Customer lifetime value (CLTV): Estimates the total value a customer can generate over time.
   - Average revenue per user (ARPU): Indicates the average revenue per user in a given period.
   - Operational efficiency: Assesses a company's ability to minimise costs and maximise productivity and profits.
3. Size:
   - Active users: Number of users actively interacting with the service in a given period.
   - Average ticket: Average value of the expenditure made by a customer in a single purchase or transaction.
   - Assets under Management (AUM): Amount of capital or financial resources managed on behalf of clients.
   - Total transaction value (TTV): Total value of transactions executed in a given period.
4. Customer:
   - Drop-out rate: Percentage of customers who stop using the company's services in a given period.

Figure 3   **Metrics driving the value of Fintech startups**

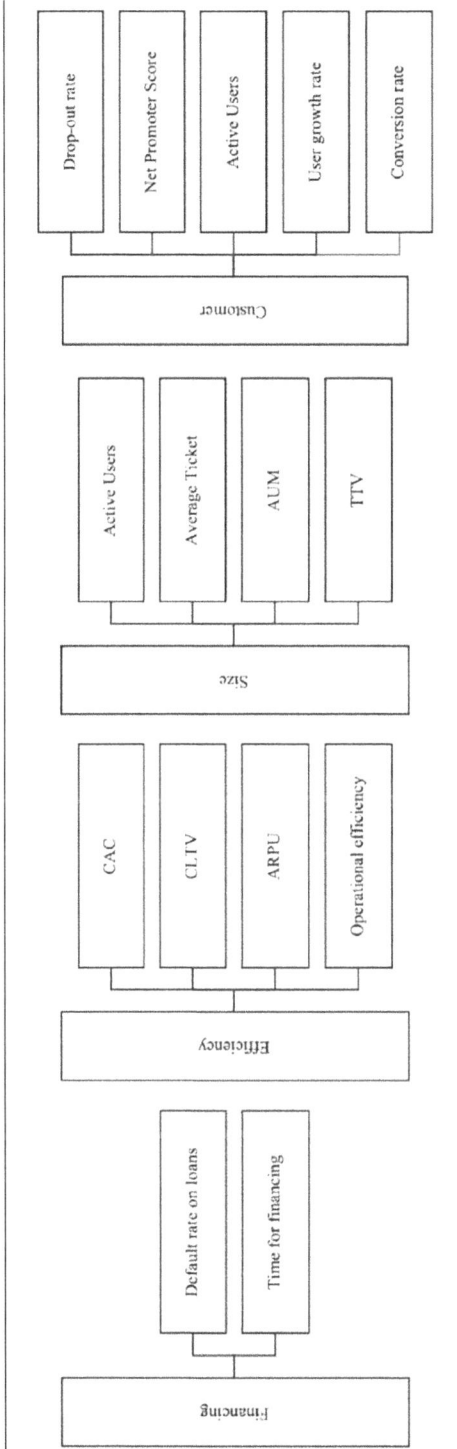

The diagram categorises Fintech valuation metrics into four areas: financing, efficiency, size and customer. Each includes sector-specific KPIs, crucial for assessing Fintech performance and sustainability.

Source: Innovation and Corporate Entrepreneurship (ICE), SDA Bocconi

Table 2   **Analysis of evaluation methods**

	Financing		Efficiency				Size	
	Default Rate on Loans	**Time for financing**	**CAC**	**CLTV**	**ARPU**	**Operational Efficiency**	**Active Users**	**Average Ticket**
DCF Method	Y	N	Y	Y	Y	Y	Y	Y
Multiples Method	N	N	N	N	N	N	Y	N
Book Valute Method	N	N	N	N	N	Y	N	N
DCF Modified Method (Damodaran)	Y	N	Y	Y	Y	Y	Y	Y
Adjusted Book Value Method	N	N	N	N	N	Y	N	N
Adjusted Revenue Multiples Method	N	N	N	N	Y	N	Y	N
Berkus Method	N	N	Y	Y	N	N	Y	N
Risk Factor Summation Method	Y	N	N	N	Y	N	Y	Y
Scorecard Valuation Method	Y	Y	Y	Y	Y	Y	Y	Y
Venture Capital Method	N	Y	Y	Y	Y	N	Y	N
First Chicago Method	N	N	Y	Y	Y	N	Y	N
Replacement Method	Y	N	Y	Y	Y	Y	Y	N
User-based Valuation Method	N	N	N	N	N	N	Y	N
Real Option Model	N	N	Y	Y	Y	N	Y	N
	36%	14%	57%	57%	64%	43%	86%	29%
	25%		55%				61%	

The table summarises the extent to which various Fintech valuation methods incorporate key metrics across financing, ● limited coverage.

Source: Innovation and Corporate Entrepreneurship (ICE), SDA Bocconi

Size			Customer					
AUM	TTV	Drop-out Rate	Net Promoter Score	Active Users	User Growth Rate	Conversion Rate		
N	Y	Y	N	Y	Y	Y	80%	42%
Y	Y	N	N	Y	N	N	27%	
Y	Y	N	N	N	N	N	20%	
N	Y	Y	N	Y	Y	Y	80%	51%
Y	Y	N	N	N	N	N	20%	
N	Y	N	N	Y	N	N	27%	
N	N	N	N	Y	N	N	27%	
N	Y	N	Y	Y	N	N	47%	
Y	Y	Y	Y	Y	Y	Y	100%	
N	Y	Y	N	Y	Y	N	60%	
Y	Y	Y	N	Y	Y	N	60%	
N	N	N	N	Y	N	N	47%	
Y	Y	N	N	Y	N	N	27%	
N	Y	Y	Y	Y	Y	Y	67%	
43%	86%	43%	21%	86%	43%	29%		
			44%					

, size and customer dimensions. The scorecard method proves most comprehensive, while traditional methods show

- Net promoter score (NPS): A measure of the likelihood that customers will recommend a company's services or products to others.
- User growth rate: Speed at which the company gains new users over time.
- Conversion rate: Percentage of users who perform a desired action, such as buying a product or subscribing to a service.

These metrics provide an overall picture of the performance and situation of the Fintech entity considered, assessing aspects ranging from financial sustainability to the effectiveness of marketing strategies and customer engagement.

Assesment of current methods

Given the valuation methods described above and the metrics guiding the valuation of Fintechs, a detailed analysis will be carried out to examine the consistency and completeness of each of the identified methodologies. This analysis aims to identify the most comprehensive method capable of serving as a solid starting point for the development of further innovative valuation methodologies. In addition, consideration will also be given to the presence of any frequently overlooked metrics, which may reveal further causes of speculative instability and emphasise the need to develop a methodology capable of also considering what is usually not analysed.

The analysis will be conducted by evaluating each of the methods considered against the previously defined metrics. For each metric, 'Y' will be used for methods that currently include or can easily include the metric without requiring major modifications. Conversely, 'N' will be used for methods that do not include the metric or would require major modifications to incorporate it.

By carefully examining the indicated percentages, one obtains a clear overview of the issues raised at the beginning of the section, while at the same time being able to deduce additional insights. In particular, the scorecard method stands out for its high degree of completeness (100% of metrics considered), as it proves capable of considering the entire set of proposed metrics. This characteristic derives mainly from its considerable flexibility, which nevertheless introduces a high degree of subjectivity into the analysis. Consequently, while representing an excellent starting point for the development of new valuation methodologies, it is essential to identify strategies to mitigate this subjectivity. At the same time, DCF methods, both in their traditional and adjusted versions, emerge for their comprehensiveness (80% of metrics considered), suggesting the possibility of being the subject of future in-depth analysis.

In the area of financial metrics, less attention is observed; on average, only a quarter (25%) of the evaluation methods currently in use consider or could consider such metrics. In particular, the time required to obtain financing turns out to be the most problematic metric to integrate in evaluation processes (14% of methods include it).

The analyses confirm the expectation that, on average, alternative evaluation methods outperform traditional ones in terms of inclusion of metrics (51% and 42%, respectively), although the former also include slightly more than half the number of metrics examined. This finding points to a marked opportunity and a real need to further refine these methodologies in order to consider a broader range of evaluation metrics.

Timing

The above considerations necessarily also require consideration of the specific stage of maturity of the company being valued, in order to identify the methodology best able to represent the value of the entity under consideration. Indeed, during the valuation phase, methodologies may vary significantly depending on the type of company and the specific circumstances. For startups, where cash flows may be negative or growing and historical financial information is limited, traditional methods such as the income, market or equity approach are not always effective. Consequently, alternative methods are used that take into account the peculiarities of these startups.

Among these methods, Venture Capital evaluates the startup based on the potential return on investment, weighing the associated risks. The scorecard approach compares the company in question with other successful ones, assigning scores to various factors such as the quality of the management team, market size and product. The DCF method, on the other hand, is adapted to include estimates of future growth and assessments of expected cash flows.

Valuation can also be influenced by external factors such as market trends, competition and general economic conditions. For example, in a fast-growing market, a startup with an innovative product may have a higher valuation than in a stagnant economy. Similarly, intense competition may reduce the perceived value of a startup, while a dominant market position may increase it. These external elements, combined with the startup's own characteristics, help to provide a more accurate and representative valuation of its true potential.

For these considerations, the choice of valuation methodology must be carefully considered according to the maturity stage of the company, its specific characteristics and the market context.

As shown in Table 3, in order to select the most suitable method for the valuation of the company under examination, it is essential to analyse the peculiarities that characterise each stage of the company's development. In particular, five main stages can be identified, each of which is associated with specific characteristics and valuation methods:

1. Idea/Seed Phase: In this initial phase, there are no cash flows, historical or forecast data, and *proof of concept* is absent. Evaluation methods used include, for example, the Cost Approach and the Scorecard Method, which are based on qualitative rather than quantitative evaluations.

Table 3   **Mapping valuation approaches across startup growth stages**

	1	2	3	4	5
Characteristics	Idea/seed	Seed/Startup	Early growth	Expansion	Sustainable growth
Cash flows	NA	Only negative	Negative (but increasing)	Positive	Stable
Proof of concept	No	No	Yes	Yes	Yes
Historical data	No	No	Limited	Yes	Yes
Forecast data	No	Limited	Limited	Yes	Yes
Valuation methods					
Cost approach					
Scorecard valuation method					
			VC method		
			Discounted cash flows		
					Market multiples

The table maps valuation methods to the company's maturity stage, from seed to sustainable growth. It highlights how early stages rely on qualitative methods (e.g., scorecard), while later stages adopt quantitative models like DCF and market multiples.
Source: Own elaboration based on data from PwC

2. Seed/Startup: Cash flows are also negative at this stage, with limited forecast data and no historical data. Qualitative methods such as the Cost Approach and the Scorecard Method continue to be used.
3. Initial growth: At this stage, cash flows are negative but increasing, with a *proof of concept* and limited historical data. Valuation methods begin to include the Venture Capital method and the DCF method, which are based on future projections.
4. Expansion: In this phase, cash flows become positive, but grow at a decreasing rate. With historical and forecast data available, valuation methods include the Venture Capital method and the DCF method.
5. Sustainable growth: When the startup achieves sustainable growth, cash flows are stable. With comprehensive historical and forecast data, more sophisticated methods such as the Discounted Cash Method (DCF) and Market Multiples are used.

This progression highlights how evaluation methods evolve from qualitative to quantitative approaches, depending on the specific characteristics of the companies under analysis.

Chart 22   **Annual average pre-money valuations, 2017–2023 ($ billion)**

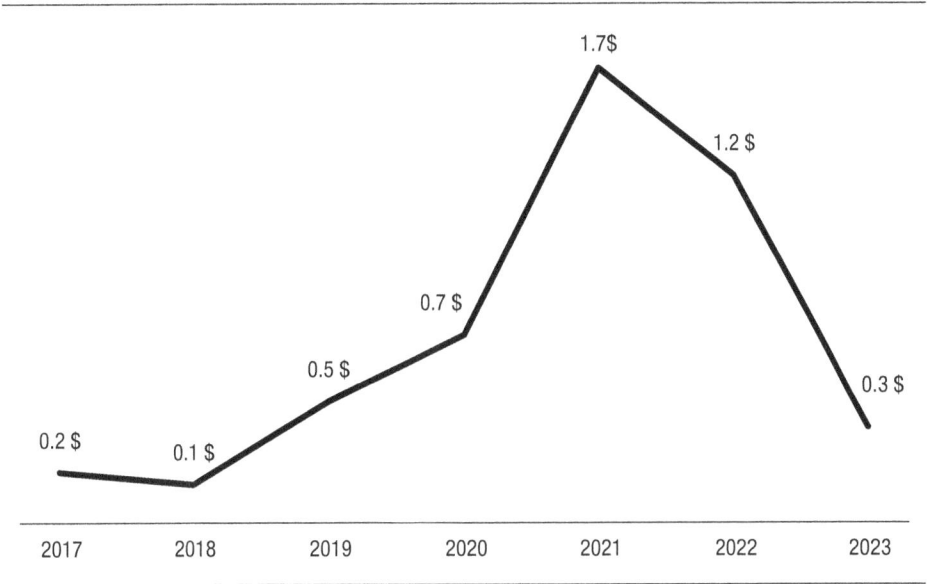

The line chart shows average pre-money valuations from 2017 to 2023. Valuations surged between 2019 and 2021, peaking at $1.7B, before declining sharply due to macroeconomic pressures such as inflation, interest rate hikes and recession fears.

Source: Own elaboration based on data from Crunchbase

Analysis of valuation trends: The 2021 speculative bubble

An analysis of the latest valuation trends has revealed a clear speculative trend. The growing enthusiasm for the sector has pushed valuations up exponentially in the two-year period 2019–2021.

However, after enthusiasm for the sector peaked in 2021, rising inflation, rising interest rates and the spectre of an impending recession have cooled valuations (Chart 22).

In addition, 2021 was a record year for unicorn startups, i.e., private startups with a valuation above $1 billion (Chart 23). In fact, there were 26 pre-money valuations (about 39% of the total) above $1 billion in 2021 (Crunchbase). Moreover, 50% of the 26 unicorns registered in the period 2017–2023 achieved status in that year.

Chart 23   Number of pre-money valuations >$1billion

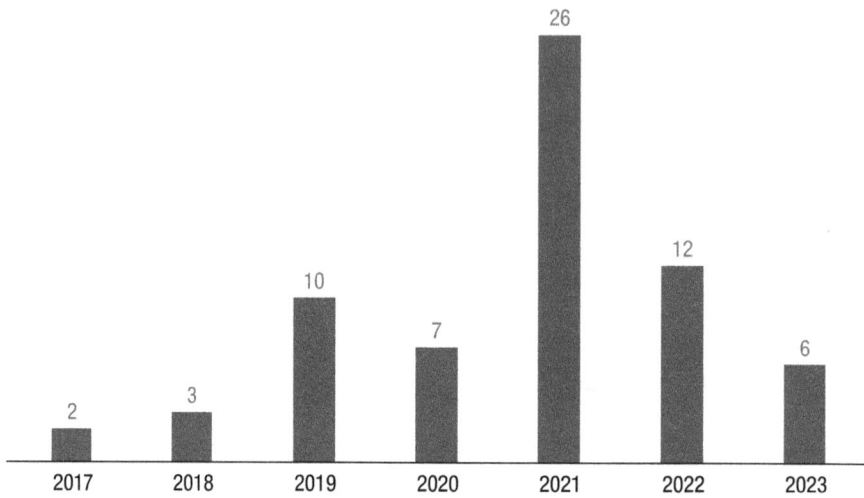

The bar chart shows the number of pre-money valuations exceeding $1B from 2017 to 2023. A record 26 occurred in 2021, accounting for nearly 50% of all such valuations in the period, underscoring the peak of investor enthusiasm during that year.

Source: Own elaboration based on data from Crunchbase

4   Case Studies

Introduction to Buy Now Pay Later (BNPL)

BNPL is a service within the digital payments sector that allows consumers to purchase products and services by paying for them in instalments (**Figure 4**). Most companies active in this sector operate in the following way: When a new user registers, he or she has to provide his or her payment details and, once approved, can start making purchases by paying in instalments, usually weekly, bi-weekly or monthly with a zero interest rate, until the balance is repaid. These businesses usually generate profits through commissions imposed on merchants and through 'late fees', i.e.,

Figure 4   **The BNPL model**

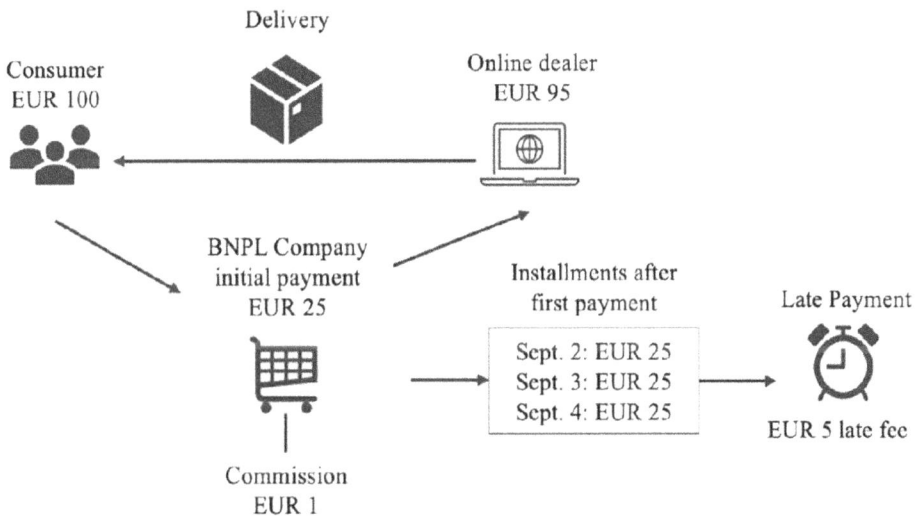

Figure 4 illustrates the BNPL model: a consumer pays in instalments, while the BNPL provider pays the merchant upfront minus a fee. Revenue is generated via merchant commissions and late payment fees, with no interest charged to the consumer.

Source: Adapted from Statista

commissions for users who fall behind on their payments. Other channels are advertisements or the introduction of membership-based models that allow, upon payment of a membership fee, access to additional services.

The advantages of BNPL, which underline the popularity of this service, are its convenience compared to credit cards and personal loans, especially considering the absence of interest rates. Moreover, given the limited level of credit control, BNPL solutions are a good option for consumers with a low credit score but who have the need to access credit in emergency situations. However, most purchases made through BNPL companies are not reported to regulators, a factor that may increase the risk of indebtedness and limit legal protections. For these reasons, the BNPL sector is likely to be affected by the new payment regulations to be introduced by the European Union.

Introduction to Klarna

Klarna is a Fintech startup, founded in 2005 in Sweden, and active in the BNPL sector. Given the trend of its valuation in recent years, it is one of the main examples of the speculative bubble that has characterised most companies active in this market segment.

Klarna's valuation has shown particular volatility since September 2020, a symbol of the transformations that have characterised the Fintech sector in the recent period. In particular, in September 2020, Klarna's valuation doubled to $10.6 billions after a $650m round in which Silver Lake Partners, BlackRock, GIC and Hmi Capital participated. During that year, Klarna's revenues grew 40% to $1 billion. Despite the strong growth results, profits declined incrementally, with the loss increasing by 50% to $109m in the same year. Despite these considerations, in March 2021, the company raised another $1 billion in a record round, tripling its valuation to $31 billion. Following the excitement resulting from this increase in valuation, in June 2021, another $639 million round raised a record valuation of $45.6 billion, making Klarna the second most valued Fintech startup in the world, after Stripe. Problems emerged in early 2022 when, in the first quarter, Klarna reported losses of $250 million, three times as much as in the same quarter of the previous year. To cover the losses, the company announced lay-offs of 10% of its staff. At that point, market sentiment towards the Fintech industry evolved, becoming very different from the enthusiasm of the first half of 2021. In July 2022, Klarna's valuation plummeted 85% to $6.7 billion.

The reasons behind the devaluation were many. In fact, the considerable change in macroeconomic conditions had a considerable impact on the realities analysed: On the one hand through the rise in interest rates from the end of 2021 onwards, which severely reduced margins, and on the other hand through the marked increase in inflation, which curbed consumption. Another reason for the slowdown *in performance* was the intensification of competition, especially resulting from the entry of banking giants such as JP Morgan Chase, Citibank and Santander, which started offering BNPL services. Apple, with its Apple Pay Later service, underwritten by

Goldman Sachs and Mastercard, is also in a particularly favourable position given its strong presence in the *digital wallet* world. Another relevant factor was the tightening of regulation, particularly in the United States and the United Kingdom, which contributed to the devaluation of the Swedish startup. In particular, more restrictions were imposed in the BNPL sector due to problems of unaffordability of loans, especially since BNPL services are mainly demanded by the less affluent classes, which are already heavily indebted. Finally, the collapse of *market sentiment* towards the Fintech industry has also been instrumental in the write-downs. In 2023, globally, funding dedicated to Fintech decreased by 42% year-on-year, reporting the worst result since 2017 (Chart 7).

Analysis of Klarna's valuation

In this section, a detailed analysis of Klarna's valuation is carried out, with a focus on the comparison between the valuation trend itself and some of the main value drivers that characterise a Fintech startup, as highlighted in the previous section. The main objective is to verify if the trend of the variables presented in the graphs below is consistent or if, on the contrary, it indicates the presence of other factors that have caused a divergence between the value attributed to the startup in the last valuation rounds and its intrinsic characteristics.

Chart 24 shows the company's valuation compared to the turnover trend, where the influence of macroeconomic conditions on company performance can be seen. In fact, a strong growth in performance was observed between 2018 and 2021, but in 2022, a year characterised by the effects of rising inflation and higher interest rates, there was a decrease in performance.

Analysing the trend in corporate valuation and performance together, consistency is noted up to 2020. However, the significant increase in valuation in 2021 and the subsequent correction in 2022 are particularly noticeable. Specifically, the turnover volume in 2023 was approximately twice as high as in 2020, but showed a lower valuation.

Continuing with the analysis of another relevant metric for Fintech startups adopting a platform-based business model, such as Klarna, a comparison of the trend in the number of annual downloads with the trend in the number of users is reported. Again, an inconsistent trend in valuation before and after the speculative bubble is evident. Starting with the observation of the downloads made each year between 2018 and 2023, it can be seen that, during the first three years, the startup valuation follows the growth in the number of downloads, showing consistency with this indicator (Chart 25). However, against a 52% increase in downloads between 2020 and 2021, the valuation increased by 330% during the same period. Furthermore, considering the current volume of downloads, the current valuation of USD 6.7 billion appears to be out of line with that before the speculative bubble. As of 2021, the number of annual downloads has stabilised at around twenty million per year, a level equal to one and a half times the level of 2020, when the valuation stood at ten and a half billion, i.e., at a higher value than the current valuation.

Chart 24   **Total income vs. Valuation 2018–2023**

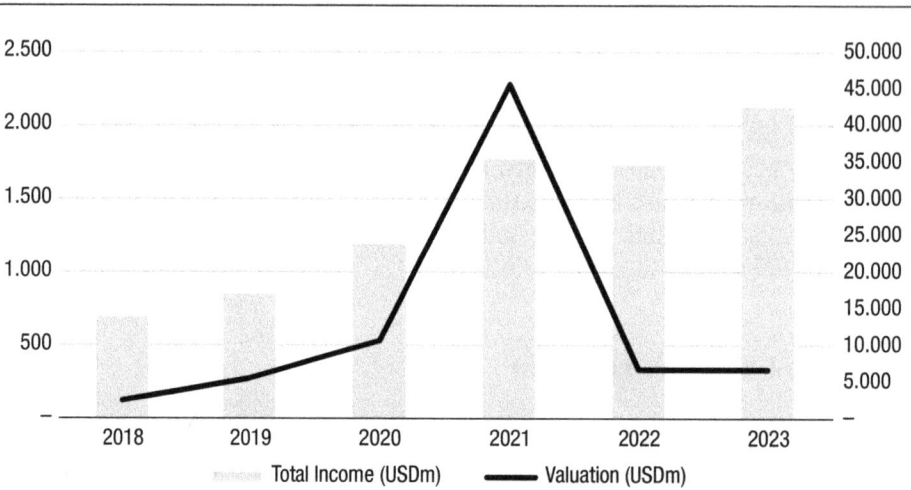

Chart 24 compares total income and valuation from 2018 to 2023. While both rose steadily until 2021, valuation dropped sharply in 2022 despite sustained income growth, reflecting the impact of inflation and interest rate hikes on market sentiment.

Source: Own elaboration based on data from Statista

Chart 25   **Number of downloads vs. Valuation 2018–2023**

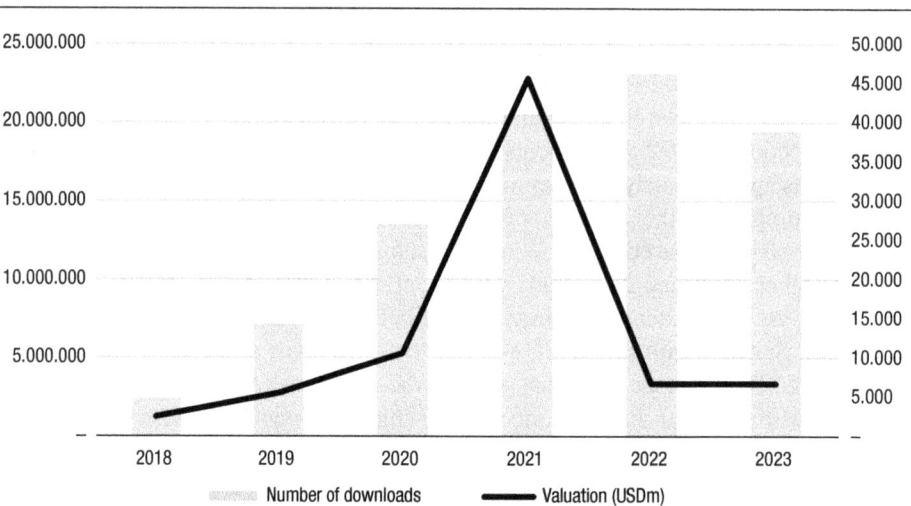

Chart 25 compares app downloads and valuation from 2018 to 2023. While downloads rose steadily, valuation surged disproportionately in 2021 and then dropped sharply, highlighting a post-bubble misalignment between market traction and perceived value.

Source: Own elaboration based on data from Statista

A further relevant metric among the main drivers of a Fintech startup's value is the total number of users (Chart 26). Here again, the lack of correlation between Klarna's valuation performance and the number of active users on the platform, an indication of the company's size, is evident.

However, when comparing Klarna's valuation with the growth rate of customers, and not with their absolute value, we observe a similar time trend, characterised by similar trends in terms of fluctuations, suggesting that changes in the company's valuation may be related to the growth dynamics of the user base (Chart 27).

GMV, i.e., the volume of transactions occurring on the platform and shown in Chart 28, is another metric that drives the value of Fintech startups. Again, the initial trend in valuation appears consistent with the increase in transactions. However, the subsequent increase in the latter is remarkable compared to the dynamics reflected by GMV.

Despite the differentiated nature of the metrics shown in the graphs above, when put in relation to the valuation trend, they provide consistent messages. A common feature of the graphs is the volatility of Klarna's valuation, which, while moving in some cases in a direction consistent with the trend of fundamentals, appears to have undergone excessive corrections.

These data, taken together, could indicate the impact of market *sentiment* on Klarna's valuation and, similarly, that of other Fintech startups, suggesting the need to consider new valuation methods than those currently applied.

Chart 26   **Number of users vs. Valuation 2019–2023**

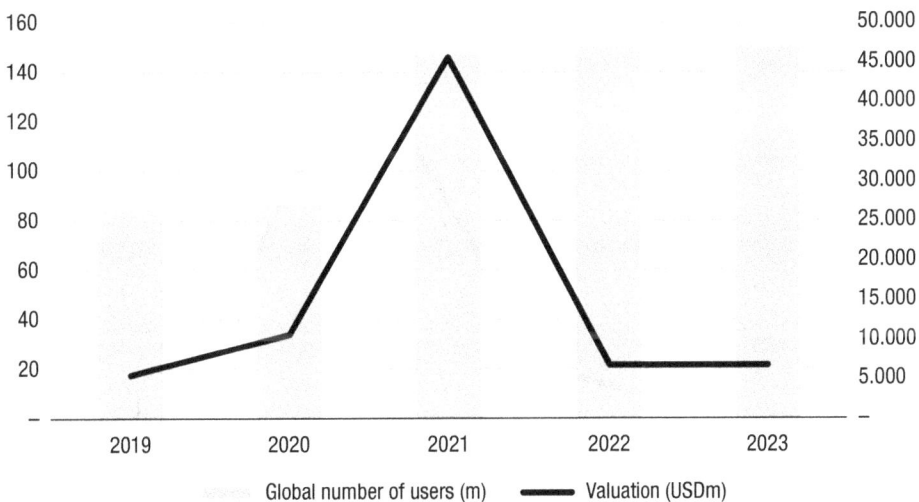

Chart 26 compares the number of users and company valuation from 2019 to 2023. While the user base remained stable post-2021, the valuation dropped sharply, highlighting a decoupling between platform size and market valuation in the post-bubble period.

Source: Own elaboration based on data from Statista, 2024b

Chart 27   **Growth rate vs. Valuation 2019–2023**

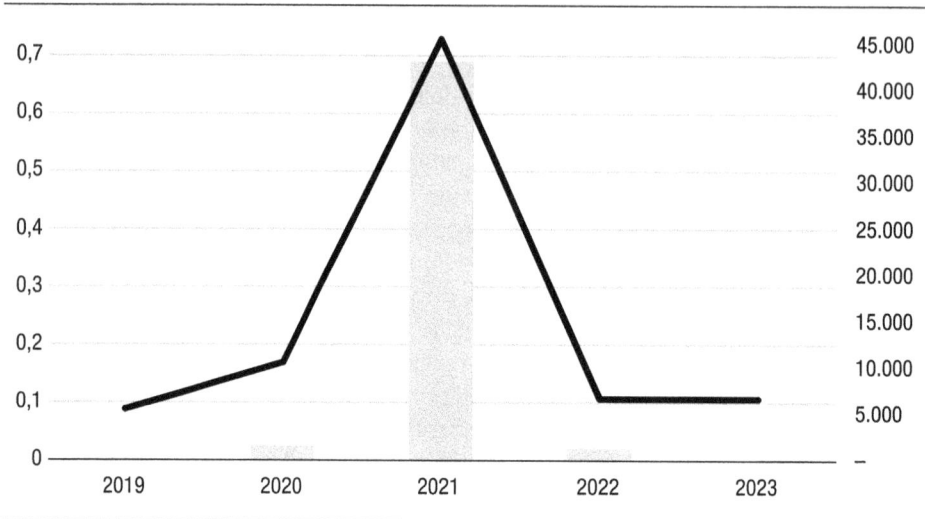

Chart 27 compares Klarna's valuation and customer growth rate from 2019 to 2023. Unlike absolute user numbers, growth dynamics align closely with valuation trends, suggesting that investor sentiment may be more responsive to growth momentum.

Source: Own elaboration based on data from Statista, 2024b

Chart 28   **GMV vs. Valuation 2019–2022**

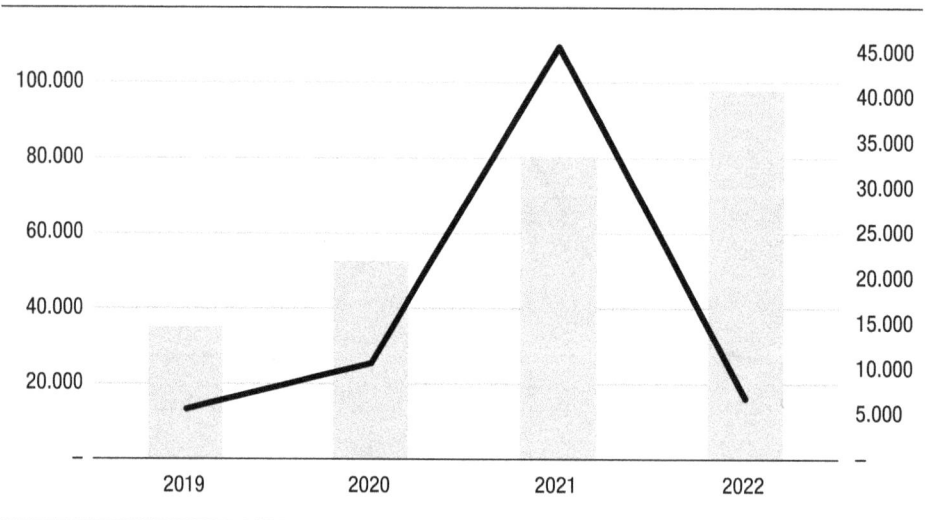

Chart 28 compares Klarna's valuation with GMV from 2019 to 2022. While valuation initially tracks GMV growth, a divergence emerges in 2022, as GMV rises but valuation drops, highlighting a decoupling between transactional volume and market value.

Source: Own elaboration based on data from Statista

Part 2
Soft Indicators

The valuation of Fintech companies, particularly during the speculative bubble period that occurred between 2021 and 2022, has been a topic of considerable interest as it was characterised by significant volatility. The difficulties encountered in the valuation of such companies are partly attributable to the inadequacy of traditional financial metrics in fully grasping the potential and risks associated with such innovative companies, and partly, instead, are related to the development phase that characterises the realities under consideration, often in early stages of growth (Visconti, 2021). In a context characterised by the growing relevance of financial technologies, technology companies, including Fintech entities, are reformulating business models through the use of innovative software, advanced algorithms, value chains based on interactive IT platforms, AI and big data. Their innovative activities in the financial services sector focus on the transmission of information through digital platforms that make extensive use of automated technologies for real-time data processing and interpretation.

In this context, traditional valuation methodologies, including DCF and market multiples, often fail to fully capture the value of Fintech realities due to their technological nature, business model and stage of maturity.

Consequently, there is a need to integrate 'soft indicators' into valuation methodologies. These indicators refer to metrics related to dimensions such as governance, management, regulation and ecosystem, the inclusion of which in valuation methodologies could provide a more holistic view of Fintech companies. The consideration of aspects beyond mere financial performance also allows for a more detailed analysis of the qualitative dimensions of such companies, leading to potentially more accurate and sustainable valuations (Visconti, 2021).

As a result, the valuation of Fintechs requires an approach that integrates both traditional financial metrics and 'soft indicators' to capture their potential and risks, improving the accuracy and sustainability of valuations. This approach not only provides a more realistic estimate of the value of Fintechs but also helps to identify and mitigate sector-specific risks, promoting a more transparent and informed investment environment.

The ability to correctly assess these realities will not only have a significant impact on investors and financial markets but will also help define the future of technological innovation in the financial sector, fostering a more dynamic and resilient ecosystem.

5 Governance

The importance of governance in Fintech companies is particularly relevant given the dynamic and often uncertain environment in which they operate. In this context, sound governance can provide a structure and guidelines that help address market challenges and exploit emerging opportunities. Indeed, effective governance not only helps improve transparency and trust among stakeholders but can also foster innovation through collaboration and the sharing of best practices.

Governance in Fintechs is, therefore, a potentially crucial determinant of their success and long-term stability. The latter significantly affects the corporate culture and strategic vision of the company. The academic literature presents two contrasting perspectives on the effect of governance on corporate value:

1. On the one hand, Agency Theory argues that governance can have a negative impact on company value, believing that investments in this area can distract managers from the goal of maximising shareholder value (Ferrell et al., 2016).
2. On the other hand, the Good Governance Theory proposes an opposite view, stating that better corporate governance strengthens the company's reputation in the eyes of investors, increasing the trust placed in the company. This is mainly based on the fact that effective corporate governance reduces information asymmetries between investors and management, decreasing risks and increasing the value of the company. Furthermore, it is necessary to consider how the relationship between the quality of corporate governance and corporate performance is bidirectional. Better performance can increase the resources available to the company, allowing more funds to be allocated to improving corporate governance. This process generates a virtuous cycle in which good governance leads to better corporate performance, which in turn enables further investment, thus creating a positive feedback loop that further strengthens the company's strength and competitiveness (Forbes, 2024).

As a result, while Fintech companies operate in an ever-changing landscape, sound governance is a key element in sustaining innovation, strengthening stakeholder trust and ensuring sustainable growth. Understanding and implementing effective governance practices can therefore be a significant competitive advantage and help build a solid foundation for long-term business success.

Agency Theory

Agency Theory is a key concept in economics and management science that explores the relationship between the owners (*principals*) of a company and the managers (*agents*) who run its operations. The theory stems from the need to resolve conflicts of interest that may arise when the agents, who are in charge of managing the company, may have personal goals that do not align perfectly with those of the principals. The central premise of Agency Theory is that both principals and agents are utility maximisers and, since principals cannot directly observe every action of agents, problems of moral hazard (such as minimum effort) and adverse selection (such as exploiting asymmetric information) may arise (Bo et al., 2012).

According to this theory, the implementation of complex and expensive governance structures can have a negative impact on company value. Indeed, Ferrell et al. (2016) argue that investments in corporate governance may divert managers' attention away from the main objective of maximising shareholder value, as the resources and time devoted to implementing and maintaining these structures could be used in activities directly related to corporate performance. Moreover, governance mechanisms may introduce additional agency costs, including monitoring costs, which reduce the overall value of the company.

An example of these costs can be observed in managers' performance-based compensation contracts, which can lead to opportunistic behaviour by managers, such as manipulating accounting results or making decisions that maximise short-term profits at the expense of long-term sustainability. An excessive focus on governance can create a rigid and bureaucratic environment that stifles innovation and the ability to respond quickly to market changes, which are crucial for Fintech companies.

This critical view of corporate governance is countered by the Good Governance Theory, which instead argues that good governance improves company reputation and investor confidence by reducing information asymmetries and perceived risks, thus leading to an increase in company value (Ferrell et al., 2016). However, Agency Theory highlights the importance of carefully balancing investments in governance with the need to maintain a clear focus on the company's operational and strategic performance.

Good Governance Theory

The Good Governance Theory argues that effective and transparent corporate governance is critical to enhancing a company's reputation and value. This theory emphasises how high-quality governance practices can create an environment of trust among investors, managers and other stakeholders, reducing information asymmetries and perceived risks. In this context, good governance is seen as a factor that can positively influence long-term corporate performance. The Good Governance Theory, in fact, is based on the idea that companies that adopt sound governance practices are able to attract more investors, obtain financing on more favourable terms and face market challenges with considerable effectiveness.

A key element of the Good Governance Theory is transparency. Companies that communicate clearly and openly with stakeholders tend to gain market trust, which can translate into lower stock volatility and a lower cost of capital. Ferrell et al. (2016) point out that robust corporate governance can reduce information asymmetries between management and investors, thereby increasing the perceived value of the company. For example, detailed financial disclosure practices and rigorous internal audits can reassure investors about the financial and operational soundness of the company, reducing perceived risk and improving market valuation.

Moreover, good governance can promote an ethical and responsible corporate culture, which is essential for the long-term sustainability of the company. Companies that invest in governance not only comply with international regulations and standards but also develop stronger relationships with their stakeholders, including employees, customers and local communities. These strong relationships can result in increased customer loyalty, reduced employee turnover and improved corporate reputation.

The Good Governance Theory also recognises the importance of the board of directors (BoD) in the supervision and strategic guidance of the company. A BoD composed of independent and qualified members can provide effective oversight of management, ensuring that business decisions are made in the interests of all stakeholders and not just a small circle of executives. The adoption of advanced governance practices can improve the quality of business decisions, reducing the risk of opportunistic behaviour and contributing to long-term value creation (Dixon et al., 2012).

The Good Governance Theory therefore argues that investment in sound corporate governance is a strategic element that can increase the value of the company by enhancing investor confidence, reducing risk and promoting a sustainable and responsible corporate culture.

Given the importance of governance in determining the value of a company, it is crucial to identify metrics to assess its quality. The Organisation for Economic Cooperation and Development (OECD) has developed a set of guidelines for judging the quality of corporate governance (OECD, 2019). According to the OECD, dimensions to focus on include anti-corruption policies, the independence of the BoD, the separation of CEO and chairman of the board and the tenure of its members (Najaf et al., 2023).

The OECD Guidelines (2023) also consider crucial aspects such as transparency and disclosure of information, accountability of directors and fair treatment of shareholders. These elements are essential to ensure that board decisions are made in the interests of all stakeholders, not just a small circle of shareholders or directors (OECD, 2023).

In the literature, the most commonly used governance quality metrics in Fintech evaluation models are the following: the profile of founders and key stakeholders, board characteristics, CEO characteristics, governance policies and the quality (or reputation) of the company's accounting firm. In fact, during the financial crisis caused by the COVID-19 pandemic, it emerged that Fintech companies with more robust governance tended to have less negative market performance than those with weaker governance (Najaf et al., 2023).

The growing importance of ESG policies and sustainability disclosure is also emphasised as factors that can significantly influence investor perception and market performance of Fintech companies (Najaf et al., 2023).

It follows that the integration of governance quality metrics into the evaluation models of Fintechs is crucial to ensure their long-term sustainability and growth, especially in times of financial crisis. The choice of auditors, the transparency of governance policies and the focus on sustainability are key factors that can determine the success or failure of these realities (Najaf et al., 2023).

Profile of founders and key stakeholders

The profile of founders and key stakeholders is of crucial importance in the evaluation of Fintech companies, as the background, experience and skills of the founding team significantly influence a company's development. Numerous studies have shown that the profile of the founder exerts a direct impact on the company's performance (Cooper et al., 1994). In particular, venture capitalists often place a higher value on founders with previous leadership experience or industry-specific knowledge (Schachel et al., 2021).

An essential element of the profile of founders lies in their ability to attract and retain relevant stakeholders. The competence of a founding team in establishing effective governance can be crucial for long-term success. Indeed, robust governance not only helps to clearly define roles and responsibilities within the organisation but also facilitates transparency and trust among investors and other external stakeholders. Transparency in governance practices is also crucial in reducing information asymmetries between founders and investors, fostering an environment of greater trust and collaboration.

The educational and professional background of founders is a significant indicator of their ability to effectively implement and manage the realities analysed. Founders with a solid academic background in relevant fields and work experience in successful companies tend to be more effective in implementing control systems that meet investors' expectations. Furthermore, the founders' prior entrepreneurial experience is a crucial factor that lenders consider during the evaluation process (Schachel et al., 2021).

Key stakeholders, besides the founders, include initial investors, board members, strategic advisors and business partners. Each stakeholder group brings specific expertise and resources that can accelerate the growth of the company in question. Initial investors, for instance, not only provide capital but often contribute their network of contacts and strategic *know-how*. Board members, selected for their experience and reputation, play a crucial role in providing guidance and strategic vision (Schachel et al., 2021).

In conclusion, the profile of founders and key stakeholders is decisive for the success of a Fintech. The ability to attract and retain quality stakeholders represents a significant competitive van tage. Investors carefully evaluate these aspects, recognising that sound governance and a competent founding team are reliable indicators of potential long-term success.

Board of directors (BoD)

The composition of the BoD represents one of the most studied dimensions in literature with reference to the governance of Fintechs. Specific board characteristics, such as size, diversity and specialisation, exert a significant influence on both risk and profitability. Board size may determine the effectiveness of the decision-making process. Indeed, larger boards may benefit from a wider variety of skills and perspectives, but may also suffer from coordination problems and a tendency towards more conservative decision-making. Diversity, in terms of gender, age and professional background, has been correlated with better governance and corporate performance, due to a plurality of viewpoints and a greater ability to respond effectively to market challenges. Finally, the specialisation of board members, especially in fields such as economics and law, contributes to more analytical and prudent risk management, although it can sometimes limit innovation and the propensity for more aggressive growth strategies.

Board size

A study conducted by Ferilli et al. (2024) on a sample of almost 600 Fintechs, reported in the 'Italian Fintech Observatory Report' published by PwC (PwC, 2020), showed that a larger BoD tends to reduce profitability due to more conservative decisions than those made by a smaller group. This phenomenon is grounded in the resource dependency theory (Pfeffer & Salancik, 1978), which suggests that increasing the number of individuals increases the depth and breadth of expertise available in the BoD, enhancing decision-making capacity and expanding the *pool of* resources accessible to the organisation. It follows that, although larger Boards may offer a greater diversity of skills and viewpoints, they also tend to introduce operational complexities that may slow down decision-making. In particular, the presence of a larger number of individuals may lead to a dilution of individual responsibility, which may increase the difficulty in reaching a quick and effective consensus. In addition, a larger board may generate additional costs, both in terms of time and resources, needed to coordinate activities and communications between members.

On the other hand, Yermack (1996) pointed out that a smaller board facilitates communication and decision-making, thus improving corporate performance. Indeed, they foster greater cohesion and more direct interaction between members, facilitating closer supervision and greater agility in strategic decision-making. This alignment with Jensen's (1993) view emphasises that a large number of subjects can increase agency problems, reducing the board's effectiveness in supervising managerial behaviour and decreasing corporate profitability.

Board diversity

Diversity within the BoD, in terms of gender, age and educational background, has been the subject of numerous studies for its impact on corporate performance. The latter have confirmed a positive correlation between gender diversity on the BoD and company performance. In particular, Erhardt et al. (2003) found that the presence of women on the BoD can increase the effectiveness of control, as women are generally more rigorous than men. Women's participation in the BoD may help to avoid risky projects, as women are generally more averse to financial risk than men (Byrness et al., 1999). Furthermore, Manetti and Toccafondi (2012) suggested that gender diversity could improve the credibility of corporate communications through reinforcement mechanisms facilitated by stakeholder engagement (Ferilli et al., 2024).

A further study by Arena et al. (2023) highlights the crucial role of independent women on the board of Italian banks in the context of Fintech governance. Independent women on the BoD help mitigate the negative relationship between Fintech and banks' asset riskiness, improving competitiveness and reducing conflicts of interest between shareholders, creditors and social governance. (Arena et al., 2023).

Furthermore, it has been observed that greater diversity in terms of age and educational background within the board can lead to a broader range of skills and perspectives, fostering corporate innovation and creativity. The combination of different backgrounds contributes to a better analysis of business issues and the formulation of more effective strategies. For instance, age diversity can lead to a balance between the propensity for innovation of younger members and the established experience of older members, creating a dynamic and well-balanced working environment.

In sum, boardroom diversity not only improves corporate performance through more effective control and reduced risk but also through more credible communication and more robust governance. These benefits also extend to the Fintech sector, where independent women on the boards of Italian banks play a crucial role in mitigating the associated risks and promoting competitiveness, thus demonstrating the importance of diverse and inclusive governance.

Board specialisation

Specialisation of board members (BoDs) in disciplines such as economics or law has been associated with greater risk management capacity and a more analytical and conservative decision-making approach. According to Ferilli et al. (2024), BoDs with directors specialised in economics or law show a higher capacity for risk management. This result is consistent with vision-based resource theory, which emphasises the importance of internal competencies and capabilities in determining corporate performance.

However, such a conservative approach could potentially stifle the innovative potential and profitability of Fintech entities, as these boards tend to avoid more aggressive growth strategies (Ferilli et al., 2024). Indeed, due to their background, directors specialised in economics and law may adopt a cautious attitude, prioritising financial stability and regulatory compliance over high risk-taking.

It follows that, while specialisation in economics or law of board directors may lead to a more conservative approach to decision-making, it also offers significant advantages in terms of risk management and corporate stability. It is therefore crucial to balance these skills with other experiences and perspectives within the board to ensure a balance between prudence and innovation, thereby maximising both the financial sustainability and growth of the company.

The composition of the BoD, in terms of size, diversity and specialisation, plays a crucial role in determining the risk and profitability of Fintechs. Although larger board sizes and high levels of specialisation may improve risk management, they may also limit innovation capacity and growth. Therefore, it is essential to strike a balance between different board characteristics to optimise both the stability and long-term profitability of Fintechs (Ferilli et al., 2024).

The main challenge for such companies is to create a BoD that balances prudence and boldness, stability and innovation. A well-balanced board can not only mitigate financial and legal risks but also promote competitiveness and sustainable growth. Furthermore, inclusive and diverse governance is crucial to meet the challenges of the modern marketplace and ensure the long-term success of Fintech companies.

Characteristics of the CEO

The characteristics of the CEO represent a key element in the evaluation of Fintechs, as they significantly influence the company's performance and strategy. The existing literature highlights how the CEO's educational background and professional experience can affect the company's approach to innovation and risk management.

Educational background

The CEO's educational background has been the subject of numerous studies that have shown its relevance for corporate performance. Ferilli et al. (2024) point out that, similar to the considerations made with regard to the BoD, CEOs with a background in economics or law tend to adopt more conservative strategies, oriented towards long-term stability rather than immediate profitability. This behaviour is attributed to the rigorous and analytical training that characterises these fields of study, which fosters an in-depth understanding of systemic risks and the long-term consequences of corporate decisions. The presence of CEOs with such characteristics can thus be positively valued by venture capitalists as an indicator of risk reduction, although it may limit short-term growth opportunities (Ferilli et al., 2024). Furthermore, it highlights how the presence of an MBA among CEOs represents a significant element in influencing the leadership of Fintech companies, contributing to the development of sustainable business models (Sannino et al. 2019).

Professional experience

The CEO's professional experience plays a crucial role in the ability to manage the company and meet market challenges. CEOs with practical experience in innovation or advanced technical skills are able to evaluate, select and implement innovative initiatives more effectively, thereby improving corporate performance. In particular, CEOs with a background in management or law demonstrate a greater capacity for risk reduction and a more prudent approach to decision-making. However, this cautiousness can sometimes limit the innovative potential and profitability of the companies considered (Ferilli et al., 2024). It is also shown that CEOs with greater seniority and previous entrepreneurial experience tend to have a positive impact on the company's ability to create and maintain sustainable business models (Sannino et al., 2019).

CEO characteristics, including educational background and professional experience, play a crucial role in determining a Fintech's growth. Although a conservative approach can reduce risks and promote long-term stability, it is essential to balance these qualities with innovative skills to ensure sustainable and competitive growth. Therefore, when evaluating Fintechs, venture capitalists should carefully consider the profile of the CEO, recognising how his or her characteristics can significantly influence profitability, risk management, innovation capacity and financial sustainability.

Governance policies

Corporate governance policies are of paramount importance for the success and sustainability of both established and emerging companies such as startups. In line with the classification proposed by the Organisation for Economic Co-operation and Development (OECD), adherence to good governance practices emerges as a determining factor in the creation of corporate value. Among the most relevant governance practices are anti-corruption policies, the independence of the BoD and the appropriate term of office for executive directors:

• Anti-corruption policies are an essential component in building a transparent and trustworthy business environment. Such policies not only reduce the risk of fraud but also contribute to building trust among investors and other stakeholders. Transparency in business operations and the adoption of anti-corruption preventive measures strengthen the company's reputation, fostering stable and lasting business relationships.

- Board independence is another key aspect of good governance practices. A BoD with a majority of independent members is able to exercise more effective control over management decisions, preventing conflicts of interest and ensuring that corporate decisions are made in the interests of all shareholders. An independent BoD promotes more balanced and objective governance, improving the quality of strategic and operational decisions.
- The length of executive directors' terms of office is a further indicator of good governance. Mandates that are too long can lead to stagnant and change-resistant corporate governance, while mandates that are too short can prevent directors from developing and implementing long-term strategies. An appropriate balance in the length of mandates allows directors to make a significant and sustainable contribution to corporate development while fostering the necessary flexibility and innovation.

Empirical studies have shown that better governance practices are usually associated with lower fraud risks, higher investor confidence and, ultimately, increased corporate value. According to research conducted by Najaf et al. (2022), there is a positive correlation between the adoption of effective governance policies and the market valuation of companies. Companies that implement rigorous governance measures tend to be more attractive to investors due to their perceived lower riskiness and more responsible and transparent management.

It follows that governance policies are not just a regulatory requirement, but a strategic lever for improving business performance and consolidating stakeholder trust. The adoption of good governance practices, such as those outlined by the OECD, contributes to a safer, more transparent and sustainable business environment, fostering the long-term growth and success of companies.

Quality of the auditing company

A frequently adopted approach in academic literature to assess the quality of a company's governance is to analyse it indirectly by examining the quality of the auditing firm the company relies on. Considering the market of auditing firms, their quality is often judged by their membership in the Big 4 group, consisting of Deloitte, Ernst & Young, KPMG and PricewaterhouseCoopers. These four firms are recognised as the audit firms with the highest reputation and are associated with a higher quality of services (Che et al., 2020).

These audit firms have established their reputation through years of experience and a wide range of services offered globally. Being a client of one of the Big 4 not only indicates a certain level of compliance with international standards but also suggests greater transparency and reliability in accounting and control processes. In addition, the Big 4 are often involved in strategic consulting and risk management, offering their client companies added value beyond simple auditing.

Therefore, the presence of an audit performed by one of the Big 4 is generally correlated with reduced risks and can, as a result, contribute to an increase in the valuation of companies. This is because investors and other stakeholders tend to have greater confidence in the financial information audited by these prestigious audit firms, perceiving a lower likelihood of errors, fraud or questionable accounting practices. As a result, companies that rely on one of the Big 4 can benefit from better access to capital and a stronger reputation in the market.

The integration of governance indicators into business valuation methodologies represents a significant advance in the analysis of Fintechs. This approach sheds light on inherent strengths and potential vulnerabilities that financial metrics alone might not highlight, offering a broader and more detailed perspective on the management quality and structural soundness of the company. In particular, examining the quality and stability of leadership, as well as governance structures, allows investors to gain a deeper understanding of the company's ability to maintain long-term sustainable growth.

The consideration of such indicators not only improves the accuracy of financial evaluations but also enriches the overall understanding of the company. This integrated approach represents significant added value for investors, contributing to a better allocation of financial resources and promoting the development of more sustainable and transparent business practices.

Fintech startups

With specific reference to the evaluation of Fintech startups, given the early development stage in which they find themselves, the analysis of the Governance variable focuses exclusively on the profile of the founders, the main stakeholders and the characteristics of the CEO. This approach is due to the absence of other components typical of more mature governance structures.

The profile of founders and key stakeholders is crucial at this stage. The background, experience and skills of the founding team significantly influence the development of the company. Investors often place a higher value on founders with previous leadership experience or industry-specific knowledge, recognising that their ability to attract and retain relevant stakeholders is crucial to long-term success.

At the same time, the characteristics of the CEO, including educational background and professional experience, are key elements in the evaluation of the startup. A CEO with a solid academic background and significant entrepreneurial experience can be an indicator of stability and potential success, capable of implementing effective strategies and handling market challenges competently.

Consequently, when evaluating Fintech startups, the main focus is on the founders, key stakeholders and the CEO. These elements provide the main indications of the company's ability to develop solid and effective governance, despite the absence of more complex structures typical of mature companies. This focus allows investors to assess the startup's potential for growth and success, based on factors that may be decisive at an early stage of development.

6 Management

Consideration of management effectiveness in managing business activities is of paramount importance for the proper evaluation of a company. Such activities include the ability to monitor performance, anticipate market changes, optimise resources and implement corrective strategies. One indicator of management quality is the presence of Management Control Systems (MCSs), defined as *'formal or informal routines and procedures that managers employ to maintain or modify organisational activities'* (Simons, 1995).

MCSs, or measurement and control systems, can vary widely depending on the type of performance they are intended to measure. In general, they can be categorised into three main types:

1. Financial CSMs focus mainly on assessing the economic and financial performance of an organisation, including indicators such as turnover, profit and return on investment.
2. HR MCSs, on the other hand, focus on measuring personnel-related performance, such as employee productivity, job satisfaction and turnover rate.
3. The MCSs of strategic planning, which concern the evaluation of the effectiveness of the strategies adopted by the company, through the use of indicators such as alignment with long-term corporate objectives, innovation and the ability to adapt to market change.

Financial management control systems

Financial MCSs are essential tools that include metrics such as cash flow projections, profitability analysis of the various products and services offered by the company and capital investment approval procedures. These systems enable continuous monitoring of financial performance through detailed analyses of income and expenditure, ensuring that the company maintains a financial balance and identifies any liquidity problems at an early stage. Cash flow projections and product profitability analyses are considered particularly important by external financiers to assess the financial sustainability of companies and their ability to generate profit (Schachel et al., 2021).

An effective MCS must be aligned with the organisation's objectives and structures, facilitate decision-making and ensure that performance metrics are measurable. In addition, effective communication of any deviations from set targets is crucial to make necessary corrections and improvements.

Financial control systems include policies and procedures that help monitor and control the allocation and utilisation of financial resources, ensuring the efficient management of resources and the integrity of financial information. Timely updating of data and analysis of all possible operational scenarios are key to implementing effective financial control strategies. These systems are particularly relevant for Fintechs, as external investors, such as equity and debt providers, consider financial MCSs crucial for the initial assessment and ongoing monitoring of investments (Schachel et al., 2021).

Human resources management control systems

Human Resources MCSs monitor crucial aspects such as codes of conduct, incentive programmes, job descriptions and orientation programmes for new employees. These systems also include performance targets for managers and individual incentive programmes that link pay to performance. Human Resources MCSs are essential for maintaining a motivating and well-organised working environment, thus improving the overall productivity of the company.

Human Resource MCSs play a significant role in human capital management, which is crucial for the growth and development of startups. These systems make it possible to centralise data, automate HR processes and improve organisational efficiency. In addition, HR MCSs are crucial for managing the relationship between employees and the organisation, including the management of labour relations and working conditions. Advanced Human Resource Information Systems (HRIS) also support the management of occupational health and safety risks, monitoring accidents and hazardous conditions, and ensuring a safe and compliant working environment.

As a result, HR MCSs not only improve the operational management of human resources but also provide strategic tools to support business growth, increase productivity and maintain a healthy and motivating work environment. These systems are indispensable for companies seeking to optimise their human resources and attract external investors interested in the strength and sustainability of the company's human capital. In an ever-changing economic environment, the ability to effectively manage human resources through advanced management control tools is a significant competitive advantage. Centralising information and automating processes not only reduces operating costs but also improves the accuracy of strategic decisions. Furthermore, the implementation of performance-related incentive programmes promotes a result-oriented corporate culture, increasing employee engagement and motivation.

HR MCSs, therefore, are not only operational tools, but are an essential component of corporate strategy, contributing decisively to the achievement of the organisation's long-term goals (Schachel et al., 2021).

Management control systems of strategic planning

Finally, the MCSs of strategic planning focus on the achievement of strategic objectives by organising the entire portfolio of products and services offered by the company. These systems include customer development plans, product portfolio plans and monitoring of investment budgets. The definition of strategic objectives and human resources development planning are key components, enabling the company to align its resources and strategies with long-term goals. Such systems are essential to ensure that the company can adapt quickly to market changes and maintain a competitive advantage.

Strategic Planning MCSs incorporate a variety of tools and methodologies to ensure that strategic objectives are achieved efficiently and effectively. Among these tools are Balanced Scorecards, which facilitate the translation of corporate strategy into measurable objectives across different perspectives: financial, customer, internal processes and learning and growth. In addition, strategic planning systems include SWOT (Strengths, Weaknesses, Opportunities, Threats) analysis to assess internal capabilities and market opportunities, helping to identify key areas to focus on for competitive advantage. This type of analysis is crucial for formulating strategies that can adapt to market changes and exploit new opportunities.

Another crucial component of Strategic Planning MCSs is the continuous monitoring of performance through KPIs. KPIs allow progress towards strategic goals to be measured and timely changes to strategies to be made when necessary. This dynamic approach allows the company to remain agile and responsive in a changing market environment. Finally, the integration of technology, such as Enterprise Resource Planning (ERP) systems, into Strategic Planning MCSs allows for greater coordination and visibility of business operations, improving decision-making and operational efficiency.

These systems are crucial not only to maintain strategic alignment within the company but also to ensure that the company in question can respond quickly to external changes, thus maintaining its competitive advantage in the market (Schachel et al., 2021).

The design of MCSs depends on the specific needs of the business and, in particular, is closely linked to the market context in which the company operates and the competitive strategy adopted by it. A higher level of competition generally requires more structured and formal MCSs, as there is a need for more accurate control of performance metrics to maintain its positioning. Expanding businesses, especially those with global ambitions, require more advanced MCSs due to the increasing operational complexity resulting from expansion. Therefore, the value placed on MCSs in Fintechs is more pronounced in highly competitive markets or those with significant growth prospects (Davila et al., 2015).

From the perspective of competitive strategy, it has been observed that investors tend to reward companies that have MCSs aligned with their strategy. In this context, Davila et al. (2015) classify MCSs into three categories: basic MCSs, differentiation MCSs and cost leadership MCSs.

1. Basic MCSs include commonly adopted systems such as financial planning, financial evaluation, human resources planning, sales targeting, investment approval, strategic planning, product development, human resources evaluation and sales pipeline management.
2. Differentiation MCSs are designed to support differentiation strategies and focus on aspects such as market analysis and customer relationship management (CRM), marketing and branding in order to attract and retain customers.
3. Cost leadership MCSs focus on quality monitoring to offer products and services comparable to those on the market, but at a competitive price.

The adoption of MCSs is also influenced by the intrinsic characteristics of the company and its growth expectations. Companies operating in highly competitive markets or with high growth prospects tend to implement more formal and sophisticated MCSs. These systems not only facilitate the management of complex operations but also serve as management quality signals to external investors. In fact, the presence of formal MCSs can increase information capacity and improve investors' perception of managerial quality, thereby increasing the value of the company.

Another crucial aspect is the ability of MCSs to support corporate strategy. Control systems that are well aligned with a company's competitive strategy can significantly improve business performance. For example, for a differentiation strategy, systems that support marketing, branding and customer relationship management are essential. For a cost leadership strategy, on the other hand, quality monitoring and cost management systems are essential. A company's ability to implement MCSs that are consistent with its competitive strategy can therefore represent a significant competitive advantage and a highly valuable asset for investors.

It follows that the design and implementation of MCSs in Fintechs not only meet immediate operational and strategic needs but also play a crucial role in the perception of the company's value by external investors. The ability of a company to adapt its MCSs to the competitive environment and its own growth ambitions can lead to a significant increase in its market value and improve its prospects for long-term success.

Main benefits

The presence of MCSs is particularly relevant in the context of a company as it strengthens internal decision-making processes and enables better coordination of resources, increasing the likelihood that the company can grow and progress to the next stages of its development (Davila et al., 2015). MCSs assist managers in focusing on key areas, facilitating a safe transition through business crises and preparing the company for future success (Davila, Foster, & Jia, 2010; Greiner, 1972). The positive relationship between the intensity of MCSs and the growth of the companies considered has been documented by a study showing that the adoption of formal systems facilitates growth (Davila & Foster, 2005, 2007; Sandino, 2007). This effect related to the presence of MCSs was further corroborated by the evidence of a positive relationship between the adoption of these systems and the valuation of a Fintech. Indeed, Davila et al. (2015) show that a 10% increase in MCSs adoption is associated with a 3.3% increase in firm value. This effect is particularly pronounced in companies operating in highly competitive and high-growth environments.

Indeed, MCSs not only support management decisions but also serve as signals of management quality and potential future growth. The voluntary adoption of MCSs can indicate to external financiers the qualification of management and the preparedness of the company to meet growth challenges. The findings of Davila et al. (2015) provide further evidence in favour of the positive and incremental role of formal control systems. These show that investors value the adoption of MCSs positively, challenging the traditional view that considers these systems as rigid and bureaucratic, and therefore detrimental to the success of startups.

The reasons for the positive association between MCSs and value are many and, in part, similar to those for which better governance is generally associated with greater corporate value. Indeed, MCSs are a crucial source for reducing information asymmetries between investors and companies. In a context where information asymmetries emerge due to managers' advantage over investors regarding the company's performance, potential, risks and real value, the adoption of MCSs can act as a signal of quality and transparency. Fintechs can implement MCSs to demonstrate higher management quality and operational transparency to the market (Schachel et al., 2021). This approach not only facilitates a better understanding of internal dynamics by investors but also improves the ability to monitor and manage business operations. MCSs, being systems based on formal information and procedures that managers use to maintain and modify organisational activity patterns, motivate employees and managers by setting challenging goals, holding them accountable for their achievement and contributing to the creation of a reliable internal information base for managerial decisions (Simons, 1995).

Lenders

Management quality, supported by well-implemented MCSs, reduces investors' decision-making uncertainties and increases companies' financing capacity, as investors perceive the adoption of MCSs as an indicator of a company's potential future growth and quality (Rahaman & Al Zaman, 2013; Strauss et al., 2013). However, the relevance of management quality varies according to the type of lender, with particular differences between equity and debt providers. In particular, debt and equity lenders assess MCSs differently. Debt financiers attach greater importance to financial control systems than other types of MCSs, as these systems ensure the long-term financial stability of the entities under consideration and reduce the perceived risk for investors (de Rassenfosse & Fischer, 2016; Garcia Osma et al., 2018). In contrast, equity financiers, while considering financial MCSs important, also place more emphasis on strategic MCSs, as these contribute to a more comprehensive management aligned with the companies' growth and development objectives (Kaplan & Strömberg, 2004). Underlying this difference is the fact that *lenders* usually encounter greater information asymmetries than Venture Capitalists because they do not enjoy the same screening capabilities in the pre-investment phase (Amabile, 1998). Furthermore, once they enter into the investment, *lenders* have only very limited screening capabilities (Kaplan & Strömberg, 2001). These important differences between the two types of lenders in fact explain why the presence of MCSs is less relevant for Venture Capitalists at the time of the investment, since once they enter the company's capital they will be able to influence its management. Differently, *lenders*, who lack decision-making powers within the company, attach more relevance to MCSs in the pre-investment phase since they will not be able to implement them once the financing has been provided (Schachel et al., 2021).

The quality of management is, therefore, a further key aspect to be taken into account when evaluating Fintechs. It is imperative to monitor such a relevant metric as the presence, extent and type of MCSs implemented by the company in the sector. The sophistication and effectiveness of such control systems not only reflect management's ability to effectively manage resources and adapt to changing market conditions but are also an indicator of a company's organisational maturity and strategic preparedness. A thorough assessment of MCSs must necessarily consider the market context in which the company operates. Each sector has specific competitive dynamics and the ability of management to configure its control systems in a manner consistent with these dynamics can make the difference between success and failure. The assessment must, therefore, take into account the competitive strategy adopted by the reality: A quality management will know how to align MCSs not only with the strategic objectives of the company but also with the opportunities and threats present in the competitive context of reference.

In conclusion, the quality of management, measured through the presence and sophistication of MCSs and contextualised within the specific sector and competitive strategy of the company, emerges as an essential criterion in the evaluation of Fintechs. Indeed, this integrated analysis provides a better understanding of the startup's ability to sustain growth and maintain a competitive advantage in the long term.

Fintech startups

With specific reference to the evaluation of Fintech startups, given the early development stage in which they find themselves, the analysis of the management variable assumes a fundamental role and is closely intertwined with that of governance. In these early stages, both assessments focus exclusively on the profile of the founders, key stakeholders and the characteristics of the CEO. This approach is crucial, since these startups have not yet developed the other components typical of more mature governance structures, including MCSs, which are absent in these emerging realities.

Fintech startups often stem from the innovative ideas of individuals or small groups of entrepreneurs. Therefore, the background, skills, experience and strategic vision of the founders and CEO become the main elements on which investors and analysts base their assessment. The ability of these leaders to guide the company through initial challenges, to adapt quickly to market changes and to attract talent and financial resources is crucial to the success of the startup.

In the absence of established governance structures, such as formal boards of directors or managerial control systems, the behaviour and decisions of the founders and CEO take on even greater importance. Transparency, integrity and the ability to effectively communicate the corporate vision become crucial factors in establishing trust among investors and other stakeholders.

In addition, the assessment of management in a Fintech startup may also include the analysis of the relationships and networks that the founders and CEO possess within the financial and technology sector. These connections can represent significant added value, facilitating strategic partnerships, access to new technologies and market opportunities.

Finally, as Fintech startups often operate in complex and rapidly changing regulatory environments, management's ability to navigate these legal and regulatory challenges is another critical aspect to consider. Understanding regulations, the ability to obtain the necessary approvals and licences, and the ability to maintain compliance with applicable laws are all elements that contribute to the overall assessment of a Fintech startup's management.

7   Regulation

The regulatory environment in which Fintech companies operate can have a significant impact on their future development and, consequently, on their valuation. Regulation is a crucial element to consider, as it can act as both a promoter and a deterrent to the evolution of the sector in question. In recent years, the rapid growth of the sector has outpaced the pace of regulatory updates, raising the risk of a possible slowdown in innovation (Ciukaj & Fowlarski, 2023). It is essential, therefore, that the sector has an appropriate and flexible regulatory structure that can provide protection for consumers and ensure the stability of the financial system without slowing down its development.

Regulatory Development and Fintech

The impact of regulation on the degree of innovation in the financial industry is debated in both academic and practical circles. On the one hand, it is argued that regulation and innovation are mutually restrictive and contradictory. According to this view, stringent regulations may limit the ability of Fintech companies to experiment with new technologies and business models, thus reducing the industry's innovative potential. On the other hand, a dialectical relationship between the two is proposed, in which regulatory development stimulates innovation and vice versa. This perspective suggests that a well-designed regulatory framework can provide a safe and stable environment, fostering the adoption of new technologies and the growth of Fintechs.

Cumming and Schwienbacher (2020) noted that, in the wake of the Global Financial Crisis, investments by Venture Capitalists shifted to countries with less stringent regulations. Fintechs took advantage of regulatory arbitrage opportunities to decide where to establish their operations, choosing jurisdictions with more favourable regulations. This phenomenon suggests a negative relationship between stringent regulation and incentives for the development of the Fintech industry, indicating that a permissive regulatory environment may be more conducive to innovation.

In contrast, Ciukaj and Fowlarski (2023) highlighted a positive relationship between regulatory development and innovation in the Fintech sector in Europe. Specifically, with reference to European countries, they studied the correlation between the Fintech Development Index proposed by the Global Fintech Index Database (2021) and the Fintech Regulation Index calculated on World Bank 2021 data. The correlation was positive and significant, suggesting that developed, clear and up-to-date regulation can create an environment of trust and security, which is essential to attract investment, promote technological development and protect end-users. In particular, a structured regulatory framework can reduce the uncertainty and risks associated with innovation, giving Fintech firms the opportunity to invest in new technologies and grow.

This discrepancy between practice (Cumming & Schwienbacher, 2020) and academia (Ciukaj & Fowlarski, 2023) reflects the complexity of the interactions between regulation and innovation. While over-regulation can stifle innovation and ease of adoption of new technologies, an absence of proper regulation can lead to systemic risks and lack of trust on the part of users and investors. Therefore, the biggest challenge for regulators is to find a balance that favours innovation while protecting public interests and the stability of the financial system.

Regulatory status

Global regulatory status

Analysing the data provided by the World Bank for 198 countries and the year 2021, it can be seen that, globally, there is a greater regulatory focus on the topics of Digital Banking (the treatment of purely digital banking as part of the normal banking licence or as a separate type of licence) and Anti-Money Laundering (regulations and standards relating to AML/CFT). As shown in **Chart 29**, 197 out of 198 countries have at least one regulation related to Digital Banking, while

Chart 29   Global Regulatory Coverage on Digital Banking and Anti-Money Laundering (2021)

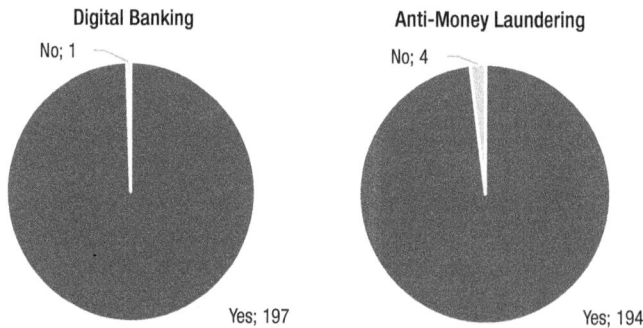

The pie charts show that in 2021, 197 out of 198 countries had regulations on Digital Banking, and 194 had frameworks addressing Anti-Money Laundering (AML), reflecting strong global regulatory attention to both areas in the financial sector.

Source: Own elaboration based on data from World Bank, 2021

194 deal with Anti-Money Laundering. In addition, the results on Data Protection (laws and regulations concerning data security and transmission) and Cyber Security (regulations or standards concerning cyber security) appear significant, highlighting the states' concern for the protection and security of individuals and their data (Chart 30).

Finally, despite the growing interest in cryptocurrencies and open banking, it is evident that these two areas lack specific regulation in most countries (Chart 31).

Chart 30   **Global Regulatory Coverage on Data Protection and Cybersecurity (2021)**

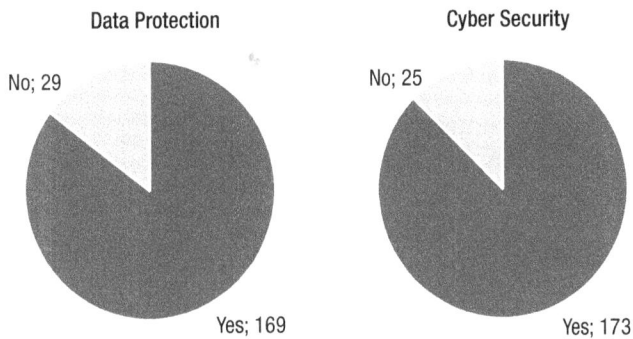

The pie charts show that, in 2021, 169 countries had data protection laws and 173 had cybersecurity regulations in place, reflecting global concern for safeguarding personal data and digital infrastructure in an increasingly interconnected world.

Source: Own elaboration based on data from World Bank, 2021

Chart 31   **Global Regulatory Adoption of Cryptocurrency and Open Banking (2021)**

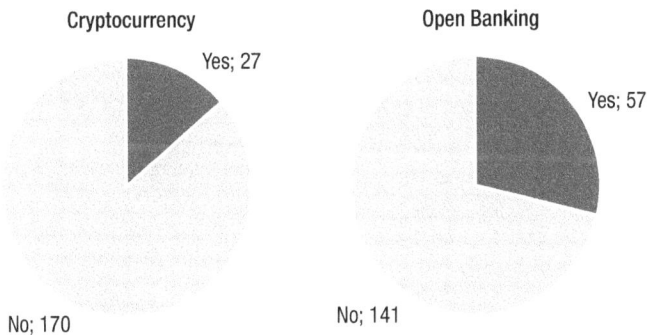

The pie charts show that as of 2021, only 27 countries had specific cryptocurrency regulations and 57 had open banking frameworks, indicating that most jurisdictions have yet to implement dedicated regulatory measures for these emerging sectors.

Source: Own elaboration based on data from World Bank, 2021

European Regulatory Status

At the European level, the heterogeneity of regulations among the various Member States has prompted the European Commission (EC) to seek a common direction. As shown in the study by Ciukaj and Fowlarski (2023) based on data provided by the World Bank (2021), at the European level there is variability in the regulatory development of the various countries. In particular, as shown in **Chart 32**, Estonia and Lithuania emerge as the most densely regulated states, while Italy ranks among the countries with the least regulatory development in Fintech.

This is derived from the determination of a *'Fintech Regulation Index'*, which, based on the World Bank *database* (2021), considers 14 regulatory areas for each state (Ciukaj & Fowlarski, 2023):

- Anti-Money Laundering
- Central Banking Digital Currencies (CBDC)
- Community-Driven Development (CDD)
- Cryptocurrency
- Cybersecurity
- Equity Crowdfunding
- Peer To Peer Lending (P2P)
- Data Protection
- Digital Banking
- Digital ID
- Electronic Money
- Electronic payments/transactions
- Innovation Facilitators, such as Innovation Hub, regulatory sandbox and regulatory accelerator
- Open Banking.

With the aim of promoting regulatory convergence across EU countries, in March 2018, the EC adopted an action plan for the Fintech sector. This action plan consists of 19 steps aimed at facilitating the adoption of new technologies, enabling Fintechs to expand Europe-wide, and strengthening cybersecurity and the integrity of the financial system (European Commission, 2018). In the same year, the European Banking Authority (EBA) identified the main challenges resulting from the introduction of technological innovation in the financial system:

- consumer protection
- prudential risk analysis
- the impact of the Fintech sector on the business models of financial institutions
- the creation of regulatory sandboxes
- the effect of technological innovation on the resolution of credit institutions.

Chart 32 Fintech Regulation Index of European countries 2021

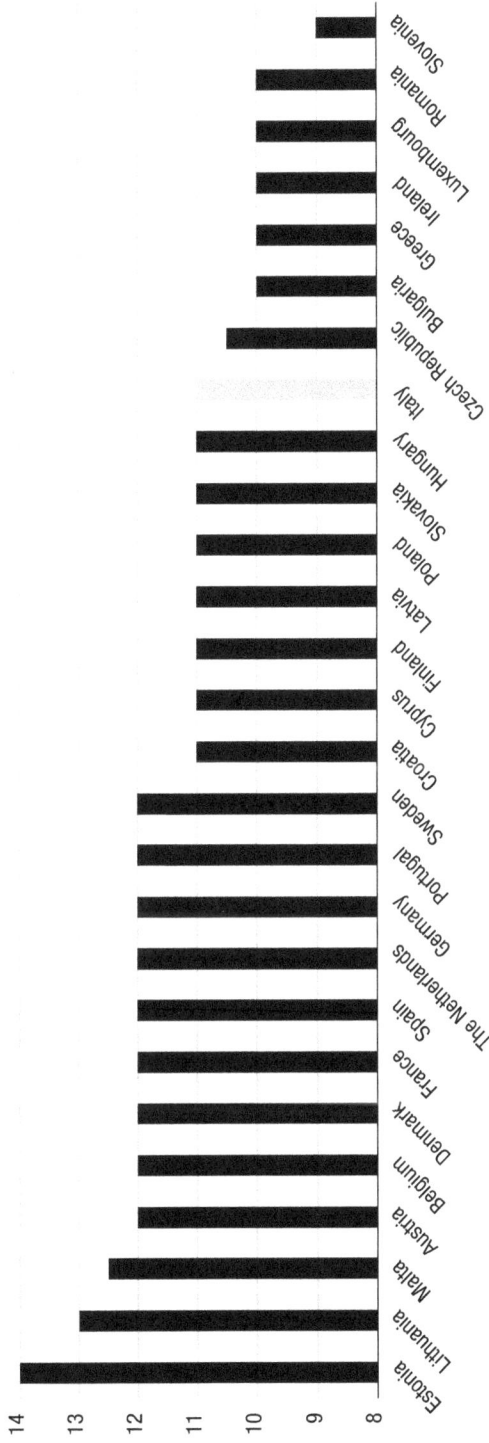

The bar chart displays the Fintech Regulation Index in Europe for 2021. Estonia and Lithuania lead in regulatory development, while Italy ranks among the countries with the least advanced regulatory frameworks, highlighting significant regional disparity.

Source: Ciukaj and Fowlarski, 2023

It is in this context that the EC launched the Digital Finance Strategy in 2020, setting out the four main priorities for digital finance (European Commission, 2020):

1. remove fragmentation within the Digital Single Market
2. adopt an EU Regulatory Framework to facilitate digital innovation
3. promote data-driven finance
4. face the challenges and risks of digital transformation.

Regulatory sandbox

In order to resolve the innovation-regulation debate, the instrument of the regulatory sandbox was established. A 'regulatory sandbox' is defined as a controlled environment in which supervised intermediaries and Fintech players can test, for a limited period of time, technologically innovative products and services in the banking, financial and insurance sectors (Bank of Italy). Access to a regulatory sandbox usually requires a preliminary application process with the regulator or market supervisor and compliance with requirements set by the regulator.

The main advantage of regulatory sandboxes is that both regulated entities (such as financial institutions) and unregulated entities (such as startups) can participate in them. In addition, regulatory sandboxes can help supervisors address the challenges of improving consumer protection in the financial market. Benefits of participating in a regulatory sandbox include (Ciukaj & Fowlarski, 2023):

- accelerating the process of introducing innovations to the market
- facilitating access to finance for Fintech companies, especially startups
- allowing more services to be tested
- promoting cooperation between the supervisor and Fintech companies in the application of consumer protection measures to the financial services offered.

Despite the fact that such an environment offers a safe environment to experiment with new technologies without exposing the financial system to the risks associated with untested changes, its diffusion is still limited. Analysing the World Bank database cited above, one can see that the regulatory sandbox is present in only 37% of countries.

Italy is among the countries that provide for such discipline, as Decree No. 100 of the Ministry of Economy and Finance No. 100 of 30 April 2021, implementing the delegation provided for by Decree-Law No. 34 of 30 April 2019 (the so-called 'Growth Decree'), defines the 'Discipline of Fintech Committee and Experimentation', i.e., the so-called 'regulatory sandbox' of Fintech activities at the supervisory authorities.

8   Ecosystem

The ecosystem is another key driver to consider when evaluating a Fintech, in order to go beyond traditional financial metrics and also focus on the operating environment and relationships that the company is able to establish. In fact, a favourable ecosystem can determine the long-term success of a company through a number of relevant factors.

The ability to integrate within the ecosystem could open the company up oppurtunities for synergies with other players, access to new markets and greater scalability. This implies that a company that is well embedded in a dynamic and collaborative ecosystem can benefit from the expertise and resources of other companies, financial institutions, regulators and innovation incubators. Such integration can lead to strategic partnerships, co-development of products and services and rapid market adoption of solutions.

Furthermore, the position of the company within the ecosystem can affect its ability to attract investment. Investors tend to prefer companies operating in environments where there is adequate infrastructure, a clear regulatory framework and incentives for innovation. Active participation in industry networks, conferences and working groups can increase the company's visibility and credibility, making it a more attractive option for potential investors.

The ecosystem also includes access to qualified talent. Fintechs operating in technology hubs or close to universities and research centres have a competitive advantage in attracting and retaining highly qualified professionals. The presence of a local talent pool can accelerate the development and innovation process, contributing to the sustainable growth of society.

Finally, it is crucial to consider the impact of local and international regulations within the ecosystem. Fintechs must navigate a complex and ever-changing regulatory landscape. An ecosystem that offers regulatory support, through specialised legal advice and partnerships with government agencies, can facilitate compliance and reduce the risks associated with legal operations.

It follows that the ecosystem is a key soft indicator that can significantly influence a Fintech's potential for success. The ability to integrate effectively in a collaborative environment can pave the way for growth opportunities, strategic partnerships, investment attraction and talent development, all of which are essential to the scalability and long-term success of Fintechs.

For these considerations, a detailed analysis and definition of the intrinsic ecosystem that characterises the Fintech sector is imperative. This ecosystem can be distinctly identified through the following key elements (Figure 5):

Figure 5   **The ecosystem of Fintech**

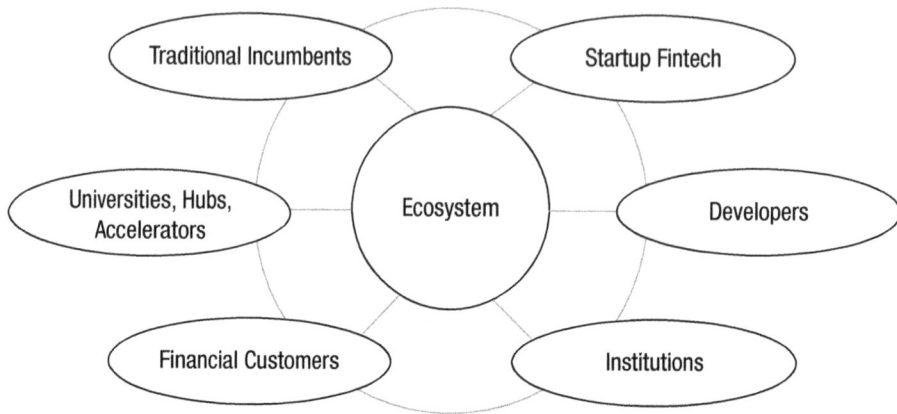

The diagram illustrates the Fintech ecosystem, comprising startups, developers, institutions, traditional incumbents, financial customers and academic entities. These actors interact to drive innovation, regulation and adoption within the financial sector.

Source: Adapted from Lee and Shin, 2018

1. Fintech startups, such as emerging startups in areas such as payments, asset management, lending and crowdfunding.
2. Technology Developers, working in cutting-edge areas such as big data analytics, cloud computing, cryptocurrency and social media.
3. Governmental entities, represented by financial regulators and legislators.
4. Universities, Hubs and Accelerators.
5. Financial Customers, which include both individuals and organisations.
6. Traditional Financial Institutions, such as banks, insurance companies, securities brokerage firms and Venture Capital.

Fintech startups

The role of Fintech startups within the ecosystem coincides with the strategy behind their disruptive character for the financial sector, namely their ability to disaggregate and redefine the services traditionally offered. Thanks to their flexibility and innovative capacity, Fintech startups allow financial customers to turn to various providers specialised in specific sub-sectors. This fragmented approach allows customers to select the best provider for each specific need, instead of relying on a single, non-specialised financial institution.

Fintech startups act as catalysts for innovation within the financial ecosystem, introducing advanced technologies such as AI, blockchain and ML. These technologies not only improve operational efficiency but also offer customised and scalable solutions that respond more precisely to customers' needs. In this way, they contribute to a more dynamic and competitive financial ecosystem.

Fintech startups also foster transparency and trust in the financial sector. Through the use of technologies such as blockchain, transactions become more traceable and secure, reducing the risk of fraud and increasing consumer trust. Moreover, the transparency in the costs and fees of the services offered by such entities is often greater than that of traditional financial institutions, a factor that improves the customer experience and their trust in the financial system.

Their role in the ecosystem also extends to collaboration with established financial institutions. Fintechs, thanks to their agility and innovative capacity, can collaborate with banks and other traditional institutions to co-develop new products and services, improve existing processes and accelerate the digitisation of the sector.

Fintech startups represent a key element within the modern financial ecosystem. Through their ability to unbundle services, introduce technological innovations, promote financial inclusion, ensure transparency and collaborate with traditional institutions, they are transforming the financial landscape, making it more efficient, accessible and customer-oriented.

Technology developers

Technology developers form the fundamental basis of the Fintech ecosystem, as they provide the *framework* on which financial technologies are based. Their contribution is essential for the development and implementation of innovative solutions that characterise the industry. Developers provide, for example, the big data analysis technologies that underpin the micro-personalisation of financial services. By processing and interpreting large volumes of data, these technologies enable Fintech companies to offer highly personalised and targeted services, improving the customer experience and increasing the effectiveness of market strategies.

Cloud computing is another pillar provided by technology developers. This allows Fintech startups to deliver services via the web without facing the costs and complexities of building and maintaining an in-house infrastructure. With cloud computing, companies can rapidly scale their operations, reduce development and deployment time, and ensure greater flexibility and resilience of their services. In addition, cloud computing facilitates collaboration and integration between different platforms and applications, promoting a more interconnected and synergistic ecosystem.

Technology developers also provide the sophisticated algorithms used in WealthTech to create robo-advisors. These algorithms automate financial advice, making investment services more accessible and convenient for a broad spectrum of clients. Robo-advisors use advanced mathematical models and AI to analyse market and client data, providing personalised and optimised investment recommendations. This not only democratises access to financial advisory services but also improves the efficiency and accuracy of investment decisions.

The role of technology developers also extends to security and regulatory compliance. By providing advanced cybersecurity solutions and compliance management tools, they help protect sensitive data and ensure that Fintech operations are aligned with current regulations. This is particularly relevant in a highly regulated industry like the financial sector, where trust and security are key.

Technology developers, therefore, are key players within the Fintech ecosystem, as they provide the technological foundation for innovation and growth in the sector. Through big data analytics, cloud computing, robo-advisors algorithms and security solutions, they enable Fintechs to develop and offer advanced, personalised and secure services. Their contribution is essential for the creation of an efficient, interconnected and resilient Fintech ecosystem, capable of responding to dynamic market and consumer needs.

Institutions

Institutions play a crucial role in creating regulatory systems within which the various players in the Fintech ecosystem can operate. As discussed in the section on regulation, each government develops different regulations, positioning itself along a dimension that ranges from fostering the development of the sector to preventing risks to consumers and the stability of the financial system. This balance is crucial to ensure a safe and innovative environment in which Fintechs can thrive.

Institutions, through the formulation and implementation of specific regulations, help shape the operating conditions of the Fintech market. This regulatory framework is essential to ensure that Fintech activities are conducted in a transparent, fair and safe manner, thereby protecting consumer interests and maintaining confidence in the financial system.

In addition, institutions play a proactive role in fostering innovation within the sector in question. Many governments and regulators have introduced initiatives such as regulatory sandboxes, which allow startups to test new products and services in a controlled and supervised environment. These sandboxes offer a unique opportunity for Fintechs to experiment and innovate without being immediately subject to all applicable regulations, thus fostering rapid development and introduction of innovative solutions to the market.

Institutions themselves have stimulated the development of Fintech companies, in part because of the stricter regulations applied to traditional operators following the Great Financial Crisis. Indeed, the stricter regulations imposed on traditional banks and other financial institutions have created a space for Fintechs, which have been able to take advantage of their greater flexibility and adaptability to offer alternative and more efficient solutions. This has led to increased competition and innovation in the financial sector, benefiting consumers and the economy as a whole. Institutions also play a key role in consumer protection, ensuring that the services they offer are safe and reliable. By overseeing and enforcing strict standards, regulators work to prevent fraud, abuse and misconduct. This helps to create an environment of trust, which is essential for the adoption and use of services by the public.

Through regulations, promotional initiatives such as regulatory sandboxes and careful supervision of Fintech activities, institutions contribute significantly to the development and stability of the sector, while ensuring consumer protection and confidence in the financial system.

Financial customers

Financial customers are the main source of revenue for the entire Fintech ecosystem. They differ substantially from those in the traditional financial ecosystem, where large companies constitute a major component of the business. In the Fintech ecosystem, however, the predominant source of revenue is consumers and SMEs. This change in customer profile is crucial to understanding the dynamics of the functioning and strategies of this market.

The demographic profile of Fintech customers differs considerably. A survey conducted by Goldman Sachs in 2015 revealed that the typical Fintech customer is a young person aged between 18 and 34. This customer segment is characterised by a greater familiarity with digital technologies and a propensity to adopt new financial solutions that offer convenience, personalisation and transparency.

Consumers are mainly looking for services that are easily accessible, user-friendly and able to respond quickly to their financial needs. They appreciate the ability to manage their finances through digital platforms, without the need to physically visit a bank branch. This has led to the development of mobile applications and online services that offer an optimised and integrated user experience.

SMEs constitute another crucial segment for Fintechs. These companies often find it difficult to access traditional financial services due to complex bureaucratic procedures and stringent requirements. Fintechs respond to these needs by offering more flexible solutions tailored to the specific needs of SMEs. Through peer-to-peer lending platforms, innovative payment services and advanced financial management tools, Fintech companies enable SMEs to obtain financing, manage cash flows and improve operational efficiency.

The role of financial customers in the ecosystem is therefore twofold: On the one hand, they represent the demand that drives innovation and the development of new products and services; on the other, through their behaviour and preferences, they influence the market strategies and operational choices of Fintechs. Their interaction with platforms generates data that, if analysed effectively, can be used to further improve the offer and customise services according to the specific needs of each customer.

Financial customers, therefore, are key players within the Fintech ecosystem. Their different composition from traditional customers, characterised by a greater presence of young people and SMEs, and their propensity to use digital technologies, determine their market dynamics and development strategies. Understanding the needs and preferences of these customers is essential for the success and sustainable growth of Fintechs, which must continue to innovate and adapt to meet changing demand.

Universities, hubs and accelerators

A key role is played by universities, hubs and accelerators, which provide advanced research and specialised training, facilitate essential connections and resources, and promote the rapid growth of Fintechs, contributing to the creation of a dynamic and innovative ecosystem.

Universities play an essential role in producing advanced knowledge and developing specialised skills in the field of financial technologies. Through dedicated research programmes and academic courses, they train new talent with the technical and analytical skills needed to innovate in the Fintech sector. Universities frequently collaborate with startups, offering access to academic resources, research labs and expert networks. This two-way exchange encourages the practical application of academic theories and stimulates innovation through experimentation and prototyping.

Hubs, often located in strategic cities and technology centres, provide physical and virtual spaces where startups can work, collaborate and grow. They offer state-of-the-art infrastructure, access to business networks, networking events and mentoring opportunities. They act as catalysts for the Fintech ecosystem, creating a fertile environment for interaction and knowledge sharing between entrepreneurs, investors and industry professionals. These spaces stimulate creativity and innovation, enabling Fintechs to develop advanced technology solutions in a collaborative environment.

Accelerators, finally, play a crucial role in supporting the rapid growth of Fintechs. They offer intensive support programmes that include training, mentorship, access to funding and strategic resources. Accelerators select promising startups and guide them through an accelerated growth path, providing management expertise, product development assistance and market opportunities.

These three actors contribute to the creation of an integrated and synergetic Fintech ecosystem. Collaborations between these actors and Fintechs facilitate knowledge and technology transfer, fostering an environment of continuous innovation. They also play a key role in attracting investment and talent to the sector, increasing the visibility and attractiveness of the Fintech ecosystem globally. Their role is crucial in creating a dynamic and innovative environment that supports the continuous evolution of the financial sector.

Incumbent

Traditional incumbents represent key players within the Fintech ecosystem, who are reacting with tactics of competition or cooperation vis-à-vis startups in the sector. The advent of Fintechs has undoubtedly stimulated a strong push for innovation within these players, who nevertheless enjoy a significant competitive advantage stemming from the economies of scale and the substantial financial resources at their disposal.

The reaction of incumbents to the sector's evolution can be mainly divided into two strategies: competition and cooperation. On the one hand, many traditional financial institutions see Fintechs as a direct threat to their established business model and respond by intensifying investments in technology and improving their digital services. Through the adoption of new technologies and the digitisation of processes, incumbents seek to maintain their market share and offer customers an experience that is competitive with that offered by Fintechs.

On the other hand, there is a growing trend towards cooperation between incumbents and Fintechs. Traditional financial institutions recognise the value of the innovation brought by these entities and, therefore, establish strategic partnerships to leverage each other's expertise and resources. These collaborations can take various forms, such as joint ventures, direct investments or the integration of Fintech solutions into their own services. Through such alliances, incumbents can accelerate their digital transformation and offer innovative products and services to their customers.

The competitive advantage of incumbents derives not only from economies of scale but also from their solid customer base, established networks and the trust they enjoy in the market. These elements allow incumbents to deploy technology solutions on a large scale, reaching a large number of customers and ensuring a high level of security and reliability. In addition, significant financial resources enable incumbents to invest in research and development, acquire promising startups and attract highly qualified talent. However, the ability of incumbents to innovate and adapt quickly to market dynamics is often limited by their complex organisational structure and bureaucratic procedures. In this context, collaborations with Fintechs are particularly beneficial, as they allow incumbents to overcome these limitations and benefit from the agility and creativity of startups.

Traditional incumbents play a key role in the Fintech ecosystem, reacting to the innovation of startups with competition and cooperation strategies. Their ability to combine significant resources with innovative approaches determines their success in a rapidly changing market. Through a balance of competition and cooperation, incumbents contribute to a more dynamic and resilient financial ecosystem, capable of responding to consumer needs and fostering continuous innovation in the industry.

Assessing ecosystem-related indicators helps investors understand the broader context in which a Fintech operates. This includes potential synergies, market opportunities and the startup's ability to leverage external resources for growth. For example, valuation prizes could be awarded to a company whose services are more easily integrated with those of a traditional player, which can provide access to a broad user base and deeper market knowledge (Forbes, 2024). Fintech itself could also gain more value if it complies with the regulations of multiple regions, a factor that would allow for faster scalability.

By considering these indicators, investors can make more informed and strategic choices, identifying those with the greatest potential for growth and success. A Fintech's ability to integrate effectively into a dynamic ecosystem and to collaborate with different players, such as traditional financial institutions, universities, technology hubs and accelerators, is a significant competitive advantage. In addition, adherence to regional regulations not only facilitates geographic expansion but also helps reduce operational and legal risks, increasing the confidence of investors and business partners.

In conclusion, the analysis of ecosystem-related indicators is essential for a complete and accurate assessment of Fintechs. By understanding ecosystem dynamics and potential synergies, investors can identify companies that not only present promising technological innovations but are also strategically positioned to exploit the resources and opportunities offered by the ecosystem. This holistic approach to assessment helps identify Fintechs with the greatest potential for success and sustainable long-term growth.

9   Sustainability and Fintech

In recent years, the Fintech sector has significantly transformed the traditional financial landscape, introducing technological innovations that increase the efficiency, accessibility and transparency of financial services. The adoption of advanced technologies such as AI, blockchain and automation has enabled the creation of new solutions that reduce costs, simplify operations and improve the user experience.

In parallel, the importance of corporate sustainability has increased significantly, influencing investor decisions and market perceptions. The growing awareness of climate change, social issues and corporate governance (ESG) has led to an increased focus on sustainable practices.

In this context, it is crucial to assess the potential impact of sustainability on the valuation of Fintechs. Indeed, companies that integrate sustainable practices into their operations can gain a competitive advantage by attracting investments from ESG funds and improving their reputation in the market. Sustainable Fintech start-ups can contribute to a more ethical and resilient financial ecosystem by fostering the development of innovative solutions that not only meet financial needs, but also address global challenges such as climate change and economic inequality.

It follows that the integration of sustainability into Fintech strategies is not a temporary trend, but a key determinant for long-term success. Examining how sustainability influences the valuation of these realities, therefore, is essential to understanding the future of the Fintech sector and promoting a more responsible and sustainable financial environment.

Main results

The literature review highlights some variables of interest in order to consider the potential impact of sustainability on the valuation of Fintechs. These variables include, among others, transparency in corporate social responsibility (CSR) practices, the presence and quality of *green certifications* and adherence to sustainable reporting guidelines such as those of the Global Reporting Initiative (GRI). Examining these variables provides a more complete view of how sustainable initiatives can influence market perception and, consequently, the value of Fintech companies. In order to analyse in greater detail what has been outlined, the following are the main results and related variables, derived from a research conducted on a sample of 95

Fintech companies, using data from the KBW and Nasdaq Fintech Indices and the NASDAQ Insurance Index (IXIS) over a 10-year period (2010–2019) (Merello et al., 2022).

The research outlined identifies the following main findings with reference to the potential impact of the *sustainability* variable on the value of the realities considered:

- Issuing a CSR Report: Issuing a CSR report is a key practice for companies wishing to demonstrate their commitment to environmental, social and economic sustainability. This document not only provides an overview of the company's sustainable initiatives and achievements but also serves as a transparency and communication tool towards stakeholders, including investors, customers, employees and local communities. In the Fintech context, the publication of a CSR report can have a significant impact on a company's valuation. The literature shows that companies that adopt CSR reporting practices tend to be more trusted by investors, improving their reputation and, consequently, their market value. This positive effect can be attributed to the fact that a well-structured and detailed CSR report increases corporate transparency, allowing investors to better assess the risks and opportunities related to the company's sustainable practices. In addition, issuing a CSR report can also help differentiate Fintechs from competitors by highlighting their commitment to responsible and sustainable business practices. This can be particularly beneficial in an increasingly environmentally and socially conscious market, where consumers and investors are inclined to reward companies that demonstrate a genuine commitment to sustainability. As a result, the publication of a CSR report not only improves transparency and corporate reputation but can also positively influence the valuation of Fintechs, making them more attractive to investors and more competitive in the global market (Merello et al., 2022).
- Green Certificates: Green certificates are official recognitions that attest to a company's commitment to sustainable and environmentally friendly practices. These certificates, which include LEED, BREEAM, Carbon Neutral, EPA Energy Star, NABERS, Carbon Disclosure Project (CDP), RE100 and ISO 14001, represent international sustainability standards covering various aspects from energy efficiency of buildings to carbon management. For Fintechs, obtaining green certificates can have a significant impact on their valuation and market perception. The presence of such certificates often indicates that the company is taking concrete steps to reduce its environmental impact, thus increasing trust and attractiveness for investors sensitive to ESG issues. In particular, green certificates can enhance corporate reputation by demonstrating a tangible commitment to sustainability.
- However, the literature suggests that the effect of green certificates on the market value of Fintech companies may be complex. While, on the one hand, these certifications may improve the perception of corporate reliability and responsibility, on the other hand, the costs associated with obtaining and maintain-

ing such certifications may not always be justified by an immediate increase in market value. In some cases, larger, more established companies may not see a significant market benefit from obtaining *green* certificates, although these certificates may still contribute to more sustainable and responsible management in the long term.

- It follows that green certificates are an important element in the sustainability strategy of Fintechs. Although they may not always translate into an immediate increase in market value, they play an important role in building a reputation for environmental responsibility and commitment, which can attract investors and customers sensitive to sustainability issues (Merello et al., 2022).
- Green Rankings: Green Rankings are rankings that assess and compare the sustainability performance of companies globally. These rankings, such as the Newsweek Green Ranking, the Corporate Knights Global 100 and the Sustainalytics ESG Rating, analyse various ESG criteria to provide a detailed picture of the sustainable practices adopted by companies.
- For Fintechs, inclusion in a Green Ranking can have a major impact on their valuation and visibility. Companies included in these rankings demonstrate that they are at the forefront of sustainable practices, a factor that can enhance their reputation and attractiveness in the eyes of investors, customers and other stakeholders. In a market increasingly focused on sustainability, being recognised in a Green Ranking can differentiate a company from its competitors and foster greater public trust and interest. Inclusion in Green Rankings can have positive effects on the market value of Fintech companies as ESG criteria become increasingly relevant in investment decisions. Investors are inclined to consider sustainability performance as an indicator of responsible, long-term corporate governance. However, it is important to note that the effect may vary depending on the specific business environment and sector. For example, for more established companies, the impact may be less pronounced than for early-stage startups trying to build a solid reputation for sustainability.
- For these considerations, inclusion in the Green Rankings is a powerful tool for Fintechs to increase their visibility and credibility in terms of sustainability. While not guaranteeing an immediate increase in market value, these recognitions can help build a solid reputation and attract investment, fostering the long-term growth and success of companies in the competitive Fintech sector.
- GRI Guidelines: The GRI Guidelines represent one of the most recognised international standards for sustainability reporting. These guidelines provide a comprehensive framework for companies to transparently and consistently communicate their economic, environmental and social impacts. Adopting the GRI guidelines means committing to rigorous reporting practices that allow companies' sustainability performance to be compared and evaluated globally.
- For Fintechs, adopting the GRI guidelines can have a significant impact on their valuation. Following these guidelines not only improves a company's transparency and credibility but also demonstrates a concrete commitment to sustainability. Investors and other stakeholders tend to positively evaluate companies that

adopt recognised reporting standards such as those of the GRI, as this reduces the uncertainty and risks associated with company management. Furthermore, transparent reporting according to GRI guidelines can facilitate access to capital markets and attract investors who favour sustainable practices.

- The literature shows that Fintech companies that follow GRI guidelines tend to see an increase in their market value. This positive effect can be attributed to the fact that accurate and detailed sustainability reporting helps build a solid corporate reputation, enhancing the trust of investors and other stakeholders. However, adopting GRI guidelines may also entail costs and operational challenges, especially for companies that may not have the resources to implement a complex reporting system.
- It follows that adopting the GRI guidelines is an important strategic step for Fintechs wishing to improve their transparency and attractiveness in the market. Although it entails initial investments, reporting according to GRI standards can lead to significant benefits in terms of corporate valuation, stakeholder trust and access to capital. Fintechs that can effectively integrate these guidelines into their business model are in a better position to compete in the global marketplace and sustain long-term growth.
- Governance (CSR committees): The presence of a CSR committee within a company is a key indicator of the organisation's commitment to sustainable practices and good governance. A dedicated CSR committee oversees and guides sustainability initiatives, ensuring that the company adopts environmentally, socially and economically responsible strategies. This committee is typically composed of board members and senior executives, who work together to integrate sustainability into the company's operations.
- For Fintechs, the establishment of a CSR committee can have a significant impact on their valuation and market perception. The presence of such a committee demonstrates a formal and structured commitment to sustainability, improving the company's transparency and credibility in the eyes of investors and other stakeholders. Furthermore, a functioning committee can help identify and manage sustainability risks, promoting more proactive and responsible management.
- Fintech companies with a CSR committee tend to benefit from increased investor confidence and a better corporate reputation. This can translate into increased market value, as investors are increasingly interested in supporting companies that demonstrate a strong commitment to sustainability. However, the effectiveness of a CSR committee also depends on its composition and activities. A committee that is inadequately resourced or not integrated into the company's strategic decisions may fail to make a significant impact. For these considerations, the presence of a CSR committee is of paramount importance for Fintechs that wish to strengthen their commitment to sustainability and improve their valuation. Such a committee not only helps to improve corporate governance but can also attract investment and enhance the company's reputation.

Added value of sustainability

Sustainable practices are becoming increasingly important not only for the positive impacts they generate on the environment and society but also for their fundamental impact on the market valuation of companies. The integration of sustainable strategies and practices into the business models of Fintechs translates into a number of tangible and intangible benefits, ranging from increased operational resilience to reduced risk and easier access to capital due to the attractiveness of ESG-oriented investment funds.

Furthermore, sustainability stimulates digital innovation, leading Fintechs to adopt advanced technologies and innovative solutions that improve energy and operational efficiency. This, in turn, fuels the improvement of corporate and brand reputation, which are key elements in attracting and retaining an increasingly ethical and sustainable clientele. Talent attraction and retention also emerge as key aspects, as professionals, particularly the younger generation, show an increasing preference for companies that demonstrate a strong commitment to sustainability. Finally, sustainable practices lead to significant improvements in operational efficiency, helping to reduce costs and optimise the use of resources.

Below, we highlight how sustainability adds value to Fintechs by analysing some of the main areas of impact:

- Resilience and risk reduction: Fintechs that adopt sustainable practices demonstrate greater resilience and a significant reduction in operational and financial risk. Sustainability, in fact, promotes responsible resource management and long-term strategic planning, which are essential elements in dealing with market uncertainties and volatilities. Companies that incorporate sustainability into their business models tend to develop a greater capacity to adapt to environmental, social and economic changes, thus reducing their vulnerability to external factors.
- This resilience is particularly important in the Fintech sector, where technological innovation and rapid regulatory changes can create a highly dynamic and uncertain environment. Sustainable companies are better prepared to handle these challenges through practices such as energy efficiency, responsible data management and carbon reduction, which not only improve operations but also corporate reputation. In addition, risk reduction is facilitated by increased transparency and robust governance, which enhance investor and stakeholder confidence. Sustainable practices also help mitigate risks related to climate change, natural resources and social dynamics, creating a more stable and predictable environment for business operations (Visconti et al., 2020).
- Access to capital: Fintechs that integrate sustainability into their operations enjoy greater access to capital. In a financial landscape where investors are increasingly oriented towards ESG criteria, companies that demonstrate a commitment to sustainable practices can attract a wider range of investments. Sustainable Fintechs can access financing on more favourable terms, due to the reduced perceived risk associated with these companies stemming from responsible sustainable practices. Investors are more likely to fund companies that demonstrate an ability to

adapt and resilience to regulatory and market changes, two factors that are often indicative of good business management and a long-term perspective. Moreover, many financial institutions and banks are required by regulation or internal policy to dedicate a significant portion of their portfolios to sustainable investments. Fintechs that embrace sustainability can therefore benefit from these policies by accessing credit lines and financial instruments designed to support sustainable development. This not only facilitates access to capital, but also allows companies to expand more rapidly and innovate, taking advantage of the opportunities offered by the global market (Visconti et al., 2020).

• Digital innovation: The adoption of sustainable practices in Fintech acts as a powerful catalyst for digital innovation. Sustainability requires the implementation of advanced technologies and innovative solutions that not only reduce environmental impact but also improve operational efficiency and company competitiveness. Sustainable digital solutions improve the internal operations of Fintech companies, opening up new market opportunities and responding to the growing demand for sustainable financial products and services. Furthermore, digital innovation fuelled by sustainability leads to greater collaboration between different entities in the financial and technology sectors. Fintechs developing sustainable solutions can establish strategic *partnerships* with traditional banks, financial institutions and other technology startups, fostering an ecosystem of collaborative innovation. This type of collaboration not only amplifies the positive impact of individual sustainable initiatives but also accelerates the adoption of sustainable practices on a global scale.

• The push towards sustainable digital innovation can also attract dedicated research and development funding from both private investors and public bodies. Governments and international organisations are increasingly interested in funding projects that combine technology and sustainability, recognising their potential for positive transformation. Fintechs that demonstrate a commitment to sustainable innovation can therefore access grants, subsidies and tax incentives that further support their growth and development (Visconti et al., 2020).

• Brand awareness: Integrating sustainability into Fintechs' business strategies has a significant impact on improving reputation and brand. At a time when consumers and investors are increasingly attentive to ethical and sustainable practices, Fintechs that demonstrate a commitment to sustainability can gain a significant competitive advantage. Sustainable practices strengthen corporate reputation, demonstrating that the company not only pursues profit but also cares about the social and environmental impact of its activities. A solid reputation, based on values of sustainability and social responsibility, can attract a broader and more diverse customer base, fostering the loyalty of existing customers and facilitating strategic alliances. A brand associated with positive and sustainable values enjoys greater recognition and differentiation in the market, helping to increase market share and improve long-term financial performance. A solid corporate reputation and a recognised brand also attract investors, especially institutional investors and ESG investment-oriented funds, facilitating access to investment capital and more favourable financing conditions. Sustainability initiatives also offer a powerful communication and marketing tool, strengthening the emotional bond with customers and improving the company's public image (Visconti et al., 2020).

- Talent: The adoption of sustainable practices in Fintechs plays a crucial role in talent attraction and retention. The younger generation of professionals, in particular, are increasingly attracted to companies that demonstrate a strong commitment to environmental and social sustainability. Working for a company that values sustainability not only improves employee satisfaction but also creates a sense of belonging. This translates into higher talent retention, reducing turnover costs and increasing overall productivity. Moreover, sustainable companies are perceived as more innovative and future-oriented, characteristics that attract highly qualified and motivated professionals to contribute to projects with a positive impact. Sustainable practices may include initiatives such as carbon footprint reduction, CSR programmes and the promotion of an inclusive and diverse corporate culture. These factors make the company more attractive to top talent seeking not only career opportunities but also to work in an environment that reflects their personal values (Visconti et al., 2020).
- Operational efficiency: Sustainability practices can help reduce operational risks for Fintechs. Careful management of environmental, social and governance issues enables companies to identify and mitigate potential risks. This proactive approach to risk management not only reduces the likelihood of incurring unexpected costs or litigation but also increases business resilience, ensuring greater operational and financial stability in the long run. Furthermore, the adoption of green technologies and sustainable processes can lead to significant improvements in operational efficiency. For example, using renewable energy sources and optimising energy consumption can reduce operating costs. Implementing circular economy practices, such as recycling and reusing materials, not only minimises waste but can also generate significant savings and increase profitability. Fintechs that integrate sustainability into their operations can also benefit from more efficient human resource management through policies that promote employee welfare and improve productivity. Finally, the adoption of sustainability standards can facilitate regulatory compliance and improve relations with regulators, reducing compliance costs and the risk of sanctions (Visconti et al., 2020, Atayah et al., 2023).
- Reducing agency problems: the adoption of ESG practices can help mitigate agency problems in Fintechs. Transparency and ESG disclosure can better align interests between executives and shareholders, reducing the risk of internal conflicts. ESG disclosure fosters greater accountability and governance, improving shareholder confidence in management decisions and protecting their long-term interests. Furthermore, the implementation of ESG standards creates a clear and transparent framework for corporate resource management and strategic decision-making, enhancing consistency and integrity. This approach reduces information asymmetries between management and shareholders, ensuring that decisions made are in line with the company's sustainable and financial objectives. As a

result, opportunities for opportunistic behaviour by management are reduced and a more collaborative and trusting working environment is promoted. Regular and detailed disclosure of ESG performance allows shareholders to monitor management performance more effectively, contributing to an overall improvement in corporate governance (Atayah et al., 2023).

In recent years, the Fintech sector has undergone a significant transformation through the adoption of advanced technologies that have improved the efficiency and transparency of financial services. In parallel, the importance of corporate sustainability has increased, influencing investors' decisions and market perceptions. Fintechs that integrate sustainable practices gain a competitive advantage, attract investors and improve their market reputation. Publishing CSR reports, obtaining *green certificates*, being included in Green Rankings and adopting GRI guidelines are key elements that help improve corporate ratings. The presence of a CSR committee within the company demonstrates a structured commitment to sustainability, increasing investor confidence. Sustainable practices lead to greater operational resilience, risk reduction and facilitate access to capital. They also stimulate digital innovation and improve operational efficiency. It follows that sustainability is a key determinant for the long-term success of Fintechs, helping to create a more ethical and resilient financial ecosystem.

Fintech startups

Integrating sustainability into the business strategies of Fintechs proves to be a crucial element in ensuring long-term success. Sustainable practices, such as publishing CSR reports, obtaining *green certificates*, inclusion in Green Rankings and adopting GRI guidelines, not only enhance corporate reputation but also attract investment and increase the market value of companies. However, for Fintech startups, which are still in their infancy, the adoption of these metrics can be a significant challenge. Limited resources, coupled with the need to balance innovation with sustainability, can make full implementation of ESG practices complex.

Despite these difficulties, a commitment to sustainability can provide a significant competitive advantage. Fintech startups that manage to overcome these challenges and effectively integrate sustainability into their operations are better positioned to attract investors, retain customers and build a solid reputation in the market. This commitment not only contributes to a more ethical and resilient financial ecosystem but also fosters the development of innovative solutions that address global financial needs while tackling critical challenges such as climate change and economic inequality.

Therefore, despite the complexities inherent in the development phase of startups, the adoption of sustainable practices represents a strategic investment that can lead to significant benefits in terms of business valuation, access to capital and long-term competitiveness. Fintechs that integrate sustainability into their business models not only improve their operational resilience and reduce risk but also help shape a more sustainable and responsible financial future.

10 Empirical Evidence

Introduction

To analyse the importance of soft indicators, a multi-level study was undertaken. The primary objective is to identify empirical evidence that confirms the relevance of soft indicators, with particular reference to the context of Fintech companies. These indicators, characterised by a predominantly qualitative nature, play a crucial role in providing complementary information to traditional financial metrics.

A second objective of the study is the definition of methodologies to translate the qualitative component of these indicators into objective and quantitative measurements, in order to make them usable in decision-making and analytical processes. In this sense, the investigation aims to fill a methodological gap by developing standardised approaches for the coding of these variables.

Finally, the analysis aims to understand the impact of soft indicators on the valuation of Fintech firms, examining both their contribution to the estimation of firm value and any correlations that may emerge between them. This study not only explores the interrelationships between the variables but also aims to investigate their role in influencing market dynamics and investors' decision-making processes.

Research hypotheses

Soft indicators

The first hypothesis of the conducted study originates in the underlying motivation of the research. Starting from the evidence of the 2021 speculative bubble, it is possible to highlight how soft indicators play a significant role in explaining the value of Fintech companies. In this context, the initial hypothesis aims to verify whether the empirical evidence is able to confirm the importance attributed to these indicators, identified in the following areas: governance, regulation, management and integration in the ecosystem.

H1: Soft indicators influence the evaluation of a Fintech company.

Governance

The study focuses on two fundamental pillars of governance: The personality that drives governance and the company's governance practices and procedures. Regarding the first aspect, the work analyses the hypothesis that the profile of the CEO is relevant in determining the value of a Fintech company. In particular, as discussed by Schachel et al. (2021), we examine the idea that a CEO of higher quality, considered as such on the basis of a higher level of education and more years of relevant experience, is, on the one hand, more capable of defining the strategic direction of a Fintech company and, on the other hand, perceived as a risk-reducing factor by investors, thus increasing the value of the company.

H2: A more qualified CEO positively influences the value of a Fintech company.

This study then examines the effect that the audit firm has on the value of the client company. Specifically, as argued by Che et al. (2019), the study is based on the theoretical idea that Big 4 audit firms are generally associated with better service quality due to their reputation. Therefore, the hypothesis to be tested investigates whether an audit performed by a Big 4 firm positively impacts the audited firm, increasing its value.

H3: An audit by a Big 4 company increases the value of the company.

Management

The research aims to find empirical evidence of the positive impact that higher-quality management has on the value of a company. First, this requires finding a suitable method to measure management quality, a complex task given the variety of aspects to be considered. Indeed, current literature has used MCSs as a proxy for management quality (Simons, 1995); however, the mere presence of MCSs does not necessarily imply higher management quality. Consequently, this study tests the hypothesis that higher-quality management increases corporate value.

H4: Superior management increases the value of Fintech companies.

Regulation

This study distinguishes between the quality, or comprehensiveness, of Fintech regulation and the extent of financial consumer protection. Indeed, these two aspects of regulation are inherently different and can have opposite effects on the ease with which a Fintech company can operate and on its success. Regarding the effect of the quality of regulation, previous literature is divided. The part that observes a positive impact of regulation focuses on Fintech-friendly regulations, as pointed out by Ciukaj and Fowlarski (2023) in the construction of their Regulation Index. However, the results of their study may be biased, as they consider regulations that promote the development of Fintechs. In contrast, Cumming and Schwienbacher (2018) found evidence showing that investor interest shifts towards countries with more lax regulations on Fintechs, taking a more neutral approach to the study of regulation. Furthermore, while regulation is necessary to ensure financial stability and consumer protection, overly rigid regulations can stifle innovation by making it difficult for Fintech companies to comply with complex legal requirements. Building on this, this study also takes a neutral approach and tests the negative effect of broader Fintech-related regulations on the value of Fintech firms.

H5: More comprehensive regulation has a negative impact on the value of Fintechs.

In contrast, financial consumer protection can have the opposite impact on corporate value. Innovations are typically adopted when consumers feel safe enough to do so. This is particularly true for financial innovations, since these concern personal finances and unclear terms or low protection can be the main cause of serious problems, such as consumer over-indebtedness. Consequently, this study supports the idea that strong consumer protection mechanisms can create a favourable environment for the growth and adoption of Fintech innovations, ultimately increasing the valuation of these firms.

H6: Increased consumer financial protection increases the value of Fintechs.

Integration into the ecosystem

The literature significantly lacks analysis on the level of integration in the ecosystem; consequently, this study presents itself as one of the first to look for evidence on the impact of greater ecosystem integration on business value. In particular, noting that much of the business of Fintech firms concerns customers of traditional banks and that the majority of revenues depend on the size of the user base, a higher level of integration should help achieve both objectives. Accordingly, this study seeks to demonstrate that a higher level of integration in the ecosystem has a positive impact on the value of Fintech firms.

H7: Greater integration of a Fintech company into its ecosystem increases its value.

Methodology

Data collection

The data collection phase included several data sources, depending on the soft indicator considered. Furthermore, to ensure the accuracy of the analysis, as this study considers company values as of the end of December 2023, all other data were collected up to December 2023, to ensure that no subsequent information, which could not have affected the company's valuation at an earlier stage, could influence the analysis. Information on each company, such as country of incorporation, turnover, profitability metrics and the name of the current auditing firm, was retrieved from the Orbis database maintained by Bureau Van Dijk.

The name of each company's CEO was retrieved through a keyword search on Google. To ensure that the correct profile was considered for subsequent research steps, each CEO's LinkedIn profile was reviewed and, if this was absent or incomplete, additional information was retrieved from each company's Corporate Governance page or their 2023 Annual Reports. As indicated, the CEO considered in the analysis is the one in office as of December 2023. Consequently, in some cases the current CEO may be different, as some companies in the sample appointed a new CEO later at the time of the analysis. Additional data, missing in the Orbis database, were retrieved from FactSet. In particular, information on the operating margins of the companies, as well as the board history of each CEO, was obtained from this database, together with data on the geographical distribution of each company's revenues, relevant for the construction of the regulatory variable, as detailed later. The Bloomberg database was used to obtain information on the companies' M&A buy-side transaction history and to assess the quality of each company's review. In addition, Bloomberg's document search (DS) function was used to collect data on how often the words 'partnership' and synonyms such as 'alliance' and 'collaboration' appeared in each company's publications during 2022 and 2023. In addition, Comparably.com and Trustpilot.com were consulted to collect customer satisfaction data, including companies' Net Promoter Scores (NPSs). The glassdoor.com platform was useful for obtaining employee reviews on each company and the CEO's satisfaction score. Finally, the World Bank's Financial Inclusion and Consumer Protection (FICP) survey was the source of data on the quality of regulation in each country included in the study.

Sample

The sample for this study was selected from a combination of the Indxx Global Fintech Thematic Index and the FactSet Global Fintech Total Return Index. These two indices were chosen to gather a set of listed Fintech companies with a broad geographic distribution. From the original sample of all 90 companies included in the 2 indices, through the different iterations of the model, the final sample size was 86 listed Fintech companies.

The observations mainly concern companies located in the United States, which makes the sample representative of the entire population, given the strong dominance of US-based companies in the global Fintech sector.

Furthermore, the sample shows a broad representation of companies operating in the Digital Payments sector, followed by those in the TechFin sector. All other sectors are generally evenly represented in the sample. Again, the selected sample represents the distribution of the population well, with the majority of Fintech companies operating in the payments sector.

Selection and processing of variables

This study analyses the effect of a set of independent or explanatory variables on the dependent variable, controlling for the impact of other factors included as control variables.

1. Dependent variable: The valuation of the Fintech companies included in the study is measured through the market capitalisation of the companies as of December 2023, the data for which were collected from the Orbis database.
2. Independent variables: Considerable effort was put into the construction of the explanatory variables, given the qualitative nature of the four soft indicators: regulation, governance, management and ecosystem.

Quality of regulation

Regulation quality is studied by means of two separate variables measuring regulation, because of the possible opposing effects they may have, as described in the section on the development of hypotheses. The first is the Regulation Quality Index (variable RQI in the regression model), while the second is the Financial Consumer Protection Index (variable FCPI). These variables were constructed from the responses of Central Banks in the World Bank's FICP 2022 survey. In the survey database, responses are coded as 1 for 'Yes' and 0 for 'No'. Based on this, the scores assigned to each Central Bank are the sum of the responses for each bank, considering a subset of questions in the survey. In summary, responses to questions related to: consumer credit providers, Nonbank E-Money Issuers (NBEIs), regulatory framework for insurance activities, e-money regulations, digital verification and digital onboarding, digital identification, data protection and Fintech innovations were considered to construct the RQI. In contrast, the FCPI was constructed by considering responses to questions on: legal framework for financial consumer protection, supervisory activities, non-supervisory activities, enforcement powers, complaint data collection and licensing criteria based on financial consumer protection. Both variables, originally measured on a range from 0 to a value other than 100, were scaled to facilitate interpretation on a range from 0 to 100.

Governance

Governance is measured on two dimensions: the quality of the CEO and the quality of the audit firm. The CEO quality variable is constructed as an index, the

CEO_q variable, which includes the key characteristics of the CEO's track record, assigning each of them a score based on their education, career and board history. Education is measured in terms of years of post-secondary education, with a range from 0 to 8 years for those who have completed a 4-year Bachelor's degree and two Master's degrees, such as the MBA. Career is measured in months of experience in sectors directly relevant to Fintech: Fintech, technology and financial services. Finally, the board history component is measured by the number of boards the CEO has served on during his or her career. This component is used to measure the level of recognition each CEO receives within their network, as a further indicator of the quality of their profile. Each of these three components has different ranges and maximum values and has therefore been scaled on a range between 0 and 100. Finally, the CEO quality index is calculated as a simple average of the scores of these three components. The audit quality variable is constructed as a dummy variable that takes value 1 if the current audit firm is one of the Big4 and 0 otherwise.

Quality of management

The management quality variable, MQI, is implemented as an index, characterised by a total of six different components, based on the 'Quality Management Principles' developed by the International Organisation for Standardisation (ISO), which awards ISO 9001 certification to companies that meet these principles. These principles are: customer focus, leadership, people involvement, process approach, improvement, evidence-based decision-making and relationship management.

- The principle of customer focus refers to the company's ability to meet customer requirements and expectations. It is measured in terms of the company's latest NPS or TrustPilot.com, or an average of the two when both are available.
- The leadership principle refers to management's ability to be united and lead the company with clarity and purpose. It was measured by looking at the number of executive changes in the last 2 years divided by the average number of executives in each company, based on the idea that a more stable management informs its ability to lead the organisation.
- The people involvement principle investigates whether the company recognises, enhances and values the skills of its employees. Engagement was measured by observing employee reviews on the Glassdoor website, where employees rate their work experience at each company, a direct proxy for their satisfaction and engagement.
- The process approach is related to the efficiency of internal processes. It was measured by the EBITDA margin of each company.
- The improvement principle recognises that successful organisations strive to improve and evolve in order to successfully respond to changing internal and external conditions. It was measured by looking at companies' expenditure on Re-

search and Development (R&D). However, due to the considerable lack of data on this aspect, this component was excluded from the MQI.
- The principle of evidence-based decision-making sees that facts, evidence and data analysis improve the quality of decisions and lead to better results. It was measured by the Bloomberg Audit Quality Score.
- Finally, the principle of relationship management is based on the idea that all stakeholders influence the performance of an organisation, which must carefully manage its relationship with these parties in order to prosper. It was measured in terms of the relevance of partnerships to each company. Specifically, a score was given based on how many times the words partnership, collaboration or alliance were mentioned in each company's publications between 2022 and 2023.

Each component was then scaled to fall within a range between 0 and 100 and the MQI was finally measured as a simple average of the 6 components, adding a minus sign in front of the leadership score, as a higher number of managerial changes indicates lower leadership stability.

Ecosystem

The ecosystem integration indicator, the Partner variable, was measured by looking at a single score that could provide information on the level of connection each company has with its ecosystem, consisting of financial customers, software developers, incumbents, Fintech companies, institutions, universities, hubs and accelerators. For this reason, this study selected the number of M&A buy-side deals to three main sectors, in which the company has been involved during its history, as a direct proxy to assess its integration into the ecosystem. First, acquisitions made in the non-cyclical consumer goods sector (which includes e-commerce platforms) inform the connection with financial customers. Second, acquisitions of financial services companies connect the Fintech Company to incumbents, other Fintech companies, as well as financial customers. Third, technology acquisitions inform about the level of integration with other Fintech companies and software developers.

Control variables

The valuation of Fintech companies, as well as other types of businesses, is a complex process influenced by numerous factors, some of which go beyond the theoretical framework of this study. It is essential to control these factors in order to avoid drawing inaccurate conclusions about the theoretical variables of interest. Therefore, the model incorporates several control variables, which include economic and company-specific factors. The measurement of these variables is simple, objective and consistent with established practices in the relevant literature.

Company size

The variable size is introduced as a control to account for the naturally positive effect that greater size has on a company's valuation. Specifically, size is measured by
looking at the turnover of the last available year for each company. This should be an
appropriate proxy for the size of a Fintech company, given the asset-light nature of
these firms, which makes asset value an inaccurate measure of their size.

Company performance

The performance variable is introduced with the aim of controlling the effect of a
company's performance on its valuation. Generally, a company is given a higher valuation the better its performance. In this study, the company's performance is represented by the average Return on Equity (ROE) of the last three years, when this figure was available.

Company sector

The industry variable is introduced to control the effect of the business in which a
company operates on its valuation. As discussed above, the Fintech industry com-
prises a variety of sectors with different characteristics and growth trajectories. As
a result, some businesses may receive higher valuations simply because they operate
in a specific sector. Therefore, the sector variable is introduced as a categorical variable, where each sub-sector represents a level, for a total of seven levels.

Regression model

With the aim of testing the described hypotheses, the following regression model
was estimated:

$$\text{Market Capitalization} = \alpha + \beta_1(\text{RQI})$$
$$+\beta_2(\text{FCPI})$$
$$+\beta_3(\text{CEO}_q)$$
$$+\beta_4(\text{Audit1})$$
$$+\beta_5(\text{MQI})$$
$$+\beta_6(\text{Partner})$$
$$+\beta_{1-K}(\text{Vector of Controls}),$$

where α is the coefficient of the intercept, β_{1-6} are the coefficients of the theoretical
variables, β_{1-k} are the coefficients of the control variables, with $k = 3$ as this model considers 3 different control variables. The model is estimated using R software.
    Subsequently, given the low degree of significance of the various levels of the

variable Sector, a control variable, this was excluded from the analysis in order to reduce the dimensionality of the model and simplify it. Furthermore, in view of a very strong positive correlation between CEO_q and Partner, a new variable was created, Average_CEO_Partner, calculated as the average of the two components, in order to avoid multicollinearity problems.

The final estimated model is therefore as follows:

$$\text{Market Capitalization} = \alpha + \beta_1(\text{RQI})$$
$$+\beta_2(\text{FCPI})$$
$$+\beta_3(\text{Average\_CEO\_Partner})$$
$$+\beta_4(\text{Audit})$$
$$+\beta_5(\text{MQI})$$
$$+\beta_6(\text{Size})$$
$$+\beta_7(\text{ROE}).$$

Analysis of results

From the results in Table 4, the coefficient of the intercept is 1415.48, which means that, when all explanatory variables are equal to 0, the market capitalisation of a Fintech company is, on average, $1,415 million. However, as expected, the estimated intercept is not statistically significant, considering that, with the exception of a few variables, most do not assume a value of 0.

The coefficient of the RQI is –33.88, with a p-value of 0.44. As the p-value exceeds the usual significance thresholds, the coefficient estimate has a low statistical

Table 4   **Regression Analysis of Key Factors Influencing Performance**

	Estimate	**Std. Error**	***t* value**	**Pr(>l*t*l)**	**Mr.**
(Intercept)	1415,47727	3533,70749	0,4006	0,68978	
RQI	−33,88045	47,56114	−0,7124	0,47827	.
FCPI	−6,12246	48,38963	−0,1265	0,89963	
Average_CEO_Partner	70,37833	31,20912	2,2551	0,02679	***
Audit	348,03923	693,02702	0,5022	0,61687	
MQI	47,04647	46,03405	1,022	0,30979	.
Size	0,98231	0,52951	1,8551	0,06717	*
ROE	3,76764	3,63413	1,0367	0,30291	.

Significance codes: 0 '*****', 0.001 '****', 0.01 '***', 0.05 '**', 0.1 '*', 0.5 '.', 1 ''
The regression output table shows coefficients, standard errors, t-values, and p-values for variables.

Source: Innovation and Corporate Entrepreneurship (ICE), SDA Bocconi

significance, although it shows a clear negative effect on the evaluation, which allows some conclusions to be drawn with the necessary precautions. The FCPI shows a negative coefficient estimate with a high p-value. Furthermore, the coefficient estimate takes a positive sign in the model specification with only regulatory factors, highlighting the difficulty of drawing conclusions on this variable and indicating the need for further studies.

The variable Average_CEO_Partner shows a coefficient estimate of 70.38 and a very low p-value of 0.01. This means that it is possible to conclude that, controlling for other variables, a unit increase in the variable Average_CEO_Partner results, on average, in a \$70.4 million increase in the valuation of a Fintech company.

The estimated audit coefficient is 348.04, although the p-value is rather high. This means that, according to the data, Fintech companies with a Big4 audit firm tend to be valued more highly than the other variables, although the result cannot be generalised, as the coefficient is not statistically significant.

Finally, the MQI has a positive coefficient of 47.05, which indicates a significant positive impact of superior management on the valuation of Fintechs. However, this coefficient should be interpreted with caution, given its low significance.

Overall, the model is very significant, as can be seen from the very low p-value of the F-test, confirming the high relevance of soft indicators in the context of Fintech company evaluation.

Discussion of results

The above analysis provided important insights into the impact of soft indicators on the value of Fintech companies.

The relationship between CEO quality and ecosystem integration

An initial insight from the study concerns the correlation between the quality of the CEO and the level of integration of a Fintech company within the Fintech ecosystem. The reasons for the strong link between the quality of a CEO and the connections the company has in the market probably lie in the networking capabilities a good CEO offers the company, as well as the greater opportunities a more interconnected company provides for a CEO to be recognised in the market.

By initially analysing the CEO-Partner direction and looking at the composition of the CEO quality index, a better score can be attributed to more years of relevant experience in Fintech-related industries. A CEO with more years of experience in the ecosystem has had more time than another CEO to build relationships and increase the opportunities his or her company has to integrate into the ecosystem. Similarly, a CEO who has served on more boards is generally more recognised in the market, an additional factor that helps the CEO build relationships for the company he or she currently leads.

Considering subsequently the opposite direction of the correlation, a CEO who joins a company with a broad set of connections within its ecosystem will more easily increase his or her fame and reputation within the network and, possibly, the number of companies that would like that CEO on their BoD.

The effect of regulation

The variables RQI and FCPI both show a coefficient estimate with low significance according to the current model specification, which could be due to sample size factors. However, some important insights can be drawn.

First, the coefficient of RQI is negative, indicating a possible negative effect of broader Fintech-related regulation on the value of Fintech firms. Considering the way the variable was defined, based on how many different aspects of the Fintech regulatory environment are covered within each jurisdiction, it could be the case that when regulation is more present and covers more aspects, this has a negative impact on the market capitalisation of a Fintech company.

One set of reasons behind this effect may be operational in nature. Broader regulation makes it more difficult for a Fintech company wishing to introduce an innovation to ensure compliance with the vast set of existing regulations. For instance, stringent rules on data privacy, customer verification (KYC/AML) and financial reporting may slow down business processes and reduce operational efficiency.

Another factor in the possible negative impact of regulation concerns higher compliance costs. More stringent regulation often requires companies to spend more on compliance, legal advice and administrative processes. This can divert resources away from innovation and growth activities, negatively affecting the overall valuation.

Moreover, Fintech companies operating in highly regulated environments may adopt a more conservative approach to avoid regulatory scrutiny and potential penalties. This lower appetite for risk may lead to fewer innovative products and slower growth.

Finally, from an investor perspective, high regulation could be perceived as a sign of a challenging business environment, leading to lower valuations. This perception might be based on the idea that stringent regulation stifles growth and increases costs.

The FCPI coefficient is also negative, signalling that broader consumer financial protection could negatively affect Fintech companies. While, as discussed above, greater consumer protection may increase consumer confidence, leading to a higher level of adoption of Fintech products and services, the negative coefficient highlights that the restrictive impact of regulation itself could be stronger.

This double impact may be one of the reasons why this coefficient shows the lowest absolute impact and significance. The reasons behind the negative impact of consumer financial protection generally overlap with those already described for Fintech-related regulation, but some additional ones can be identified.

For instance, consumer protection laws may impose limits on the fees and interest rates that Fintech companies can charge, directly affecting their revenue models. In addition, broader consumer financial protection may impose strict limitations on how Fintech companies can advertise and promote their products. This may hinder their ability to attract new customers and grow their user base.

The effect of CEO quality and ecosystem integration

The combined effect of the quality of a company's CEO and its level of integration within the ecosystem is positive. A company with a higher quality CEO and more integrated in its network is generally associated with a higher valuation, controlling for size, profitability and other soft indicators. This is an expected result, but surprisingly also very statistically significant.

Given the way the variable is constructed, an experienced CEO may be able to navigate complex regulatory environments, attract top talent and implement innovative strategies that drive growth and profitability. Strong CEOs may have a more robust strategic vision, which can help position the company effectively in the marketplace.

A robust network within the ecosystem, achieved through acquisitions in the financial services, technology and non-cyclical consumer goods sectors, can lead to synergies, improved service offerings and access to new markets. This can happen through cross-selling opportunities, advanced technological capabilities and an expansion of the customer base.

A larger network can also mean a larger market share and a stronger competitive position. A high-quality CEO and a stronger network presence also favour diversification, which can reduce risk and improve growth potential.

In line with this, investors tend to consider companies with experienced leadership and active acquisition strategies as lower-risk investments with higher return potential.

The effect of a Big4 audit firm

Audit firm quality shows a large positive effect on valuations of Fintech companies, although the significance of the variable is rather low. The reasons behind the positive effect are manifold, e.g., related to higher credibility and reputation, which positively influence investors' opinion on the quality of the company. Moreover, a Big4 audit firm also certifies higher-quality internal governance systems.

The lack of significance of the estimation of this coefficient could stem from the fact that the sample analysed does not show much variability between auditing firms, with a large part of the sample audited by a Big4 firm, making it more difficult to achieve high levels of significance.

The effect of management quality

The quality of management has a positive impact on the valuation of a Fintech company. Considering the structure of the management quality index (MQI), this includes a set of factors that help define quality management and explain why this variable positively drives value.

First of all, a higher customer focus score indicates that the company is able to meet customer requirements and expectations. This leads to higher customer satisfaction and loyalty, which can foster growth and revenue stability. Companies with high NPS scores and positive reviews on TrustPilot are more likely to retain customers and attract new ones through positive word-of-mouth, contributing to higher ratings.

More effective leadership with a stable management team ensures that the company has a clear direction and purpose, which can increase investor confidence and contribute to a higher company valuation.

High employee engagement, as measured by positive reviews on Glassdoor, indicates that employees are satisfied, motivated and productive. Engaged employees are usually associated with low turnover, higher productivity and a positive company culture, all of which can improve company ratings.

A focus on internal process efficiency, reflected in a higher EBITDA margin, indicates that the company is effective in managing its resources and operations. This efficiency can lead to cost savings and higher profitability, making Fintech companies more attractive to investors and driving higher valuations.

Effective relationship management, indicated by the relevance of partnerships and collaborations, helps companies harness external expertise and resources. Strong stakeholder relationships can enhance a company's capabilities and market position, creating expanded opportunities and ultimately contributing to higher valuations.

Implications of the results

The analysis provides critical insights that can help analysts refine valuation models for Fintech companies by incorporating adjustments for various factors. The different ways in which the findings of this study can be applied in practice are outlined in this section.

Adjustments for regulatory weight

The negative ratios of the RQI and the FCPI suggest that higher levels of regulation may reduce corporate value. Analysts should apply a discount to valuations of Fintech companies operating in highly regulated environments. This could be implemented in the form of a regulatory discount rate in the DCF model for companies operating in jurisdictions with high RQI and FCPI scores. The proposed RQI and FCPI indices can be taken as a benchmark to determine how much additional discount to apply given a given RQI and FCPI value.

Awards for high-quality CEOs and ecosystem integration

The significant positive impact of the variable Average_CEO_Partner indicates that companies with better CEOs and greater ecosystem integration are more valuable, suggesting that a premium should be applied for these companies. One way to include this could be to increase valuation multiples (such as P/E or EV/EBITDA) for companies with high scores in CEO quality and ecosystem integration. For example, a 1% increase in the Average_CEO_Partner score could result in a 0.7% increase in company value due to better strategic vision, network benefits and greater operational efficiency.

Furthermore, given the results of the model, it is advisable for analysts to consider CEO and integration metrics as proxies for each other. Analysts should use these metrics to adjust the risk premium in valuation models. For example, a company with a high CEO quality is likely to have strong ties to the ecosystem, resulting in a lower-risk premium. Again, the CEO quality index appears as a good indicator of CEO quality and can be taken as a benchmark in valuation models to include this soft indicator in quantitative models.

Incorporating management quality into evaluations

The positive impact of the MQI indicates that companies with higher management quality scores are more valuable. Ratings should be adjusted according to the MQI score. For example, a 1% increase in the MQI could result in a 0.5% increase in company value due to improved customer satisfaction, leadership stability, employee engagement and process efficiency.

Again, the MQI can be regarded as a good indicator of management quality and can be included in evaluation models, either in its current form or by adding the seventh dimension, currently missing from the MQI due to a lack of data, related to process improvement.

Part 3
The Relationship between Incumbents and Fintech

In recent years, the financial sector has undergone a radical transformation, thanks to the advent of digitisation, with a significant impact not only on operational processes but also on the structure of the market itself. Financial technologies, commonly known as Fintech, have accelerated this process by introducing new business models that challenge traditional financial institutions. Digitalisation has reduced operating costs, improved service efficiency and increased transparency in financial transactions. As highlighted in the GFT report of the Banking Disruption Index 2024, *banks' ability to adapt to new technologies is appreciated by consumers, but at the same time there is still room for improvement, particularly in the* user experience *and security of digital services (GFT, 2024).*

The evolution of Fintech has allowed new players *to enter the financial sector, especially technology companies operating outside traditional banking channels, posing a direct challenge to banks and creating a highly competitive environment (Bussoli, Conte, & Barone, 2023). The innovation process, fuelled by Fintech realities, has lowered barriers to entry, allowing new firms to compete directly with the sector's incumbents. However, this growing competition has forced traditional banks to review their operating models and invest in new technologies to maintain competitiveness. It is no coincidence that many financial institutions have responded to this technological* disruption *through merger and acquisition (M&A) transactions with Fintech firms, seeking to bridge the technology gap and exploit the synergies arising from such transactions (Bussoli, Conte, & Barone, 2023).*

Mergers and acquisitions between banks and Fintechs have emerged as a key strategy to meet the challenges of the new competitive environment. Recent studies show that M&As in the Fintech sector have led to significant improvements in the financial performance of the institutions involved, highlighting how such collaborations allow not only to integrate new technologies but also to reduce costs and improve operational efficiency (Bussoli, Conte, & Barone, 2023). The adoption of advanced technologies such as AI and ML has helped to improve service delivery, particularly in the areas of lending and credit risk assessment.

Strategic alliances between incumbents and Fintechs are not simply a defensive response to competition, but represent an opportunity for growth and innovation. As empirical studies have shown, financial institutions that have taken a proactive approach to Fintech M&As have benefited from increased profitability and greater operational efficiency. Such transactions not only allow them to cope with competi-

tive market pressures, but also achieve significant cost savings, improve the quality of service offered to customers and generate shareholder value (Bussoli, Conte, & Barone, 2023).

In this context, there is a need to examine not only whether but also how traditional banks should ally with Fintechs to maximise benefits. The research question therefore focuses on the conditions that make it advantageous for financial institutions to establish strategic alliances with Fintechs, with a focus on M&As as a means to stabilise performance and increase valuation in the medium to long term.

11 The Digitisation of the Banking Sector

Digitalisation has profoundly revolutionised the banking sector, imposing a radical rethinking of traditional business models, competitiveness and operational efficiency. The rise of digital technologies has changed the competitive landscape, leading banks to face unprecedented challenges. In particular, customer interactions have increasingly shifted to technology-mediated modes, reducing traditional contact channels and increasing the use of digital platforms to manage banking services (Sia, Soh, & Weill, 2016). This transition has pushed incumbents to modernise both their internal organisation and product offerings, with a significant impact on business models, which have been forced to adapt in order to maintain competitive sustainability (Björkdahl & Holmén, 2018; Cappa et al., 2021).

The concept of '*bankruption*', introduced by Waupsh (2016), describes this radical transformation of the banking sector due to digitalisation, which has made the traditional banking system more vulnerable and less responsive to new market *players*, such as Fintechs. The latter, by exploiting digitised business models and advanced technologies, have managed to gain ground rapidly in contrast to traditional banks, which, due to their rigidity and over-regulation, have failed to respond to market changes in a timely manner (Anagnostopoulos, 2018; Ayadi et al., 2021). The Fintech phenomenon represented a real discontinuity in the industry, introducing new standards of efficiency and customer interaction, particularly through the use of *user-friendly* and automated technologies (Gomber et al., 2018; Lee & Shin, 2018).

The adoption of Open Innovation models has been one of the banking sector's strategic responses to the pressure of digitisation. In this context, Open Innovation refers to the acquisition of external knowledge through M&As with Fintechs, a strategy aimed at fostering collaboration with external entities and integrating innovative technologies within the banks themselves (Cappa et al., 2022). In this way, banks try to bridge the digital divide with Fintechs, which have introduced much more efficient and lower-cost products and services to the market than traditional banking systems. Mergers with Fintech companies give banks access to new technologies, increased digital knowledge and new ways of interacting with customers, which are crucial for improving operational efficiency and competitiveness (Dao & Strobl, 2019).

Mergers and acquisitions with Fintechs are therefore seen as a way to generate positive synergies, reducing operating costs and improving long-term financial performance. However, the benefits of such transactions depend on the specific characteristics of the acquisition. As highlighted by recent studies, full mergers can be more complex than partial mergers, as they require the rapid integration of different business models, with the risk of cannibalising existing products and creating internal cultural conflicts (Pinelli et al., 2022). This risk can undermine the achievement of sustainable competitive advantage if not managed properly (Bauer & Matzler, 2014; Weber, Shenkar, & Raveh, 1996). For this reason, many banks prefer partial acquisitions, which allow a more gradual transition to the new digital models and reduce the risks associated with too rapid an integration (Folta, 1998).

Digitalisation in the banking sector has necessitated a change in business models, pushing banks to embrace open innovation practices through M&A with Fintechs to improve their competitiveness, efficiency and sustainability in the long run. However, the success of these transactions is highly dependent on the ability to effectively integrate new technologies without compromising the integrity and efficiency of existing banking operations (Cappa et al., 2022).

The role of incumbents in digital transformation

In the context of digital transformation, traditional companies, known as incumbents (e.g., banks, insurance companies, structured companies offering financial services), play an increasingly central role, especially due to the need to compete with new technological players, such as Fintechs and BigTechs. Although they maintain an established position in the financial sector, incumbents are facing increasing competition based on technological innovation and digital information management. This competitive pressure has prompted incumbents to re-evaluate their strategies, seeking partnerships with Fintechs to accelerate digital transformation, improve operational efficiency and offer innovative services.

A crucial aspect of this transformation is partnerships with Fintechs, initially perceived as competitors, but now seen as strategic partners for the adoption of new technologies. These *partnerships* not only enhance banks' ability to provide more efficient services but also allow them to respond to the new expectations of consumers, who are increasingly oriented towards digital experiences and fast transactions. Indeed, banks have often found it difficult to upgrade their legacy systems, being less agile in adopting advanced technologies such as AI and *big data* (Valverde & Fernández, 2020).

Competition between banks, Fintechs and BigTech is strongly influenced by the ability to effectively manage and share digital information. Incumbents face significant challenges in implementing information management technologies, which now represent the core of competition in the financial sector. In particular, the use of technologies based on *big data* and ML by Fintechs significantly improves service customisation and operational efficiency (Valverde & Fernández, 2020). This is a key point for the future of banks, which have to compete not only with Fintechs but also with BigTechs, companies that have an unprecedented ability to collect, analyse and exploit large volumes of data (Valverde & Fernández, 2020).

Against this backdrop, the World Bank pointed out that the pandemic of COV-

ID-19 has accelerated the adoption of digital technologies by banks, forcing them to review their business models and implement tools to provide remote financial services. Collaborations with Fintechs have proven to be crucial in addressing these challenges, enabling incumbents to adapt quickly to the changes imposed by the new economic and technological environment (World Bank, 2022).

Collaborations between banks and Fintechs, however, are not limited to the adoption of new technologies, but also extend to the creation of new business models. Examples in this regard are digital payment platforms and *robo-advisory*, which allow banks to reduce operating costs and access new markets, particularly those related to financial inclusion in emerging countries (Valverde & Fernández, 2020). Indeed, Fintechs, due to their greater technological agility and the absence of heavy legacy infrastructures, can often offer financial services at a lower cost than traditional banks.

The growing role of BigTech in the financial sector is also generating new regulatory challenges. Although BigTechs have not yet entered the banking market directly, their influence through payment services and credit platforms poses a threat to traditional banks. According to Valverde and Fernández (2020), BigTechs have the potential to radically reshape the competitive landscape, thanks to their superiority in data management and the use of advanced technologies such as *cloud computing* and AI. However, the regulatory framework still needs to evolve to ensure fair competition and protect financial stability.

In light of these dynamics, the role of incumbents in digital transformation is complex and constantly evolving. Fintech partnerships and the ability to address the challenges posed by BigTech will be key levers for the future success of traditional banks in the context of the increasing digitisation of the financial sector (Valverde & Fernández, 2020).

Advantages of incumbent and Fintech alliances: The incumbents' perspective

Partnerships between traditional (incumbent) financial institutions and Fintech companies are becoming increasingly strategic in the context of the digitisation of the financial sector. These partnerships not only offer operational and innovative advantages but also enable effective responses to challenges such as margin compression, pressure on profitability and the growing need for scalability and agility. Fintech and incumbents join forces to meet the demand of an increasingly demanding and technologically advanced clientele (PwC, 2023).

Fintechs, being more agile and focused on innovation, offer incumbents advanced technological solutions that enable them to develop and launch new products faster than traditional in-house systems. This is particularly important for improving efficiency and reducing operating costs, e.g., through process automation and the use of digital platforms (EY, 2022).

Access to technologies such as AI, blockchain and ML also enables incumbents to improve data analysis and the provision of customised services. One of the successful examples is the *Banking-as-a-Service* (BaaS) model, in which banks provide Fintechs with access to their infrastructure and APIs, facilitating the development of new financial services for a broader customer base. This model is particularly useful for Fintechs that wish to scale up quickly without having to invest directly in banks' regulated infrastructures. Collaborations between incumbents and Fintechs also prove effective in expanding the customer base. Fintechs, with their digital models, often attract young, technologically advanced customers that incumbents might not easily reach. This synergy allows incumbents to enter new markets, expand distribution channels and offer services on more modern and flexible platforms (Bain, 2023)

In addition, a partnership with a Fintech company accelerates digital transformation, improving the speed of transactions and the quality of service, a factor of paramount importance in the digital and international payments sector, where speed and efficiency have become imperative requirements (Barisaac, 2022).

However, these partnerships are not without their challenges: Technology integration, cultural alignment and regulatory risk management are critical factors that require careful planning and continuous monitoring to prevent partnerships from failing.

These considerations highlight how incumbents are beginning to see Fintechs not just as suppliers or competitors but as strategic partners; a factor corroborated by empirical evidence that, according to Gartner, points to an average of around nine Fintech collaborations per bank (Jeffery, Szmukler, & Egner, 2023). This trend underlines how digitisation and innovation are increasingly moving towards collaborative models rather than internally developed solutions.

Operational efficiency and process automation

One of the primary and most tangible benefits of incumbent-Fintech alliances is the increase in operational efficiency. In a context where the pressure on profit margins and the need for greater operational agility are increasingly evident, these collaborations prove to be an effective means of responding to the challenges posed by a competitive and rapidly changing environment. Indeed, the introduction of advanced technology solutions by Fintechs allows them to overcome the limitations imposed by legacy systems, which often slow down the decision-making and operational processes of established financial institutions (Jeffery, Szmukler, & Egner, 2023; Finastra, 2023).

According to the Fintech Observatory 2023, partnerships between incumbents and Fintechs are becoming more and more common and are a key factor in improving day-to-day operations, particularly in the area of digital payments and risk management. Consider, for instance, banks that have chosen to partner with innovative Fintechs and have been able to implement advanced algorithms for credit risk assessment, using unconventional and innovative data for real-time analysis of customers' creditworthiness. This has led to a significant reduction in the time to access liquidity, accelerating the decision-making process and reducing the so-called '*time to cash*', a crucial advantage in an increasingly competitive market (PwC, 2023).

Furthermore, another key aspect of partnerships between incumbents and Fintechs is the latter's ability to provide incumbents with flexible and easily integrated technology tools to enhance the customer experience, an increasingly relevant aspect in the financial services industry. According to recent research, 60% of global financial institutions have already entered into partnerships with third-party providers, including Fintechs, to address customers' growing digital needs. These partnerships have accelerated innovation and reformulated traditional business models, making incumbents more prepared to handle the challenges of the future (Finastra, 2023).

Fintechs operate on modern technology infrastructures that are not subject to the rigidities typical of legacy systems, enabling them to develop intuitive, fast and intelligent products. This technological agility allows them to bring innovative solutions to market quickly, meeting the needs of increasingly demanding customers accustomed to *user-friendly* digital interfaces. The ability to leverage systems such as the regulatory sandbox allows Fintechs to experiment and develop new ideas more easily.

According to a study conducted by Bain & Company, many banks see these partnerships as a solution to meet growing customer expectations and new market challenges, which require not only innovation but also a more flexible and dynamic approach to operational management (Jeffery, Szmukler, & Egner, 2023).

Partnerships between incumbents and Fintechs not only improve operational efficiency but also offer significant opportunities for the development of new products and services. For instance, many incumbents are using these partnerships to introduce innovative solutions in areas such as digital lending, risk management and digital customer *onboarding*. In particular, the simplification of account-opening processes and the digitisation of lending services are significantly reducing customer churn rates while improving banks' overall operational effectiveness.

In addition to operational and technological benefits, partnerships with Fintechs enable incumbents to better address regulatory challenges. For instance, the emerging open banking regulation, which obliges banks to share financial data with qualified third parties, requires close collaboration between banks and Fintechs to ensure compliance with such regulations. Such entities, through the use of flexible APIs and advanced digital solutions, can help banks adhere to regulations more efficiently.

It follows that alliances between incumbents and Fintechs represent one of the most effective strategies to address the challenges of the modern financial sector, combining the flexibility and innovation of Fintechs with the financial strength and regulatory expertise of banks. These collaborations not only improve the efficiency and customisation of services offered but also allow incumbents to remain competitive and meet the growing expectations of customers in an increasingly digitised and sustainability-oriented world (Jeffery, Szmukler, & Egner, 2023).

Flexibility and scalability: Upgrading IT infrastructure

An increasingly important aspect of collaborations between traditional (incumbent) financial institutions and Fintechs concerns the increased flexibility and scalability of incumbents' IT infrastructures. These collaborations are based on the adoption of innovative technologies such as cloud computing and APIs, which allow banks to upgrade their platforms faster and more efficiently than traditional legacy systems. Traditional IT infrastructures, characterised by rigidity and complexity, are often an obstacle to incumbents' agility and competitiveness in a market that requires rapid adaptation to change. Overcoming these limitations is essential for incumbents wishing to remain relevant and competitive in an increasingly digitised and fragmented environment (McKinsey & Company, 2016b; PwC).

The move to the cloud represents a fundamental paradigm shift in this context. Indeed, this technology enables incumbents to adopt more elastic infrastructures, capable of responding in real time to changes in market demand. This not only reduces operating costs, thanks to automation and efficient resource management but also allows for faster innovation and experimentation processes. A significant example is a North American bank that managed to migrate 70% of its applications to the cloud within three years, improving its ability to integrate new technologies and respond more quickly to market needs. This approach has also significantly reduced the time to release new products, leading to greater customer satisfaction and consolidating the bank's competitive advantage (McKinsey & Company, 2022).

Cloud adoption not only facilitates more efficient management but also offers new opportunities for scalability and adaptability. Indeed, cloud technologies have contributed to the growth of Fintech companies, which have harnessed these capabilities to manage increasingly complex operations while simultaneously improving efficiency and service quality for customers. The interoperability provided by the cloud allows Fintechs and traditional banks to collaborate more seamlessly, exchanging data and services in a secure and highly scalable environment. Furthermore, the adoption of flexible pricing models such as *'pay-per-use'* allows banks to reduce the costs associated with the purchase of technology and optimise the use of resources, ensuring greater operational efficiency (Bain & Company, 2022).

Partnerships between Fintechs and incumbents are not limited to technological aspects. These collaborations extend to the creation of innovative business models, underpinned by advanced data analysis and AI, which allow for increasing customisation of services offered to customers. This approach not only improves operational efficiency but also enables incumbents to respond with greater agility to regulatory changes and new customer needs. The integration of advanced Fintech solutions also reduces the time to market for new products, thereby increasing market competitiveness and creating opportunities for long-term sustainable growth (PwC).

The use of the cloud also promotes greater resilience of IT infrastructures, allowing incumbents to proactively manage any security and regulatory compliance issues. Concerns about data security and regulatory compliance can be effectively addressed through advanced encryption solutions and the ability to implement security controls globally. This increases confidence in cloud solutions, making them an increasingly attractive option for financial institutions (Baecker, Ebener, Ford, Mueller, & Wuest, 2022).

The adoption of cloud and Fintech technologies also has a significant impact on cost management and efficiency. Incumbents that have adopted the cloud have been able to reduce operating costs, consolidate their data centres and improve energy efficiency. The ability to rapidly scale IT resources according to market needs reduces the risk of waste and optimises the use of existing infrastructure, making the entire banking ecosystem more agile and competitive (McKinsey & Company, 2016b; PwC).

Ultimately, partnerships between incumbents and Fintechs are redefining the landscape of the financial sector. These partnerships, based on the adoption of innovative technologies, enable banks to overcome the historical rigidities of their IT infrastructures, embracing a new operating model based on flexibility, scalability and innovation capabilities. This approach not only strengthens banks' competitiveness but also contributes to a more dynamic financial ecosystem, capable of responding to future industry challenges and meeting changing customer needs (Baecker, Ebener, Ford, Mueller, & Wuest, 2022).

Accelerating digital transformation

Today, collaborations between incumbents and Fintechs are an indispensable element in the evolution of the financial system, particularly with regard to the acceleration of digital transformation. In a global context characterised by rapid technological innovation and constantly changing consumer expectations, traditional financial institutions are under pressure to adapt quickly. In this scenario, Fintech companies, with their flexibility, speed of innovation and ability to manage technological risks, assume a central role in facilitating and speeding up this process.

One of the central aspects that emerges is that Fintechs act as real catalysts for the adoption of advanced technologies, such as AI, blockchain and big data analytics. These technologies, when integrated within the incumbents' infrastructures, enable traditionally complex and costly processes to be optimised. For instance, AI finds wide application in the automation of credit risk assessment processes and the personalisation of financial services, while blockchain provides transparency and security in transactions. Fintechs, therefore, not only facilitate the adoption of these technologies, but also accelerate their implementation, significantly reducing the time it takes to develop and bring new digital products to market (McKinsey & Company, 2016b; Jeffery, Szmukler, & Egner, 2023).

Moreover, partnerships with Fintechs enable incumbents to respond quickly to new market and consumer needs. Indeed, the pandemic of COVID-19 has accelerated consumer demand for digital interactions, forcing incumbents to radically review their approach to digital services. In this context, partnerships with Fintechs have become essential to ensure operational flexibility and agility in resource management, which are crucial in an environment of increasing volatility. Such partnerships allow incumbents to benefit from the technological expertise of Fintechs while maintaining control over customers and operations (Jeffery, Szmukler, & Egner, 2023).

A tangible example of the effectiveness of these partnerships is the adoption of the Buy Now, Pay Later (BNPL) model, which has been very successful in the digital payments sector. By partnering with innovative Fintechs, banks have been able to rapidly integrate deferred payment solutions that meet new consumer expectations for flexibility. This model, which is expected to grow by around 24% annually until 2025, not only improves the shopping experience but also allows banks to remain competitive in an environment increasingly dominated by native digital players (McKinsey & Company, 2016b).

Despite the many benefits, these partnerships are not without their challenges. One of the main difficulties lies in the cultural gap between Fintechs, which are oriented towards an agile and innovative business model and traditional banks, which often adopt a more prudent and regulated approach. Overcoming these cultural barriers and operating in synergy requires considerable effort in terms of managing organisational differences and strategic alignment. Another significant obstacle is the banks' legacy systems, which are often poorly compatible with newer technologies and require continuous upgrades to support growth and cost optimisation. The ability to integrate new technologies on a large scale is therefore a major technical challenge (EY, 2021; PwC, 2016).

From a strategic point of view, banks that manage to establish effective partnerships with Fintechs can take advantage of multiple opportunities. Indeed, they help to improve not only operating costs and capital management but also the generation of new sources of income. However, choosing the right Fintech partner is crucial for long-term success. Collaboration options can range from strategic acquisitions to joint ventures or simple business partnerships but always require a careful assessment of the in-house technical capabilities and solutions offered by Fintechs (McKinsey & Company, 2016b).

Partnerships between incumbents and Fintechs do not only facilitate the digital transformation of banks, but represent a real strategy for sustainable growth. These partnerships allow incumbents to harness the technological innovation of Fintechs to meet the challenges of a rapidly changing market while improving operational efficiency and creating new development opportunities. However, maximising the benefits of these partnerships requires a strategic approach that aims to overcome cultural and technical barriers, ensuring effective alignment between the needs of both parties involved (EY, 2021; Jeffery, Szmukler, & Egner, 2023; PwC, 2016).

These considerations underline how partnerships between incumbents and Fintechs represent an indispensable strategic lever for traditional financial institutions, offering them the opportunity to respond more effectively to the challenges posed by technological evolution and the increasing digitisation of the sector. These partnerships allow banks to significantly improve operational efficiency, overcoming the limitations imposed by obsolete and rigid technological infrastructures, and to accelerate the process of digital transformation, a factor that is now crucial for maintaining competitiveness in an ever-changing global market.

Such collaborations are not limited to the mere adoption of innovative technological solutions, but represent an opportunity to rethink and redesign traditional business and operational models. Integrating the skills of Fintechs, characterised by agility, flexibility and a propensity for innovation, with the robustness, experience and risk management capabilities of traditional banks, creates an ecosystem in which both parties can benefit from each other's distinctive competencies. In this context, the adoption of advanced technologies such as AI, cloud computing, blockchain and ML makes it possible not only to improve internal processes and reduce operating costs but also to develop new products and services capable of responding to the needs of an increasingly sophisticated and digitally aware clientele.

However, for such collaborations to reach their full potential, banks need to tackle some critical challenges head-on. First, a culture of innovation must be fostered within financial institutions, overcoming the resistance to change often present in long-established organisations. Cultural transformation, in fact, is a crucial element in creating a favourable environment for the integration of the new technologies introduced by Fintechs, which are based on principles of speed, flexibility and continuous experimentation. Banks must also invest in upgrading their internal skills, creating teams capable of interfacing with Fintech players and understanding the evolving technological and market dynamics.

Another major challenge is the need to ensure effective management of risks, particularly those related to cyber security and regulatory compliance. Indeed, working with such entities requires banks to address complex issues related to data protection, privacy and security of digital transactions, as well as to ensure compliance with applicable regulations in the financial sector. An integrated approach to risk management, involving both parties and based on a clear definition of responsibilities, is crucial to avoid partnerships becoming a source of vulnerability rather than growth.

Finally, the success of these partnerships will also depend on the banks' ability to adopt a strategic and forward-looking approach when choosing Fintech partners. Banks must therefore develop capacities to strategically assess Fintechs, considering not only their technological potential but also their financial strength and ability to adapt to a complex regulatory environment.

It follows that partnerships with Fintechs represent a historic opportunity for incumbents, allowing them to evolve and adapt to the new dynamics of the financial sector. However, such opportunities can only be seized by institutions capable of tackling with determination the cultural, operational and regulatory challenges that such partnerships entail. Only through strategic commitment and a long-term vision will it be possible to turn these partnerships into a sustainable growth engine, ensuring that banks are not only able to compete effectively but also to thrive in an increasingly digitised and globalised market.

Benefits of alliances between incumbents and Fintechs: The Fintech perspective

In order to conduct a comprehensive analysis, it is necessary to consider the perspective of Fintechs and, in particular, the benefits they can gain from collaborating with incumbents. These partnerships represent a strategic tool to tackle innovation challenges, allowing the parties involved to make the most of their respective expertise and resources. From the perspective of Fintechs, the main advantages of these alliances include core business growth, expansion into new markets, access to larger investment budgets and the transfer of specific know-how.

Consolidated customer base

One of the main assets that incumbent companies bring to alliances with Fintechs is an already established customer base. This gives Fintechs the opportunity to grow their core business, expanding the scope of their services and accelerating market penetration. Thanks to the already-established trust between the incumbent and the end customers, Fintechs can more easily overcome initial barriers related to credibility and adoption of new technology services.

Expansion into new markets

Fintechs, due to their flexibility and capacity for innovation, have proven that they can successfully diversify their business. However, collaboration with an incumbent can amplify this potential. According to recent data, Fintechs that collaborate with incumbents are between 1.2 and 1.3 times more likely to generate substantial returns in new markets. The incumbent, for its part, benefits from access to cutting-edge technologies and more agile business models.

Stamp of trust

A further key advantage of alliances between incumbents and Fintechs is the 'Stamp of Trust'. Working with an incumbent, already recognised as a trustworthy and legitimate player in the industry, lends additional credibility to the services offered by Fintechs. This not only facilitates the acquisition of new customers but also helps to strengthen trust in innovative technologies that are often new to the market.

Investment budget

Incumbent companies often have significant financial resources that can be made available to finance the development and expansion of Fintech activities. These investment budgets are a key lever for growth, enabling Fintechs to scale their services and tackle development initiatives that would otherwise be out of reach. For the incumbent, on the other hand, the allocation of capital in Fintech partnerships represents an opportunity to diversify the portfolio and access new innovative lines of business.

In-house know-how

Finally, incumbents bring highly specialised in-house *know-how* to their Fintech alliances, which is particularly useful in areas such as legal and regulatory compliance and risk management. This expertise can be essential for Fintechs, which often lack sufficient internal resources to tackle complex issues such as customer due diligence or regulatory compliance. Integrating this knowledge allows Fintechs to operate more safely and efficiently while reducing operational risks.

Incumbent and Fintech collaboration models

Collaboration models between traditional (incumbent) financial institutions and Fintechs represent a central element in the adaptation and innovation strategies of the modern financial sector. In an environment characterised by increasing competitive pressure and accelerating digitisation processes, incumbents are often faced with a choice between different ways of integrating with Fintechs in order to remain competitive and improve operational efficiency. The three main types of collaborations identified and analysed in this work are *Cooperate*, *Buy* and *Make* (PwC, 2023), each with distinct characteristics and purposes, but united by the objective of maximising the benefits from technological innovation.

The '*Cooperate*' model is emerging as a particularly effective strategy for banks wishing to exploit innovation without having to bear the risk or burden of acquiring or developing Fintech solutions themselves. This mode of collaboration includes the creation of partnerships through incubators, accelerators or the use of licences. Such strategic alliances allow incumbents to gain rapid access to the most advanced Fintech technologies, integrating them into their existing platforms and enriching their service offerings with new digital functionalities, capable of responding more dynamically and customised to customers' needs. An emblematic example is the rise of strategic partnerships in the digital payments sector, where traditional banks take advantage of the speed and innovation capacity of Fintech startups (EY, 2021).

This growing interdependence between incumbents and Fintechs reflects an awareness on the part of traditional financial institutions of the need to transform their business model in order to respond to a market demand that is increasingly oriented towards digital solutions and to a customer base that demands a more seamless, efficient and personalised banking experience. Collaboration enables banks to adopt innovative technologies such as AI, ML, blockchain and process automation, significantly improving the user experience and reducing operational costs (World Economic Forum, 2017).

The '*Buy*' model, on the other hand, is characterised by the strategy of acquiring Fintechs or significant stakes in them, with the aim of embedding innovation and digital expertise within the bank's corporate structure. This allows incumbents to avoid the risks associated with the development of technology solutions while benefiting from direct control over the acquired technologies. The consolidation of these acquisitions has led to an accelerated digital transformation (Jeffery, Szmukler, & Egner, 2023).

Finally, the *'Make'* model is based on the banks' ability to develop innovative technology solutions in-house, thus retaining complete control over the digitisation process and retaining know-how in-house. Although this strategy offers the advantage of preserving technological independence and the ability to customise solutions according to the specific needs of the financial institution, it also presents considerable challenges. Firstly, the development costs and necessary infrastructure investments are particularly high. Moreover, the internal innovation process tends to be slower than the rapid technological evolution driven by the Fintech market, a factor that may reduce banks' ability to respond to changes in the industry in a timely manner (World Economic Forum, 2017).

As a result, collaborations between Fintechs and incumbents are emerging as a strategic pillar for the future of the banking and financial sector. These alliances not only allow banks to remain competitive in an increasingly digitised market but also enable Fintechs to leverage the established customer base and regulatory expertise of incumbents. This synergy is transforming the entire financial ecosystem, pushing towards more flexible and innovation-driven business models. The choice between *Cooperate*, *Buy* and *Make* strategies is not only dictated by economic considerations but also by the need to adapt to an ever-changing technological landscape, where the ability to innovate quickly is a key factor for future success.

Cooperate

The *'Cooperate'* model between incumbents and Fintechs emerges as one of the most flexible and functional strategies to address the rapid digital transformation of the financial sector. This form of collaboration is characterised by structured partnerships, such as joint ventures, corporate incubator programmes and the outsourcing of specific activities to external subsidiaries, which allow traditional banks to take advantage of the agility and technological innovation of Fintechs, without incurring the risks and costs associated with the internalisation of technological development.

Cooperate partnerships offer significant advantages to financial institutions, especially in the context of increasing competitive pressure and rising expectations from customers in terms of digital experience. Indeed, incumbents can enhance their digital service offerings by integrating innovative solutions proposed by Fintechs, such as digital wallets, contactless payment systems and open banking platforms. This allows banks to remain competitive without having to deal with costly infrastructure upgrades or lengthy internal development processes (McKinsey & Company, 2016b).

Another crucial advantage of this model is its strategic flexibility. Banks can decide to partner with Fintechs in specific areas, according to contingent needs and long-term objectives. This type of alliance not only gives banks access to cutting-edge technologies but also improves operational efficiency and reduces development costs. In particular, corporate ventures and incubation programmes allow incumbents to explore new business models and develop innovative technologies with limited risks. According to a McKinsey study, about 47% of recently founded Fintechs have a B2B (business-to-business) business model, focusing on providing technology solutions directly to banks, rather than competing with them (McKinsey & Company, 2016b).

However, one of the main obstacles to large-scale adoption of the *'Cooperate'* model is the complexity of incumbents' legacy infrastructures. Banks' core systems, while reliable and secure, are often not designed to easily support the integration of new API-based technologies and cloud-native platforms. As a result, many financial institutions face significant investments to modernise their IT architectures and facilitate effective cooperation with Fintechs.

Moreover, risk management is a critical aspect in Fintech-incumbent partnerships. Banks, being heavily regulated, have to ensure that each partnership complies with regulatory requirements and compliance guidelines. This often results in longer decision-making and sales cycles, which can slow down the adoption of innovations. Therefore, it is essential that objectives, expectations and implementation timeframes are clearly defined early on in the partnership to ensure a smoother process and optimise the use of resources.

The digital payments sector is a prime example of how the *'Cooperate'* model can lead to successful solutions. Many banks have chosen to cooperate with Fintechs specialising in this field, integrating functionalities such as peer-to-peer (P2P) payments and mobile banking solutions into their platforms. In this way, banks not only improve the customer experience but are also able to respond more quickly to the needs of an evolving market (McKinsey & Company, 2016b).

In conclusion, the *'Cooperate'* model offers incumbents a unique opportunity to modernise their services, reduce operating costs and improve customer satisfaction, without the need to undertake complex internal technology developments. However, to ensure the success of such collaborations, it is essential that banks and Fintechs adopt a clear strategic approach, including risk management, the definition of appropriate KPIs and a shared commitment to technology integration.

Buy

The *'Buy'* model, i.e., the process of traditional financial institutions acquiring Fintech startups, represents one of the most advanced and strategic forms of collaboration between the established banking sector and the world of innovative financial technologies. This approach is distinguished by its ability to create a direct bridge between technological innovation and traditional infrastructures, allowing banks to quickly acquire specialised skills, advanced digital platforms and new business models that would otherwise require years of in-house development (KPMG, 2020).

By acquiring full or partial stakes in these emerging companies, incumbents can take direct control over key technology assets, improving their competitiveness in the digital market. This approach offers several strategic advantages: on the one hand, it allows banks to reduce the time-to-market for new digital solutions, and on the other hand, it provides access to specialised skills and talent that traditional financial institutions may not possess in-house.

A crucial aspect of this model is that it allows banks to overcome the limitations imposed by legacy infrastructures, i.e., those dated and complex IT systems that often hinder the rapid adoption of new technologies. Indeed, acquiring Fintechs gives incumbents access to scalable and modern platforms, accelerating the adoption of solutions such as cloud computing, AI and blockchain, technologies that underpin the digital revolution in the financial sector. Many banks see Fintechs not only as an opportunity to improve their services, but also as a way to embrace a new technological paradigm that provides greater efficiency, speed and operational flexibility (KPMG, 2020).

Fintech acquisitions are particularly attractive when startups operate in areas critical to banks' digital transformation, such as digital payments, lending and wealth management. These areas represent focal points for the customer experience and for banks' ability to meet growing customer expectations in terms of speed, personalisation and accessibility of services (KPMG, 2020).

An emblematic example of a successful '*Buy*' model is Visa's acquisition of Plaid, which took place with the aim of strengthening Visa's position in the digital payments market. Plaid, a startup specialising in connectivity between bank accounts and financial applications, enabled Visa to expand its technology offering, improving its ability to integrate its services with modern Fintech applications. This transaction not only consolidated Visa's leadership in the sector but also demonstrated how financial institutions can gain a competitive advantage by acquiring established innovative platforms with high growth potential (KPMG, 2020).

Another significant case is that of JPMorgan Chase, which acquired the startup 55ip, a platform specialising in optimising financial advisory operations. This acquisition allowed JPMorgan to accelerate the digitisation of its wealth management services, integrating automation solutions and improving the efficiency of investment management operations. The example of 55ip demonstrates how M&As not only help bridge technology gaps but are also tools to enrich the financial services offering in line with the needs of an increasingly digitally oriented clientele.

One of the main advantages of the '*Buy*' model is the possibility to access scalable, market-ready technologies, avoiding the costs and time associated with in-house development. By acquiring Fintech startups, banks can quickly implement new solutions and business models that have already been successfully tested in the market, significantly reducing the risk of failure. In addition, the acquisition allows them to integrate specialised talent into their workforce, bringing expertise in areas such as cybersecurity, AI, big data analysis and mobile app development, all areas where traditional banks may be less competitive.

In terms of customer experience, this model allows banks to substantially improve the quality of services offered, thanks to the integration of more user-friendly and digitally oriented technologies. Fintechs, in fact, are known for their ability to innovate rapidly and develop solutions central to customer needs, such as mobile banking apps, peer-to-peer payment platforms and personal financial management tools. Through acquisition, banks can therefore offer their customers a more seamless, personalised and accessible experience.

However, the model is not without its challenges. One of the main obstacles is post-acquisition integration, which can be particularly complex both technologically and culturally. The fusion between a traditionally conservative and highly regulated banking culture and the more dynamic and innovation-oriented culture typical of Fintech startups can generate internal frictions. These contrasts often manifest themselves in differences in decision-making processes, organisational structures and approach to risk. For the acquisition to be successful, it is necessary for incumbents to adopt change management strategies that facilitate the integration of the two corporate cultures, enhancing the strengths of both.

From a technological point of view, the integration of IT systems is another critical issue. Fintechs' technology platforms are often built on agile and modern architectures, while banks still rely on complex and rigid legacy systems. This can make it difficult to connect the two infrastructures, requiring significant investments to harmonise the different systems. Studies have shown that around 70% of M&A transactions in the financial sector fail to achieve their objectives precisely because of technology integration issues (Deloitte, 2018).

The '*Buy*' model therefore offers banks a powerful lever to accelerate innovation and maintain competitiveness in an increasingly digitised financial market. However, to maximise the benefits of this strategy, it is crucial that financial institutions carefully plan the integration of acquired Fintech technologies and competencies, ensuring that they are in line with long-term business objectives. A clear roadmap and efficient management of merger processes are essential elements to overcome cultural and technological challenges, enabling incumbents to fully exploit the potential of M&As.

Make

The '*Make*' model represents an ambitious and conservative strategy, mainly adopted by large financial institutions that have the resources to develop innovative technological solutions in-house. This approach is characterised by the desire to retain full control of the innovation process, while minimising dependence on external suppliers. This strategy enables banks not only to protect their know-how but also to respond more quickly and effectively to changing market needs and the challenges posed by increasing competition in the sector. The internalisation of technology development processes allows financial institutions to maintain greater flexibility in the management of their solutions, ensuring a better ability to react to regulatory changes and the need for regulatory compliance, which are crucial in today's environment.

One of the main advantages of this model lies in the ability to thoroughly customise the technology solutions developed, ensuring seamless integration with existing IT infrastructures. This is particularly strategic in complex and highly regulated sectors, such as blockchain and open banking, where security and operational efficiency are top priorities. In this context, in-house management of technology development enables the design and implementation of high-security platforms, with the aim of ensuring the protection of sensitive information and optimising financial operations. A significant example is offered by JPMorgan, which has internally developed a blockchain solution called JPM Coin, aimed at improving operational efficiency and enhancing the security of international financial transactions (McKinsey & Company, 2018–2021).

Despite the obvious benefits, the adoption of the *'Make'* model entails a number of considerable challenges that financial institutions must be prepared to face. First, the in-house development of technologies requires huge investments, both in terms of economic resources and specialised expertise. The high cost of the resources needed to support such projects, coupled with the long development time required, is one of the main challenges of this approach. Banks that choose to adopt the *'Make'* model must take into account the possibility of suffering a slowdown in their ability to compete in the market, especially when compared with Fintechs, which are characterised by a leaner organisational structure and a greater ability to adapt to technological innovations. Fintechs, thanks to their agility, are able to quickly bring innovative solutions to the market, often at a lower cost, thus succeeding in attracting an increasingly demanding clientele eager to access advanced financial services quickly (BCG, 2023b).

A further obstacle financial institutions face when adopting the *'Make'* model is the management of legacy IT infrastructures, which often act as a brake on the integration of new technologies. Legacy infrastructures, typical of large banks, have a number of structural limitations that make the transition to more modern and flexible platforms complex. In fact, implementing new technological solutions on outdated systems entails a number of significant operational risks, including the difficulty of ensuring interoperability between new and existing tools, as well as the risk of increasing the management complexity of internal IT systems. Banks adopting this strategy must be prepared to embark on a path of modernisation of their technological infrastructures, investing both in the overhaul of IT platforms and in staff training in order to develop the skills needed to manage new technologies effectively and reduce the associated risks.

It follows that, although the *'Make'* model has significant advantages in terms of controlling the innovation process and customising technological solutions, it requires significant investment capacity and a long-term strategic vision. Financial institutions that choose to adopt this approach must be able to balance high costs and long development times with the need to remain competitive in an ever-changing market. The ability to effectively manage these challenges can ensure a lasting competitive advantage in the long run, allowing banks to differentiate themselves from competitors by creating tailor-made solutions that precisely meet their customers' needs and regulatory requirements. However, for this model to be truly effective, it is crucial that financial institutions are prepared to carefully manage the operational risks associated with legacy infrastructure management and to bear the substantial development costs.

It is important to emphasise that the choice between the *Cooperate*, *Buy* and *Make* models is neither rigid nor exclusive. In fact, many financial institutions adopt a hybrid strategy, combining different approaches depending on their strategic needs and the market environment in which they operate. This flexibility allows incumbents to balance the benefits of external Fintech partnerships and in-house expertise, creating a dynamic and adaptable operating model. The decision on which model to favour depends on multiple factors, including the availability of financial resources, internal innovation capacity, corporate culture and the degree of urgency in implementing new technologies. For instance, in highly regulated industries such as *RegTech* or fast-growing areas such as *WealthTech*, incumbents may prefer flexible collaboration strategies such as the *Cooperate* model, which allows them to access innovative solutions without compromising the stability of their core operations or incurring internal development costs and risks.

In addition to addressing specific operational and market needs, the adoption of a hybrid collaboration model enables financial institutions to be more agile and competitive in a rapidly digitising environment. The combination of strategic partnerships with targeted acquisitions and investments in in-house technology development capabilities enables banks to improve their resilience, keeping pace with technological evolution and increasing customer demands for personalised, efficient and digitally advanced services. This approach offers greater flexibility, allowing incumbents to experiment with new solutions in a controlled manner, mitigate the risks associated with innovation and ensure rapid scalability of new services.

Moreover, the competitive landscape of the financial sector is increasingly characterised by the coexistence and cooperation between traditional players and new digital entrants. Fintechs, with their ability to introduce disruptive innovations and meet the needs of digital-first customers, represent a valuable opportunity for incumbents. However, the most interesting aspect is not just the technological innovation, but the synergy created between two seemingly different realities: Fintechs bring agility, speed of execution and cutting-edge solutions, while incumbents provide stability, significant financial resources and a deep understanding of markets and regulations. This integration of their respective strengths creates a richer financial ecosystem, capable of delivering better solutions for both businesses and consumers.

In conclusion, collaboration between incumbents and Fintechs is today an essential pillar for the transformation of the financial sector. It not only facilitates the adoption of new technologies and business models but also allows for optimising operational efficiency, enhancing the customer experience and maintaining competitiveness in an increasingly digital-driven market. Financial institutions that are able to fully exploit the opportunities offered by these collaborations, and adapt readily to technological and market challenges, will be those best positioned to thrive in an ever-changing landscape. The synergies created not only generate value for both parties but also contribute to the growth of a more innovative, resilient and inclusive financial system, capable of responding dynamically to the evolving needs of customers, regulators and stakeholders.

12 M&A between Incumbents and Fintechs

The transformation of incumbents: The rise of Fintechs and the need to innovate and compete

The digitisation process in the Italian banking sector represents a crucial challenge for traditional (incumbent) intermediaries, which aim to strengthen their competitiveness in a context characterised by rapid technological change and growing customer expectations. In this context, strategic participations and collaborations with Fintech companies emerge as fundamental tools to guarantee access to advanced technological skills and highly specialised personnel.

Participations and collaborations: The numbers in 2023

According to the Bank of Italy report, in 2023, Italian intermediaries undertook a significant number of strategic initiatives through participations and collaborations. Equity investments involved a total value of €1,114 million, distributed among 36 intermediaries that held at least one equity investment. In total, 97 companies were involved in such investments, highlighting a consistent commitment to supporting innovation and digital transformation.

At the same time, 51% of intermediaries participated in at least one collaboration, with a total of 470 agreements involving 274 companies. These collaborations represent a strategic pillar to foster the rapid implementation of innovative solutions, enabling incumbents to fill technology gaps and improve their service offerings. The main motivations driving these initiatives include access to technologies that are not available in-house (51.2%), accelerating implementation times (18.4%) and acquiring skills not present within organisations (10.2%).

As can be seen from the data, incumbents showed a preference for collaborations over participations. This approach allows them to start working with Fintechs by reducing the risk associated with the introduction of new technologies and business models, while providing greater flexibility in exploring synergy opportunities.

The evolution of M&A transactions in Fintech

Over the last decade, the Italian M&As landscape in the Fintech sector has been growing steadily, culminating in a significant peak in 2022. This trend reflects the growing need for incumbents to innovate and compete in a highly dynamic market. M&A is a key strategy for acquiring cutting-edge technologies, entering new market segments and strengthening one's competitive position.

In order to understand M&A trends in the Fintech sector, a sample of deals was analysed that exclusively considers transactions involving Italian-based Fintech targets and Italian incumbent investors, offering a specific perspective on the domestic context. **Chart 33** shows that minority deals outnumber majority deals. This trend suggests that incumbents prefer to start the collaboration path by entering the capital of Fintechs through minority transactions. This approach allows them to explore possible synergy and development opportunities without immediately committing to full integration.

As collaboration evolves and technology developed by Fintechs consolidates in the market, incumbents tend to gradually increase their shareholding, often culminating in majority acquisitions. This gradual path reduces the risks associated with innovation and allows incumbents to more confidently integrate technology solutions that have already proven their value.

Despite the decline in 2023 from its 2022 peak, the number of deals remains significantly above pre-2020 levels, indicating a consolidation of M&A strategies as a key lever for innovation.

The digitisation process of Italian incumbents is strongly influenced by their ability to establish strategic relationships with Fintech companies, through participations, collaborations and M&A transactions. These instruments represent an effective and increasingly widespread response to the growing demand for innovation, allowing incumbents to overcome internal limitations and adapt to an evolving market. At the same time, these dynamics foster the growth of the Fintech sector, creating a more integrated and resilient financial ecosystem.

Challenges in Fintech integration: Why have expectations not been met?

Fintech acquisitions by incumbents have often been seen as a quick way to modernise services, access new technologies and accelerate innovation. However, despite the growing interest in this mode of collaboration, many of them do not achieve the expected results. This failure can be attributed to several reasons, each of which reveals specific challenges that arise in the course of integration between Fintech incumbents. The main reasons why these acquisitions fail to generate value include scalability issues, lack of strategic vision, cultural incompatibility, buyer amnesia and unclear compliance requirements.

Failure of scalability: A technological and organisational challenge

Scalability is one of the central elements attracting banks to acquire Fintech realities. Banks see Fintechs as an opportunity to access innovative and agile technologies that can potentially be scaled up to meet the large customer base and operational requirements of a large financial institution. However, this goal often comes up against several obstacles (KPMG, 2022a).

1. Misalignment between Technological Infrastructures. Fintechs, by their nature, tend to operate on new technology systems, often built on modern, modular *cloud* infrastructures that are easily adaptable to small or niche sectors. In contrast, banks operate on legacy systems that are complex, rigid and highly integrated with stringent security procedures and regulations. The scalability of a Fintech technology, designed for a *startup* or a small user group, clashes with the need to integrate with the banks' solid and established infrastructures.
2. This leads to the emergence of several difficulties:
   - Systems Incompatibility: Fintech platforms, designed to operate on light and flexible architectures, may not be compatible with banks' legacy systems.
   - Unforeseen integration costs: Integrating Fintech technology into a large bank often requires significant investments in terms of time and resources, with the need for customisation that can slow down the whole process.
   - Interruptions in services: When attempting to scale Fintech technology across a large banking network, interruptions or malfunctions in services can occur, negatively impacting both the bank's customers and the reputation of the acquisition.
3. Limited Fintech Resources. Fintechs are often small organisations with small teams, working in a very concentrated manner and with great operational flexibility. This approach allows them to move quickly, but does not prepare them for large-scale operations, such as those required by a bank. The lack of human and technical resources results in:
   - Inability to handle a larger load: Fintechs may find themselves unprepared to handle a much larger volume of users than originally planned. Managing large numbers of bank customers is a completely different challenge than managing a small group of early adopters.
   - Lack of structured processes: Fintechs tend to work in non-bureaucratic environments, often with agile and informal approaches. However, to scale into a large bank, well-defined structures and processes are needed to ensure that services work smoothly on a large scale.
4. Difficulties in Expanding Operational Processes. Scalability is not only about technology but also about operational and management processes. Fintechs operate with much simpler and leaner processes than banks, which allows them to be flexible and responsive. However, when these organisations are integrated into a broader banking environment, several problems can arise:
   - Lack of structure in operations: Fintechs, lacking experience in managing

large-scale operations, may not be prepared to handle complex and highly regulated workflows typical of banks.
   – Inadequate control processes: Fintechs may not have robust control and gov-
     ernance systems, which creates risks in terms of security, compliance and op-
     erational management when exposed to a larger environment.
5. Banks' rigidity in adapting. Banks, on the other hand, have a strong organisational inertia. They tend to operate with a very pronounced internal bureaucracy
   and time-consuming validation processes. When they try to scale a Fintech, this
   rigidity often clashes with the agility and operational flexibility of the Fintechs
   themselves. This results in:
   – Brakes on innovation: Fintechs operate in rapid development cycles, but banks
     impose numerous layers of control and approval, slowing down the process
     and nullifying the competitive advantage offered by acquisition.
   – Technology trade-offs: In order to adapt to banks' security and compliance
     needs, Fintechs often have to give up some of their technological flexibil-
     ity, which has a negative impact on their ability to effectively scale their
     solutions.

The difficulty of scalability is one of the main reasons why many Fintech deals do
not achieve the desired results. The differences between small, agile Fintech structures and large, complex banking organisations create significant technological, operational and organisational challenges. To overcome these hurdles, banks need to
carefully assess the compatibility of technological infrastructures, prepare to invest
in the resources needed to handle a larger size and strike a balance between the agility of Fintechs and the structural requirements of banks (KPMG, 2022a).

Lack of strategic vision

Lack of strategic vision is one of the main causes of failure in Fintech acquisitions.
Banks often fail to integrate Fintechs into a broader strategy, limiting themselves to
treating them as single, isolated transactions. This approach prevents the growth and
innovation potential of such realities from being fully exploited.

1. Isolated Operations and Lack of Long-Term Plans. When banks acquire Fintechs,
   they sometimes view the acquisition as a strategic transaction rather than as a key
   element of a long-term strategy. This 'short-term view' prevents banks from effectively integrating the new technologies and innovative business models of Fintechs into their broader operations. A Fintech acquisition should be seen as part
   of an ongoing growth platform or broader ecosystem. However, many banks treat
   these transactions as single events, without a plan to further grow the company or
   use its capabilities to improve the overall group offering. This strategic error is
   evident when banks fail to turn the acquisition into an innovation engine for the
   entire organisation (KPMG, 2022a; Wyman, 2024).

2. Failure to Create Synergies between Products and Services. A successful strategic acquisition requires banks to develop a clear vision of how the acquired Fintech can be integrated to improve or expand their products and services. However, this is often not the case. Banks tend not to exploit the synergies between their existing product lines and the capabilities of the Fintech, missing opportunities to expand their offerings significantly.

3. Focus on Non-Strategic Objectives. Another critical aspect of the lack of strategic vision is that banks sometimes acquire Fintechs for non-strategic reasons, such as blocking competitors or simply entering a trendy sector. This lack of clear and measurable objectives greatly reduces the chances of long-term success. An acquisition motivated solely by competition often lacks solid direction on how to integrate and grow Fintech organically (McKinsey & Company, 2023a).

4. Inadequate Business Models for Growth. Some banks acquire Fintechs without carefully evaluating whether the business model of the company in question can be expanded to meet the needs of a large bank. Often, these companies are optimised for a small user group, with operational structures and business models that are not easily adaptable to a large organisation. If the bank does not have a clear strategic plan on how to adapt and scale the Fintech business model, the acquisition is likely to fail.

5. Lack of a Coherent Vision for Technology Integration. Technology integration also requires a strategic vision. Without a clear plan on how Fintech technology platforms can integrate with the bank's existing infrastructure, the transition can become chaotic and costly. In many cases, banks underestimate the complexity of this process, with the result that integration takes much longer than expected or fails altogether.

Without a clear plan on how to integrate, grow and fully exploit Fintech, banks risk losing both financial investment and innovation opportunities. It is crucial that banks develop a holistic, long-term vision to maximise the potential of Fintechs within a broader banking ecosystem.

Cultural incompatibility

Cultural incompatibility between traditional banks and Fintechs is one of the main causes of acquisition failure. Banks and Fintechs operate in very different cultural and organisational contexts, and these differences create difficulties when trying to integrate the two.

1. Differences in Mentality and Operating Styles. Traditional banks tend to be large, highly structured organisations with a strong risk management orientation and an often bureaucratic culture. These institutions are regulated, risk-averse and operate according to rigid procedures. In contrast, Fintechs are typically smaller, agile and innovative organisations with an entrepreneurial culture focused on rapid innovation and continuous adaptation to market needs (Jinasena et al., 2020).

2. This divergence in operating models and mindsets creates friction during integration:
   – Bureaucracy versus agility: Banks follow slow and highly regulated decision-making processes, whereas Fintechs are used to fast and flexible decision-making cycles. The imposition of bureaucratic practices can slow down innovation and limit adaptability.
   – Risk aversion vs. innovation propensity: Banks, being subject to strict regulations, are very cautious about risk. Fintechs, on the other hand, operate with a higher risk tolerance and adopt experimental approaches to innovate quickly. This contrast may limit the adoption of new ideas within the bank.
3. Divergence in Decision-Making Processes. Banks have centralised decision-making structures, where decisions pass through multiple hierarchical levels and departments, such as compliance and legal, slowing down the implementation of Fintech projects. The latter, on the other hand, are used to making decisions quickly and decentralised, often through smaller, autonomous teams. This divergence leads to frustration and misalignment between teams (Wyman, 2024; McKinsey & Company, 2023a).
4. Creativity and Innovation Management. Fintechs thrive in environments where creativity is encouraged, and where new products or solutions are rapidly experimented with. In banks, on the other hand, innovation is often hampered by regulatory constraints and the obligation to maintain operational stability. This creates a tense dynamic, where innovative ideas proposed by Fintechs are slowed down or even blocked by banks' approval processes (McKinsey & Company, 2023a). In many cases, Fintechs perceive that their ability to innovate is being stifled by integration with the banking organisation, leading to a loss of motivation and a drop in productivity.
5. Misalignment of Values and Priorities. Fintechs tend to have a culture based on their *mission*, with a strong sense of purpose linked to innovation and digital transformation. Banks, on the other hand, have values that are more oriented towards stability, risk control and investor protection. This mismatch in core values can generate internal conflicts, especially when it comes to making strategic decisions involving the balance between innovation and compliance.

Cultural incompatibility represents one of the most complex challenges in Fintech acquisitions. Differences in decision-making structures, values and operational processes can seriously jeopardise the success of the integration. However, with a strategic approach that recognises and addresses these differences, banks can create a more collaborative environment that can preserve the innovation of Fintechs and, at the same time, leverage their resources and capabilities.

Buyer's amnesia

Acquirer amnesia is one of the most insidious reasons for the failure of Fintech acquisitions. This phenomenon occurs when the acquiring company, after completing the acquisition, loses sight of the strategic motivations and objectives that led to the decision to acquire the reality.

1. Loss of Focus on the Purpose of the Acquisition. Banks often acquire Fintechs with specific objectives, such as improving technological capabilities, reducing operating costs, filling a gap in their product portfolio or acquiring new digital skills. However, once the acquisition is complete, these priorities can take a back seat, especially when the focus shifts to day-to-day operations or integration. The pressure to align Fintech with the bank's existing practices and structures can lead to an excessive focus on operational integration rather than growth and strategic enhancement.

2. For instance, some banks tend to treat Fintech as a subordinate division, imposing their own management and bureaucratic practices, rather than allowing the acquired entity to operate more independently in order to make the most of its innovative capabilities (KPMG, 2022a; Jinasena et al., 2020).

3. Excessive Focus on Integration. One of the main factors contributing to buyer amnesia is an excessive focus on operational integration. Banks, which are often risk-averse and highly regulated, focus their resources on ensuring that the Fintech complies with their regulatory and operational standards. However, this focus on integration can distract from the strategic objectives that motivated the acquisition (Oliver Wyman, 2024).

4. Failure to Capitalise on Fintech Skills. Often, Fintechs are acquired to gain access to specific technological skills or unique talent. However, over time, banks can lose sight of these crucial resources. In some cases, key Fintech employees may become frustrated with the bank's bureaucratic environment and leave the company, leading to a dissipation of human capital that was one of the most valuable assets of the acquisition (Jinasena et al., 2020).

5. Banks also tend not to capitalise on the distinctive technical skills of Fintechs, trying to force the integration of their technologies with existing banking systems. This process not only hampers innovation but can also make acquired technology obsolete, with a negative impact on return on investment.

6. Change of Priorities and Leadership. Another factor contributing to buyer amnesia is a change in leadership or corporate priorities. In many cases, banks change strategies in response to market conditions or regulatory pressures. These changes can lead to a revision of post-acquisition priorities, resulting in a loss of focus on the initial acquisition objectives.

7. Moreover, the lack of dedicated leadership to oversee and guide the integration and development of Fintech may create additional difficulties. Without a clear vision and strong leadership, this reality risks being assimilated into the wider bank organisation without being able to retain its distinctive value.

Acquirer amnesia represents a critical challenge in Fintech acquisitions. Without a clear focus on strategic objectives and strong leadership, banks risk losing sight of the original reasons for the acquisition, undermining the overall value created by the deal. Only with a clear strategy and proactive integration management can banks avoid these risks.

Unclear compliance requirements

Another reason for the failure of Fintech acquisitions relates to unclear compliance requirements. This problem emerges when banks, operating in a highly regulated environment, find it difficult to align their own regulatory requirements with those of Fintechs, which are often less regulated. This difference creates significant operational and strategic obstacles.

1. Differences in regulatory requirements: Banks are subject to very stringent and specific regulations governing every aspect of their operations, from capitalisation requirements and risk management systems to AML and know your customer (KYC) rules. Fintechs, on the other hand, being generally younger and less structured, are not always subject to the same regulatory requirements. When a bank acquires a Fintech, it is often necessary to adapt the latter to the bank's compliance standards, a process that can prove complex and costly (KPMG, 2022a).
2. This difference creates problems when Fintechs have not developed sufficiently robust compliance processes to meet banks' requirements. Fintechs, in many cases, are not prepared to operate under the intense regulatory supervision that banks are subject to.
3. Lack of regulatory experience in Fintechs: Many Fintechs are born in environments with minimal or technology-specific regulation. This allows them to focus on innovation and rapid development but makes them vulnerable when they have to adapt to banks' stricter requirements, especially in areas such as sensitive data management and financial security. Integration with strict banking regulatory protocols can significantly slow down the implementation of new products or innovation.
4. Banks, on the other hand, have to manage a very complex set of regulatory standards covering security, data protection and risk management. This can create a gap between the two business models that is difficult to bridge without a clear compliance plan and coordinated integration.
5. Inadequate compliance and documentation: Another frequent problem concerns insufficient documentation maintained by Fintechs. Banks are used to maintaining detailed and constant documentation to meet regulatory and auditing requirements. Fintechs, operating leaner and with fewer internal controls, may not have the same attention to detail in terms of compliance and risk management. This results in significant hurdles during integration, as the bank has to address these shortcomings to avoid regulatory sanctions (Jinasena et al., 2020).
6. Furthermore, Fintechs may not have anticipated the need to comply with much stricter regulations, as they are not used to the auditing regimes, inspections or constant monitoring typical of the banking sector. This takes time and resources

to resolve, reducing the effectiveness of integration and slowing down overall operations.

7. Legal and reputational risks: Banks are very sensitive to the risk of non-compliance, as they can face serious legal consequences and fines if they do not comply with regulations. Integrating a non-compliant Fintech can expose the bank to significant risks, including compliance costs, fines and reputational damage. A single error in data management, security or AML practices can result in long-term damage for the bank.

8. The perception of inadequate compliance may also have a negative impact on the confidence of investors and customers, who may see the acquisition as a risk rather than an opportunity.

9. Complications arising from the lack of clear guidelines: One of the key problems is that there are no clear or universal guidelines for regulatory integration between banks and Fintechs, as regulations vary widely across sectors and jurisdictions. Each market has its own data management, privacy protection and financial security laws, which makes integration even more complicated when Fintechs operate on an international scale. Regulatory uncertainty can delay the integration process, requiring banks and Fintechs to navigate a maze of legal requirements and interpretations, which varies from market to market.

Unclear compliance requirements represent a significant challenge in Fintech acquisitions. Differences in regulatory regimes and compliance culture between banks and Fintechs can generate friction that undermines the success of the integration. Only through careful planning, rigorous due diligence and a collaborative approach can these issues be effectively addressed and the success of the acquisition ensured.

Fintech acquisitions offer great opportunities for innovation and growth for incumbents, but also considerable risks. As highlighted, challenges such as the difficulty of scaling Fintech technologies, the absence of a clear strategic vision, cultural differences, acquirer amnesia and unclear compliance requirements are the main reasons that undermine the success of these transactions. Overcoming these obstacles requires meticulous strategic planning, dedicated leadership and the ability to effectively manage cultural and operational change. Only with a holistic and proactive approach can banks avoid the most common pitfalls and maximise the value of their Fintech acquisitions, building an integration that is not only operational but also a source of continuous innovation.

Strategies for effective incumbent and Fintech integration: How to maximise acquisition value

In recent years, integration between incumbents and Fintechs has become an increasingly relevant strategy to foster innovation and remain competitive in the financial sector. The correct identification of the Target, thorough due diligence, a clear pre-acquisition strategy and the adoption of an appropriate post-acquisition integration model are key factors to ensure that the transaction generates the highest possible value for both parties involved. Therefore, there are key steps that incumbents must follow in order to successfully manage such transactions, paying particular attention to the importance of strategic, cultural and technological alignment.

Identification of targets

The process of identifying the appropriate Target is the first essential factor in ensuring the success of a deal between an Incumbent and Fintech. It is not just about analysing financial statements or making comparisons between possible deals, but finding Fintech companies that closely align with the bank's long-term strategic ambitions and that pass a rigorous set of qualitative and quantitative criteria. To begin with, incumbents need to establish a list of potential candidates, asking some basic questions:

1. Strategic alignment: It is essential that the acquisition or partnership fits into the growth and innovation strategy of the incumbent. The latter must ask how Fintech can help fill an existing gap, expand product offerings or improve internal processes through new technologies (McKinsey & Company, 2019).
2. Unique offering: the Fintech entity must provide something distinctive that the incumbent does not currently possess, such as innovative technology, a new business model or a customer base that is difficult to reach by traditional means. This competitive differential is crucial to justify the acquisition and to ensure that the bank can exploit the resulting advantage.
3. Cultural compatibility: One of the biggest challenges in bank-Fintech arrangements is cultural divergence. Banks tend to be more bureaucratic, slow in decision-making and heavily regulated, while Fintechs are often more agile, lean and entrepreneurial. Assessing whether the two organisations can effectively collaborate is crucial to avoid integration problems that may emerge after the deal (McKinsey & Company, 2019).
4. Scalability and technological sustainability: Another essential criterion is the assessment of the scalability of Fintech technologies. The bank has to check whether the systems and infrastructure are sustainable in the long term and able to support potential integration with the incumbent's customers and systems (Kwon et al., 2023)

Therefore, identifying the Target most closely aligned with one's needs does not only mean looking at numbers but also carefully assessing strategic alignment, differentiating value, cultural compatibility and technological robustness. Only by carefully selecting companies that meet these criteria can incumbents maximise the potential success of the collaboration or acquisition (KPMG, 2022a).

Due diligence

Due diligence is an essential step to ensure that the acquisition of a Fintech company is successful. It involves an in-depth analysis of the Target to assess its strategic, cultural, technological and financial compatibility with the acquirer.

1. Checking the strategy and objectives: Due diligence should start with a clear strategic assessment. Incumbents must assess the value of the acquisition against other options, such as partnerships or internal development of solutions, and identify potential synergies. The success of an acquisition is based on a strong strategic justification, such as access to new technologies or market expansion (McKinsey & Company, 2019).
2. Corporate culture analysis: One of the most sensitive aspects of due diligence concerns cultural compatibility. Differences between the agile and lean culture of Fintechs and the traditional structure of banks can lead to conflicts during integration. It is essential that due diligence identifies these differences in advance to ensure a smoother integration (Oliver Wyman, 2024).
3. Technology infrastructure assessment: Due diligence must include a thorough analysis of the Fintech's technology platform. Banks need to check whether the technology is scalable and sustainable. It is important to assess not only the current state of the technology but also its ability to grow and adapt to the bank's customers (McKinsey & Company, 2019).
4. Geography and governance: The geographic location of the Fintech can also influence the success of the acquisition, especially if cross-border transactions are involved. Due diligence should consider local regulations and governance differences. Clear and well-defined governance should be included in the process to determine who will make decisions and how the integration will be managed.
5. Financial and legal analysis: Financial due diligence is crucial to ensure that the price paid is justified by the expected benefits. A thorough analysis must include an assessment of the Fintech's business model, financial sustainability and cash flows (Oliver Wyman, 2024).

Effective due diligence, therefore, is not limited to financial analysis, but encompasses a 360-degree assessment involving strategic, cultural, technological and geographical aspects, ensuring that Fintech is suited to the bank's needs and objectives.

Defining the pre-acquisition strategy

The pre-acquisition strategy phase is crucial to ensure that the Fintech operation is well planned and leads to the desired results. It is important that both parties are aligned on strategies and objectives, and that the bank puts in place a detailed plan for the integration.

1. Transparency and clarity of objectives: Before concluding the deal, the Incumbent must establish a clear plan for what it intends to achieve from the acquisition. It is essential that Incumbents openly communicate their long-term vision, making it clear how the acquisition will fit into their future strategies and what the integration path will be (McKinsey & Company, 2019). This allows the Fintech to prepare for future changes and facilitates the transition to the new operational structure of the bank.

2. Integration Planning: Planning must include a clear integration strategy. During this phase, incumbents must define in advance the integration model that will be adopted. This planning is crucial to prevent confusion and conflicts during the post-acquisition process (McKinsey & Company, 2019). Furthermore, it is crucial to define roles and responsibilities, especially regarding governance and decision-making processes, thus reducing uncertainties during the transition.

3. Involvement of key leaders: Another important step is to ensure that Fintech leaders remain involved in the process and feel part of the project. Indeed, retaining and involving key members of Fintech management is crucial to ensure that the innovative culture and agility of Fintech are not lost (Oliver Wyman, 2024). This helps to preserve business continuity and maintain the motivation of Fintech teams, reducing the risk of turnover of key personnel.

4. Sharing regulatory expectations: As Fintechs often operate in less stringent regulatory environments than banks, it is crucial that the bank communicates in advance what changes will need to be adopted, in terms of compliance and governance. Discussions on regulatory requirements and operational changes should take place before the deal closes (KPMG, 2022a).

5. Creation of a defined reporting structure: The strategy must include the definition of a clear reporting structure, which outlines how responsibilities will be managed and how Fintech will be integrated into the bank's corporate hierarchy. A clear definition of roles avoids overlaps and creates a more efficient working environment post-acquisition (KPMG, 2022a).

Consequently, the definition of a pre-acquisition strategy must be detailed and involve strategic, operational, cultural and regulatory aspects, with the aim of preparing both parties for a smooth and successful integration.

Post-acquisition integration models

Post-acquisition integration models play a key role in determining the success of an operation. Several approaches can be used, each with its own advantages and risks. The choice of integration model depends on the objectives of the incumbent, the Fintech culture and the need to preserve innovation.

1. Complete autonomy: In this model, the Fintech operates independently even after the acquisition, while the incumbent only provides financial support and re-

sources. This approach is often used to preserve the agility and innovation of the acquired entity. A successful example is the acquisition of WePay by JPMorgan Chase, in which the bank allowed the Fintech to continue operating autonomously to ensure that operational flexibility was not lost (KPMG, 2022a). Autonomy is useful when the Fintech has a well-defined business model, which can grow further with the support of the incumbent (McKinsey & Company, 2019).

2. Hybrid model: This model allows Fintech to operate autonomously initially, but with the aim of being gradually integrated. This process minimises the risk of culture clashes and allows for the careful introduction of more complex processes or banking regulations (KPMG, 2022a). Moreover, a gradual integration also helps to preserve staff motivation, reducing the risk of talent leaving.

3. Immediate integration: In this case, the Fintech is immediately integrated into the incumbent, taking over its processes, regulations and governance structures. This model is suitable when the bank wants to quickly acquire the technical capabilities or customer base of the Fintech to achieve immediate synergies (KPMG, 2022a). This type of integration can be successful when the Fintech is acquired primarily for its technologies and not for its independent operational structure (Oliver Wyman, 2024).

The success of an integration does not depend solely on the model chosen, but on the bank's ability to adapt to circumstances and problems that may arise. Flexibility in execution is crucial to address unforeseen challenges and maximise synergies, especially in the first few months post-acquisition (McKinsey & Company, 2019; Oliver Wyman, 2024). For these considerations, the post-acquisition integration model must be chosen based on the nature of the acquisition, strategic objectives and cultural compatibility between incumbent and Fintech.

The integration of incumbents and Fintechs requires a well-defined and carefully planned strategic approach to avoid failure and ensure long-term success. From the identification of the most suitable Target, through exhaustive due diligence, to the creation of a solid pre-acquisition strategy and the choice of an appropriate integration model, each step plays an essential role in determining the final outcome of the transaction. Only with thorough preparation and flexible process management can incumbents maximise the value of Fintech acquisitions while maintaining innovation and exploiting synergies from the deal.

13 Empirical Evidence

Introduction

In order to investigate the dynamics that characterise the relationship between incumbents and Fintechs, a study focused on value creation in M&A transactions was carried out. The main objective is to investigate a recurring issue in the literature on M&A activity, contextualising it in the specific context of Fintech transactions in Europe. This approach aims to fill knowledge gaps and offer new perspectives on the interactions between traditional and innovative actors in the financial landscape.

Traditionally, research on M&A activity has focused on analysing short-term value creation for shareholders, often using event study methodologies to assess stock market reactions in the period immediately following the announcement of transactions. Previous studies have shown that while shareholders of target companies tend to benefit from M&A transactions, those of acquiring companies frequently experience no or negative returns in both the short and long terms (Agrawal & Jaffé, 1992; Cosh & Hughes, 2008; Mandelker, 1974; Langetieg, 1978; Dodd, 1980). Jensen and Ruback (1983) identified various determinants of value creation, such as economies of scale, improved management efficiency and financial synergies.

In recent years, these analyses have been extended to the Fintech M&A context, with often mixed results that suggest the need for further investigation. Dranev et al. (2019), for instance, found a positive value increase in the short term for Fintech M&A, but pointed out that these benefits were not sustained in the long term. This phenomenon was attributed to factors such as the size effect, according to which the size of the acquirer negatively affects abnormal returns, and the bidder's experience in Fintech markets, as well as sector correlation. Similarly, Wang et al. (2023) and Kohers and Kohers (2001) observed positive reactions in the short term, but accompanied by lower performance in the long term. Notably, in the European context, studies such as those by Cappa et al. (2022) and Carlini et al. (2022) showed negative market reactions to bank–Fintech transactions.

A significant aspect emerging from the literature is the limited focus on the European M&A market in Fintech. While most research focuses on the US context, there is a growing need to investigate the regulatory, structural and cultural peculiarities that characterise the European landscape. Indeed, the European market presents unique challenges and opportunities compared to the US market, making an in-depth understanding of how these factors influence M&A outcomes crucial.

Moreover, despite the extensive literature devoted to traditional M&A, there is limited understanding of the specific dynamics that apply to Fintech transactions. The integration of technological innovations in the financial services sector introduces novel challenges and opportunities that have yet to be explored. In particular, there is a need to analyse the impact of acquiring technological expertise on the long-term performance of acquirers, the role of cultural and organisational integration and the influence of regulatory environments on deal outcomes.

The study aims to provide a detailed analysis of shareholder value creation in incumbent-Fintech M&A deals, with a focus on the European context. By examining 107 transactions conducted between 2013 and 2023, the investigation assesses short-term stock market reactions to M&A announcements, analysing the cumulative abnormal returns (CARs) of acquirers. Using a linear regression model, it explores deal-specific and firm-specific characteristics that may influence post-announcement value creation.

Analysis of literature

Traditionally, academic research uses the event study methodology to analyse the short-term impact of M&As on stock market reactions before and after the announcement. According to existing literature on the topic, the most common motivation behind an M&A transaction is the exploitation of synergies resulting from combining the resources and capabilities of the two companies (Damodaran, 2005; DePhampilis, 2010). With the increasing speed of digitisation, the acquisition of specific resources, such as new technological skills or intellectual property rights, has become a common feature in M&A transactions (Hitt et al., 1996). This aspect is one of the main reasons why banks are involved in M&As with Fintech companies (El-said, 2021).

Studies show that such transactions benefit shareholders of target companies, while acquiring companies often do not experience a significant increase in share prices (Agrawal & Jaffé, 1992; Cosh & Hughes, 2008). One of the earliest studies on the measurement of M&A value was conducted by Mandelker (1974), who showed no substantial gains for shareholders of bidding companies following a takeover, assuming that markets were efficient and share prices adjusted to reflect all publicly available information. This conclusion has been confirmed by several other authors (Langetieg, 1978; Dodd, 1980). In particular, Dodd (1980) considered a sample of transactions and observed that the announcement of the transaction generated positive CARs for the shareholders of the target companies, while the impact on the shareholders of the bidding companies showed significantly negative values, regardless of the outcome of the transaction.

In addition, some factors have been shown to have a significant impact on CARs, such as economies of scale (Jensen & Ruback, 1983), the size of the target companies relative to the bidder and the premium paid (Loughran & Vijh, 1997; Dranev, 2019), leading to a hypothesis on the size effect. Rau and Vermaelen (1998) found that companies with high P/BV (price to book value) ratios have lower abnormal returns. Following this trend, M&A transactions tend to benefit only the shareholders of target companies, while acquiring companies experience negative CARs in both short and long terms (Rosen, 2006).

Focusing on the post-2009 period, Alexandridis et al. (2017) point to improvements in M&A performance, linked to better corporate governance and strategic alignment. After 2009, acquiring companies showed positive abnormal returns for the first time, averaging 1.05%, compared to an average of –1.08% over the 1990–2009 period. This improvement is particularly evident in 'mega-deals' in excess of $500 million, which generate significant earnings. The study attributes these positive changes to better corporate governance practices and a decline in excessive optimism towards CEOs, leading to more rational investment decisions.

Analysing the excess returns to shareholders of the top 1,000 non-banking companies that completed more than 15,000 deals in the last decade, Rehm et al. (2012) show that companies that undertake numerous small deals, representing 19% or more of their market capitalisation, generally perform better than those that rely on organic growth, with a higher probability of positive returns. For example, 75% of companies remaining in the top 500 use active M&A programmes, and 91% of those in the top 100 engage in programmatic M&A. Large deals are successful in mature sectors, while they appear less profitable in fast-growing sectors. Companies in mature sectors achieved a TRS (total shareholder return) of 4% five years after the deal, while those in growth sectors saw a TRS of –12%. Smaller, more strategic deals proved particularly successful in the technology and industrial sectors, while companies with occasional M&A activity often saw returns driven more by organic growth than by M&A, indicating the absence of a clear M&A strategy.

M&A in the Fintech sector

The analysis of value creation in bank M&A is a growing area of study. According to Cybo-Ottone et al. (2000), the main reason why banks decide to merge is to achieve greater efficiency and performance, while Hankir et al. (2011) pointed out that M&As in the banking sector are mainly driven by the desire to expand market share through size growth. The analysis of value creation regarding M&As between banks is a recently developed line of research. The first event study was conducted by Cybo-Ottone and Murgia (2000) in the European banking sector and showed positive CARs in domestic transactions and diversified bank acquisitions in the insurance sector. In contrast, De Long (2001), focusing on the US banking market, found negative CARs for bidding companies.

With regard to European banks, Beitel et al. (2004) reported CARs for bidding companies that were not significantly different from zero, while Beltratti and Palladino (2013) documented an average positive CAR of 0.99%, in contrast to the existing literature. Therefore, the conducted study extends the investigation on the hypothesis that bidding companies may experience positive CARs.

Research on M&A activities involving Fintech companies is limited, mainly because Fintech is a new phenomenon that has emerged in the last decade, especially in Europe. According to existing literature, the most common reason for acquiring a Fintech company is access to complementary resources, especially technological expertise. Consistent with this idea, King et al. (2008) suggested that companies characterised by low levels of research and development expenditures benefit more by acquiring technology through a merger than by investing internally. Dranev et al. (2019) demonstrated value creation in the short term but not in BHARs (Buy and Hold Abnormal Returns), due to 'managerial hubris', according to which managers pay excessive premiums by overestimating the successful outcome of the transaction.

Furthermore, Dranev et al. (2019) noted a negative correlation between acquirer size and CARs (the so-called size effect) and higher CARs for acquiring companies from developed countries and those entering the Fintech market. According to Dranev (2019), acquirers new to the Fintech M&A market show higher positive CARs, making the acquirers' prior experience significant. Dranev et al. (2019) documented a second effect, of industry correlation, according to which companies operating in the same industry as the targets achieve higher CARs by exploiting combined synergies.

Wang et al. (2023) examined the impact of Fintech acquisitions on a sample of cross-border deals involving Chinese listed companies over the period 2011–2019, observing higher returns for acquirers after the announcement of the acquisitions. They also provided a list of variables to explain acquirers' performance, including size, market-to-book value ratio, leverage and regional characteristics (GDP, deposit and loan levels), as well as deal-specific characteristics such as cultural distance between the host country and China. The latter is crucial, as cultural distances can complicate the integration of acquired technology, which, according to Burke and Kovela (2017), is the key to a successful merger.

As far as bank technology acquisitions are concerned, research is limited. Cappa et al. (2022) recorded negative CARs, and Carlini et al. (2022), analysing a sample of Fintech companies with at least one European or US bank as acquirer, observed negative market reactions, particularly for targets in the 'Tech' versus 'Fin' sectors, in line with the industry correlation effect. In addition, they noted a positive 'learning' effect for banks conducting multiple deals with the same Fintech Company. Hornuf et al. (2020) pointed out that alliances between banks and Fintechs tend to lead to negative CARs, suggesting a development of in-house digital capabilities.

Building on existing research, the conducted study aims to investigate whether Fintech M&As benefit the bidding banks in the short term. The first hypothesis to be tested is whether Fintech M&A leads to the creation of positive value for the bidders' shareholders, or alternatively, whether such acquisitions lead to positive CARs in the short term, through a t-test on average CARs in five time windows: (–20;20), (–10;10), (–3;3), (–1;1), (0;1).

Additional hypotheses were tested, such as the impact of cross-border versus domestic acquisitions, deal-specific factors and prior experience of the acquirer. Finally, the effects of the COVID-19 pandemic are considered, distinguishing between pre-COVID and post-COVID deals, in recognition of the significant increase in deals between banks and Fintech companies after the outbreak of the pandemic.

Methodology

Sample

The sample covers the period from 21 November 2013 to 19 April 2023 and includes only announced and subsequently completed transactions. It includes a total of 107 deals, with Fintech companies as targets and banks as buyers, involving 38 bidders and 41 Fintech companies. Some transactions include multiple bidders, as in the case of financing rounds with groups of investors. Geographically, target companies are limited to Europe, while bidders come from all over the world. The specific focus on Europe is aimed at studying the recent development of the Fintech sector in the region, which has grown later than in the United States. Only listed bidders were considered due to the need to collect share price data in order to calculate CARs. The data came from the Refinitiv, MergerMarket, MarketLine and Preqin databases. To ensure an adequate sample, all types of bank investments in Fintechs, such as Private Equity, Venture Financing and partnerships between Fintechs and lending institutions were included, excluding duplicates and bidders without share price information. After cleaning the database, Fintech companies were categorised as 'High Technology' or 'Financials' according to Refinitiv's classification, and both bidders and targets were further categorised as 'Emerging' or 'Developed', depending on their market, using MSCI's classification.

Data collection and processing

To conduct the analysis, the daily share prices of the bidding banks were retrieved from the Thomson Reuters—Refinitiv database. Abnormal returns are defined as the difference between the actual returns observed in the market and the expected returns, calculated according to the CAPM market model $\left(ER_i = \alpha + \beta_i \times R_m \right)$. To estimate β, an OLS regression was run on a 252-day time window, excluding the month prior to the announcement. The KBW Nasdaq Bank Index was chosen as a proxy for market returns, considered reliable to represent a consistent market, even in the presence of bidders from emerging markets. Expected returns were calculated as

$$ER_i = \beta_i \times R_m$$

since the intercept α is insignificant for analytical purposes. The anomalous returns were obtained as the difference between the expected and actual returns.

$$AR_i = R_i - ER_i.$$

CARs represent the aggregate sum of ARs over various time windows.

$$CAR_i = \sum_{t1}^{t2} AR_i.$$

The mean CARs (CAARs) for the sample were calculated and their significance was tested by means of a t-test.

$$\overline{CAAR} = \frac{1}{N} \sum_N CAR_i.$$

Regression model

To test which variables influenced the CARs of the bidding banks, an OLS linear regression model was used. The regression was run only on those observations for which CARs were statistically significant, reducing the sample from 107 to 42 transactions. This introduced a limitation, which was mitigated through the analysis of heteroschedasticity. Highly correlated variables were excluded, such as the type of transaction and the type of market, developed or emerging, to which the target company belongs. Two regression models were formulated to test the influence of several variables, including the size and experience of the bidder and the industry to which the target belongs. Finally, an F-test was performed to check the overall significance of the models. The final regressions, therefore, break down as follows:

$$CARi = \beta0 + \beta1 \times \text{Bidder developed} + \beta2 \times \text{Target Industry} + \beta3 \times \text{Covid} + \beta4 \times \text{Change of Control (CoC)} + \beta5 \times \text{Bidder P/BV},$$

$$CARi = \beta0 + \beta1 \times \text{Bidder developed} + \beta2 \times \text{Target Industry} + \beta3 \times \text{Covid} + \beta4 \times \text{Change of Control (CoC)} + \beta5 \times \text{Previous experience}.$$

Analysis of results

The mean and median values of CARs are similar, indicating low overall variance. The means hover around zero and the t-test is not significant for all time windows, suggesting that the hypothesis that buyers' CARs are zero cannot be rejected. Therefore, we conclude that Fintech acquisitions do not create significant short-term value for buyers. This result is in line with existing literature, which often suggests that acquiring firms do not make substantial gains after the announcement of M&A deals. Previous studies, such as those of Mandelker (1974) and Dodd (1980), show similar results, supporting the market efficiency hypothesis. The concentration of average CARs around zero could reflect the fact that any expected synergies from Fintech acquisitions are already embedded in share prices, as argued by Agrawal and Jaffé (1992) and Conh and Hughes (2008).

The analysis shows negative CAR levels for longer time windows (–20;+20) and (–10;+10), and positive for shorter windows (–3;+3) and (–1;+1), with a return to negative values in the (0;+1) window, indicating an initially positive market response, followed by scepticism. This pattern has been observed in previous studies, such as those by Cappa et al. (2022) and De Long (2003), who reported negative CARs over longer periods due to integration difficulties and concerns about the possible overvaluation of the acquisition.

In addition, the impacts of buyer characteristics and deal specifications on CARs were assessed. In the first model, three variables were found to be statistically significant: '*Bidder developed*', 'Covid' and '*Change of Control*'. The negative coefficient of '*Bidder developed*' supports the size effect hypothesis, whereby larger buyers tend to experience lower abnormal returns, consistent with the difficulties of integration in large groups, as noted by Dranev et al. (2019). The variable 'Change of Control' suggests that acquisitions with changes in management control are perceived less favourably due to higher integration risks. The positive coefficient of the variable 'Covid' indicates an improved market perception for Fintech M&A in the post-pandemic context, reflecting a growing trust in digital financial instruments during the pandemic, as argued by Elsaid (2021) and Wang et al. (2023).

In the second model, the P/BV ratio of the acquirer is replaced by the variable '*prior experience*', improving the explanatory power of the model. The significance of this variable suggests that companies with experience in Fintech acquisitions are perceived positively by investors, due to their ability to successfully pursue acquisitions and reduce perceived risks.

Discussion and implications

The research therefore aimed to investigate the profitability of banks acquiring Fintech companies in Europe by analysing a sample of 107 transactions. The analysis of CARs revealed non-statistically significant abnormal returns in all time windows, in line with previous studies that did not detect value creation for acquirers' shareholders. Initial studies showing positive and significant CARs in Fintech transactions (Dranev, 2019; Akhtar, 2022) may have resulted from the novelty of the phenomenon, which has diminished with the spread of investment banking in Fintech. New studies have highlighted negative CARs (Carlini, 2022; Cappa, 2022; Hornuf, 2020), and the results confirm this trend, indicating a lack of value creation in M&A transactions over longer time windows. However, it is important to emphasise that for incumbent banks, M&A transactions in the Fintech sector are of key strategic significance. Indeed, these transactions allow them to keep up with the technology and financial innovations introduced by Fintech startups, thus avoiding losing market share and competitiveness to the latter. In this context, it is not so much crucial that banks achieve positive abnormal returns in the short term, but that they manage to avoid negative abnormal returns, as this implies safeguarding their market positioning. Among the determinants, acquirer size and change of control were found to be negatively correlated with CARs, as documented in the literature, while prior experience is positively correlated confirming Carlini's (2022) findings. The significance of the Covid variable represents the new contribution made by the present research. The limited significance of other regression coefficients and the low R^2 are attributed to low CAR in the short term and a limited sample. Future research could benefit from more observations, including the study of abnormal returns of target companies.

Conclusions

This study focuses on the analysis of the Fintech sector, highlighting the crucial role of technological innovation in the transformation of financial services globally. Fintech is not only a fast-growing segment but also a driver of change capable of redefining traditional operating models, promoting the entry of new players and fostering the establishment of unprecedented competitive dynamics. This phenomenon requires a rigorous analytical approach, capable of identifying both opportunities and criticalities within a complex and constantly evolving ecosystem.

A fundamental aspect that emerged as a starting point for the analysis concerns the need to arrive at a clear and shared definition of the concept of Fintech, which is often interpreted in a heterogeneous manner by both the academic community and market operators. In this context, the definition provided by the Bank of Italy proved to be exhaustive and consistent with the representation of the phenomenon analysed within this report. In particular, Bank of Italy defines Fintech as the *'financial innovation made possible by technological innovation, which can manifest itself through new business models, processes or products, significantly influencing financial markets, institutions or the range of services offered'* (Bank of Italy, 2017).

A further important element concerns the way in which Fintech companies are evaluated, especially in a context characterised by high volatility and the inadequacy of traditional metrics in fully capturing the growth potential of such realities. The empirical analysis conducted has highlighted the importance of integrating established quantitative methods with the analysis of qualitative indicators, such as governance, management, regulation, ecosystem and sustainability, in order to develop more balanced and realistic assessments. This multidimensional approach is crucial not only for investors but also for policy-makers engaged in the regulation of a rapidly changing industry.

In addition, special attention was paid to the interactions between Fintechs and traditional players, known as incumbents. The results of the analysis indicate that the industry is going through a phase of convergence, characterised by strategic collaborations and M&As, which are essential tools to face the challenges of digital transformation. However, it is important to consider how the integration between Fintechs and incumbents also presents critical issues, including the scalability of technology solutions, regulatory compliance, cultural differences and divergences in business strategies, factors that need to be analysed in order to address them through collaboration.

Overall, this study aims to contribute to the academic debate not only by describing the transformations taking place, but by providing an analytical framework geared towards answering specific research questions. The aim is to promote a resilient, transparent and sustainable Fintech development, able to face future challenges with robustness and foresight. Finally, it is hoped that the evidence that has emerged may stimulate further in-depth studies and guide the strategic choices of sector operators, fostering the creation of a Fintech ecosystem capable of generating value not only for the financial markets but also for society as a whole.

Bibliography

Agrawal, A., Jaffè, J.F., & Mandelker, G.N. (1992). The post-merger performance of acquiring firms: A reexamination of an anomaly. *Journal of Finance*, 47(4), 1605–1621. https://doi.org/10.2307/2328956

Akhtar, Q., & Nosheen, S. (2022). The impact of fintech and banks M&A on Acquirer's performance: A strategic win or loss? *Borsa Istanbul Review*, 22(6), 1195–1208. https://doi.org/10.1016/j.bir.2022.08.007

Alexandridis, G., Antypas, N., & Travlos, N. (2017). Value creation from M&As: New evidence. *Journal of Corporate Finance*, 45, 632–650. https://doi.org/10.1016/j.jcorpfin.2017.05.010

Amabile, T. M. (1998). How to kill creativity. *Harvard Business Review*, 76(5), 76–87. https://hbr.org/1998/09/how-to-kill-creativity

Anagnostopoulos, I. (2018). Fintech and regtech: Impact on regulators and banks. *Journal of Economics and Business*, 100, 7–25. https://doi.org/10.1016/j.jeconbus.2018.07.003

Arena, C., Catougno, S., & Naciti, V. (2023). Governing fintech for performance: The monitoring role of female independent directors. *European Journal of Innovation Management*, 26(7), 591–610. https://doi.org/10.1108/EJIM-11-2022-0621

Atayah, O. F., Najaf, K., Hakim Ali, M., & Marashdeh, H. (2023). Sustainability, market performance and FinTech firms. *Meditari Accountancy Research*, 32(2), 317–345. https://doi.org/10.1108/MEDAR-08-2021-1405

Ayadi, R., Bonghini, P., Casu, B., & Cucinelli, D. (2021). Bank business model migrations in Europe: Determinants and effects. *British Journal of Management*, 32(4), 1007–1026. https://doi.org/10.1111/1467-8551.12437

Bain & Company (2022). Countering the myths that hinder cloud adoption in financial services.

Bain & Company (2023). United we thrive: The untapped power of bank-Fintech partnerships.

Bank of Italy (2017). Fintech in Italy: Survey on the adoption of technological innovations applied to financial services.

Bank of Italy (2021). Fintech survey in the Italian financial system.

Bank of Italy (2023). Open Banking in the payments system: Infrastructural evolution, innovation and security, supervisory and oversight practices.

Bank of Italy (n.d.). Regulatory sandbox. Available at: https://www.bancaditalia.it/focus/sandbox/?dotcache=refresh

Bauer, F., & Matzler, K. (2014). Antecedents of M&A success: The role of strategic complementarity, cultural fit, and degree and speed of integration. *Strategic Management Journal*, 35(2), 269–291. https://doi.org/10.1002/smj.2091

BCG (2023a). Reimagining the future of finance.

BCG (2023b). Financial institutions must get serious about digital ecosystems.

Beitel, P., Schiereck, D., Wahrenburg, M. (2004). Explaining M&A success in European banks. *European Financial Management*, 1(10), 109–139. https://doi.org/10.1111/j.1468-036X.2004.00242.x

Beltratti, A., & Paladino, G. (2013). Is M&A different during a crisis? Evidence from the European banking sector. *Journal of Banking and Finance*, 37(2), 5394–5405. https://doi.org/10.1016/j.jbankfin.2013.02.004

Björkdahl, J., & Holmèn, M. (2018). Exploiting the control revolution by means of digitalization: Value creation, value capture, and downstream movements. *Industrial and Corporate Change*, 28(3). https://doi.org/10.1093/icc/dty022

Bloomberg (2023). Prosus agrees to sell part of PayU to Rapyd for $610 million.

Bo, H., & Driver, C. (2012). Agency theory, corporate governance and finance.

Burke, D., & Kovela, S. (2017). ITMA – IT integration in mergers and acquisitions. *International Journal of Business and Management*, 12(11), 16–40. https://doi.org/10.5539/ijbm.v12n11p16

Bussoli, C., Conte, D., & Barone, M. (2023). The impact of FinTech merge operation on financial performance: Evidence from a banking international sample. *International Journal of Business and Management*, 18(2), 72–86. https://doi.org/10.5539/ijbm.v18n2p72

Capgemini (2023). Wealth management.

Cappa, F., Oriani, R., Peruffo, E., & McCarthy, I. (2021). Big data for creating and capturing value in the digitalized environment: Unpacking the effects of volume, variety, and veracity on firm performance. *Journal of Product Innovation Management*, 38(1), 49–67. https://doi.org/10.1111/jpim.12545

Cappa, F., Collevecchio, F., Oriani, R., & Peruffo, E. (2022). Banks responding to the digital surge through Open Innovation: Stock market performance effects of M&As with fintech firms. *Journal of Economics and Business*, 121, 106079. https://doi.org/10.1016/j.jeconbus.2022.106079

Carlini, F., Del Gaudio, B.L., Porzio, C., & Previtali, D. (2022). Banks, FinTech and stock returns. *Finance Research Letters*, 45. https://doi.org/10.1016/j.frl.2021.102252

CB Insights (2023). State of Fintech.

Che, L., Hope, O.-K., & Langli, J. C. (2020). How Big-4 firms improve audit quality. *Management Science*, 66(3), 1276–1297.

Ciukaj, R., & Folwarski, M. (2023). Fintech regulation and the development of the fintech sector in the European Union. *Journal of Banking and Financial Economics*, 2023(19), 44–56. https://doi.org/10.7172/2353-6845.jbfe.2023.1.3

Consob (2018). The development of Fintech: Opportunities and risks for the financial industry in the digital age.

Consob (2021). Fintech: Attention profiles and opportunities for issuers and national savings.

Cooper, A. C., Gimeno-Gascon, F. J., & Woo, C. Y. (1994). Initial human and financial capital as predictors of new venture performance. *Journal of Business Venturing*, 9(5), 371–395. https://doi.org/10.1016/0883-9026(94)90013-2

Cornelli, G., Doerr, S., Franco, L., & Frost, J. (2021). Funding for Fintechs: Patterns and drivers. *BIS Quarterly Review*, September, 31–43. https://www.bis.org/publ/qtrpdf/r_qt2109c.pdf

Corporate Financial Institute (n.d.). Modified Book Value. https://corporatefinanceinstitute.com/resources/valuation/modified-book-value/

Cosh, A. D., & Hughes, A. (2008). Takeovers after "Takeovers". Working Papers wp363, Centre for Business Research, University of Cambridge.

Cumming, D., & Schwienbacher, A. (2020). Fintech venture capital. In D. Arner, R. P. Buckley, & E. Avgouleas (Eds.), *The Routledge Handbook of Fintech* (47–62). Routledge.

Cybo-Ottone, A., & Murgia, M. (2000). Mergers and shareholder wealth in European banking. *Journal of Banking and Finance*, 24(6), 831–859. https://doi.org/10.1016/S0378-4266(99)00109-0

Damodaran, A. (2005). The value of synergy. http://dx.doi.org/10.2139/ssrn.841486

Damodaran, A. (2009). Valuing young, start-up and growth companies: Estimation issues and valuation challenges. https://doi.org/10.2139/ssrn.1418687

Dao, M. A., & Strobl, A. (2019). Exploration outcomes of M&A: The interplay between co-ordination mechanisms and acquisition experience. *R&D Management*, 49(1), 86–102. https://doi.org/10.1111/radm.12314

Davila, A., Foster, G., & Jia, N. (2015). The valuation of management control systems in start-up companies: International field-based evidence. *European Accounting Review*, 24(2), 207–239. https://doi.org/10.1080/09638180.2014.965720

Deloitte (n.d.). FIDA: Open Finance is coming.

Deloitte (2018). Closing the gap in fintech collaboration: Overcoming obstacles to a symbiotic relationship.

Deloitte (2023). Tech Trends 2023: An insurance industry perspective.

Deloitte (2024a). Definitions of fintech have evolved over time.

Deloitte (2024b). The evolution of Fintech.

Delong, G. (2001). Focusing versus diversifying bank mergers: Analysis of market reaction and long-term performance. https://doi.org/10.2139/ssrn.256164

DeLong, G. (2003). Does long-term performance of mergers match market expectations? Evidence from the U.S. banking industry. *Financial Management*, 32(2), 5–25. https://doi.org/10.2307/3666334

DePamphilis, D. (2010). *Mergers and Acquisitions Basics: All You Need to Know.* Academic Press.

Dixon, J., & Frolova, Y. (2012). Accounting for good governance: The fair value challenge. *Corporate Governance*, 13(3), 318–331. https://doi.org/10.1108/CG-10-2011-0078

Dodd, P. (1980). Merger proposals, management discretion and stockholder wealth. *Journal of Financial Economics*, 8(2), 105–137.

Dranev, Y., Frolova, K., & Ochirova, E. (2019). The impact of fintech M&A on stock returns. *Research in International Business and Finance*, 48, 353–364.

Elsaid, H.M. (2021). A review of literature directions regarding the impact of fintech firms on the banking industry. *Qualitative Research in Financial Markets*, 15(5), 693–711. https://doi.org/10.1108/QRFM-10-2020-0197

European Commission (2018). Fintech action plan: For a more competitive and innovative European financial sector. https://finance.ec.europa.eu/publications/fintech-action-plan-more-competitive-and-innovative-european-financial-sector_en

European Commission (2020). Digital finance strategy. https://finance.ec.europa.eu/publications/digital-finance-package_en

European Parliament (2020). Che cos'è l'intelligenza artificiale? https://www.europarl.europa.eu/topics/it/article/20200827STO85804/che-cos-e-l-intelligenza-artificiale-e-come-viene-usata

Evertec (2023). EVERTEC closes on the acquisition of Sinqia, a leading provider of software solutions for financial institutions in Brazil.

EY (2021). Collaboration between banks and FinTechs is evolving, driven by the rise of digital ecosystems, regulatory changes and increasing customer adoption.

EY (2022). The FinTech Pledge has helped support stronger FinTech and financial services relationships that will ultimately benefit consumers.

Ferilli, G., Altunbas, Y., Stefanelli, V., Palmieri, E., & Boscia, V. (2024). Fintech governance and performance: Implications for banking and financial stability. *Research in International Business and Finance*, 70(B), 102349. https://doi.org/10.1016/j.ribaf.2024.102349

Ferrell, A., Liang, H., & Renneboog, L. (2016). Socially responsible firms. *Journal of Financial Economics*, 122(3), 585–606. https://doi.org/10.1016/j.jfineco.2015.12.003

Finance Magnate (2023). The evolution of Regtech—Will it continue in 2023?

Financial Times (2023). Buyout group Francisco Partners to acquire Macrobond for almost $700mn.

Finastra (2023). Global banks turn to fintechs to cut operational costs and pursue innovation, Finastra research reveals.

Fintech Futures, Barisaac (2022). Collaboration between banks and fintechs can bring faster speeds to the international payments.

Folta, T. B. (1998). Governance and uncertainty: The trade-off between administrative control and commitment. *Strategic Management Journal*, 19(11), 1007–1028. https://doi.org/10.1002/(SICI)1097-0266(1998110)19:11%3C1007::AID-SMJ999%3E3.0.CO;2-8

Forbes Finance Council (2024). Collaboration paves the way for next big innovation in fintech.

GFT (2024). Banking Disruption Index.

Giglio, F. (2021). Fintech: A literature review. *European Research Studies Journal*, XXIV(2B), 600–627. https://doi.org/10.35808/ersj/2254

Global Payments (2023). Form 10-Q—Quarterly report pursuant to section 13 or 15(d) of the Securities Exchange Act of 1934 for the quarterly period ended March 31, 2023.

Gomber, P., Kauffman, R. J., Parker, C., & Weber, B. W. (2018). On the Fintech revolution: Interpreting the forces of innovation, disruption, and transformation in financial services. *Journal of Management Information Systems*, 35(1), 220–265. https://doi.org/10.1080/07421222.2018.1440766

Hankir, Y., Rauch, C., & Umber, M. (2009). Bank M&A: A market power story? *Journal of Banking & Finance*, 35, 2341–2354. https://doi.org/10.1016/j.jbankfin.2011.01.030

Hitt, M.A., Hoskisson, R.E., & Kim, H. (1997). International diversification: Effects on innovation and firm performance in product-diversified firms. *Academy of Management Journal*, 40(4), 767–798.

Hornuf, L., Klus, M., Lohwasser, T., & Schwienbacher, A. (2020). How Do Banks Interact with Fintechs? *Small Business Economics*, 57, 1505–1526.

Insurtech Insights (2023). Insurtech trends leading market disruption in 2023.

ISACA (2023). An executive view of key cybersecurity trends and challenges in 2023.

Jensen, M.C., & Ruback, R.S. (1983). The market for corporate control: The scientific evidence. *Journal of Financial Economics*, 11(1–4), 5–50.

Jinasena, D. N., Spanaki, K., Papadopoulos, T., & Balta, M. E. (2020). Success and failure retrospectives of FinTech projects: A case study approach. *Information Systems Frontiers*, 25(3), 1–16. https://doi.org/10.1007/s10796-020-10079-4

Jreisat, A., Bashar, A., Alshaikh, A., Rabbani, M. R., & Ali, M. A. M. (2021). Is Fintech Valuation an Art of Science? Exploring the Innovative Methods for the Valuation of Fintech Start-ups. 2021 International Conference on Decision Aid Sciences and Application (DASA), Sakheer, Bahrain, 922–925. https://doi.org/10.1109/DASA53625.2021.9681922

Kamal, I., & Firmansyah, E. A. (2021). Optimizing fintech startup seed funding valuation. *The International Journal of Social Sciences World (TIJOSSW)*, 3(2), 124–141.

Kaplan, S. N., & Strömberg, P. (2001). Venture capitalists as principals: Contracting, screening, and monitoring. *American Economic Review*, 91(2), 426–430. https://www.jstor.org/
stable/2677802

Kohers, N., & Kohers, T. (2001). The value creation potential of high-tech mergers. *Financial
Analysts Journal*, 56(3), 40–51. https://www.jstor.org/stable/4480246

KPMG (2022a). How banks can maximise the value of fintech acquisitions.

KPMG (2022b). Venture Pulse Q4 2021.

KPMG (2023). Pulse of Fintech H1'2023: Global analysis of Fintech funding.

KPMG (2024). Pulse of Fintech H2'2023: Global analysis of Fintech funding.

Kwon, K. Y., Molyneux, P., Pancotto, L., & Reghezza, A. (2023). Banks and FinTech acquisitions. *Journal of Financial Services Research*, 65(1), 41–75. https://doi.org/10.1007/
s10693-022-00396-x

Langetieg, T.C. (1978). An application of a three-factor performance index to measure stockholder gains from merger. *Journal of Financial Economics*, 6(4), 365–383. https://doi.
org/10.1016/0304-405X(78)90010-7

Lee, I., & Shin, Y. J. (2018). Fintech: Ecosystems, business models, investment decisions, and
challenges. *Business Horizons*, 61(1), 35–46. https://doi.org/10.1016/j.bushor.2017.09.003

Loughran, T., & Vijh, A.M. (1997). Do long-term shareholders benefit from corporate acquisitions? *The Journal of Finance*, 52(5), 1765–1790. https://doi.org/10.2307/2329464

Mandelker, G. (1974). Risk and return: The case of merging firms. *Journal of Financial Economics*, 1(4), 303–335. https://doi.org/10.1016/0304-405X(74)90012-9

McKinsey & Company (2016a). Bracing for seven critical changes as fintech matures.

McKinsey & Company (2016b). Fintechs can help incumbents, not just disrupt them.

McKinsey & Company (2018). Six digital growth strategies for banks.

McKinsey & Company (2019). Realising M&A value creation in US banking and fintech:
Nine steps for success.

McKinsey & Company (2021a). Seven technologies shaping the future of Fintech.

McKinsey & Company (2021b). Disrupting the disruptors: Business building for banks.

McKinsey & Company (2022). Three big moves that can decide a financial institution's future in the cloud.

McKinsey & Company (2023a). Why most digital banking transformations fail-and how to
flip the odds.

McKinsey & Company (2023b). Fintechs: A new paradigm of growth.

Merello, P., Barberà, A., & De la Poza, E. (2022). Is the sustainability profile of fintech companies a key driver of their value? *Technological Forecasting and Social Change*, 174,
121290. https://doi.org/10.1016/j.techfore.2021.121290

Mergermarket (n.d.).

Milian, E. Z., Spinola, M. D. M., & Carvalho, M. M. D. (2019). Fintechs: A literature review and research agenda, *Electronic Commerce Research and Applications*, 34, 100833.
https://doi.org/10.1016/j.elerap.2019.100833

Moro Visconti, R. (2020). FinTech valuation. https://dx.doi.org/10.2139/ssrn.4132428

Najaf, K., Chin A., Lean Wan Fook, A., Dhiaf, M., & Asiaei, K. (2023). Fintech and corporate governance: At times of financial crisis. *Journal of Financial Services Marketing*,
24, 605–628. https://doi.org/10.1007/s10660-023-09733-1

OECD (2019). OECD Corporate Governance Factbook 2019. https://doi.org/10.1787/d3aaf1e1-
en

OECD (2023). OECD Corporate Governance Factbook 2023. https://doi.org/10.1787/6d912314-
en

Oliver Wyman (2024). A comprehensive analysis of Bank-Fintech M&A: How bank-fintech synergy can drive M&A success.

Pinelli, M., Cappa, F., Peruffo, E., & Oriani, R. (2022). Acquisitions of non-controlling equity stakes: Agency conflicts and profitability. *Strategic Organization*, 20(5), 147612702092667. https://doi.org/10.1177/1476127020926672

PwC (2016). Blurred lines: How Fintech is shaping Financial Services.

PwC (2020a). Digital payments in Italy: Evolution or revolution?

PwC (2020b). Fintech calls for fuel: To exploit a great, maturing and increasing potential.

PwC (2023). FinTech Observatory 2023: Italian market and main trends.

PwC (n.d.). Bitcoin, cryptocurrency, blockchain... So what does it all mean? https://www.pwc.com/us/en/industries/financial-services/Fintech/bitcoin-blockchain-cryptocurrency.html

PwC (n.d.). Deals insights: How to value a start-up business. https://www.pwc.com/lv/en/news/how-to-value-start-up-business.html

PwC (n.d.). Fintech: From disruption to collaboration. https://www.pwc.nl/en/insights-and-publications/services-and-industries/deals/fintech-from-disruption-to-collaboration.html

Rahaman, M. M., & Al Zaman, A. (2013). Management quality and the cost of debt: Does management matter to lenders? *Journal of Banking and Finance*, 37(3), 854–874. https://doi.org/10.1016/j.jbankfin.2012.10.011

Rau, R., & Vermaelen, T. (1998). Glamour, value and the post-acquisition performance of acquiring firms. *Journal of Financial Economics*, 49, 223–253. https://doi.org/10.1016/S0304-405X(98)00023-3

Reuters (2023). Brazil's QI Tech raises $200 million in General Atlantic-led round.

Rehm, W., Uhlaner, R., & West, A. (2012). Taking a longer-term look at M&A value creation. *McKinsey Quarterly*, 2.

Rosen, R.J. (2006). Merger momentum and investor sentiment: The stock market reaction to merger announcements. *Journal of Business*, 79(2), 987–1017. https://doi.org/10.1086/499146

Sannino, G., Di Carlo, F., & Lucchese, M. (2019). CEO characteristics and sustainability business model in financial technologies firms: Primary evidence from the utilization of innovative platforms. *Management Decision*, 58(8), 1779–1799. https://doi.org/10.1108/MD-10-2019-1360

Schachel, H., Lachmann, M., Endenich, C., & Breucker, O. (2021). The importance of management control systems for start-up funding—empirical evidence from external financiers. *Journal of Accounting & Organizational Change*, 17(5), 660–685. https://doi.org/10.1108/JAOC-07-2020-0089

Sia, S. K., Soh, C., & Weill, P. (2016). How DBS Bank pursued a digital business strategy. *MIS Quarterly Executive*, 15(2). https://aisel.aisnet.org/misqe/vol15/iss2/4

Simons, R. (1995). *Levers of Control: How Managers Use Innovative Control Systems to Drive Strategic Renewal*. Boston: Harvard Business School Press.

Smith, J. E., & Nau, R. F. (1995). Valuing risky projects: Option pricing theory and decision analysis. *Management Science*, 41(5), 749–936. https://doi.org/10.1287/mnsc.41.5.795

Zetzsche, D. A., Buckley, R. P., Arner, D. W., & Barberis, J. N. (2017). From FinTech to TechFin: The regulatory challenges of data-driven finance. http://dx.doi.org/10.2139/ssrn.2959925

Statista (2023a). Fintech: In-depth market analysis.

Statista (2023b). Number of Fintech unicorns worldwide as of April 2023, by country.

Statista (2023c). Largest Fintech companies in the United States in 2023, by value (in billion U.S. dollars).

Statista (2024a). Number of Fintechs worldwide from 2018 to 2024, by region.

Statista (2024b). Value of investment in Fintech worldwide from 2019 to 2023, by region.

Statista (2024c). Global market volume of neobanks 2017-2028.

Tabby (2023). Tabby secures $200M in Series D funding at $1.5B valuation.

Terry, H.P., Schwartz, D., & Sun, T. (2015). The future of finance: The socialization of finance. Goldman Sachs Global Investment Research.

Thomson Reuters (2023). Fintech, Regtech, and the role of compliance in 2023: Addressing deployment & management.

Valverde S. C., & Fernández F. R. (2020). Financial digitalization: Banks, fintech, bigtech, and consumers. *Journal of Financial Management, Markets and Institutions*, 8(1), 2040001. https://doi.org/10.1142/S2282717X20400010

Vention (n.d.). Blockchain in Fintech. https://ventionteam.com/Fintech/blockchain/guide

Visa (2024). Visa completes acquisition of Pismo.

Visconti, R. M. (2020a). The valuation of Fintechs.

Visconti, R. M. (2020b). *The Valuation of Digital Intangibles: Technology, Marketing and Internet*. Palgrave Macmillan.

Visconti, R. M., Cruz Rambaud, S., & López Pascual, J. (2020). Sustainability in FinTechs: An explanation through business model scalability and market valuation. *Sustainability*, 12(24), 10316. https://doi.org/10.3390/su122410316

Visconti, R. M. (2021). Fintech valuation. In R. M. Visconti (Ed.), *The Valuation of Digital Intangibles* (197–221). Palgrave Macmillan.

Wang, Y., Hu, J., & Chen, J. (2023). Does Fintech facilitate cross-border M&As? Evidence from Chinese A-share listed firms. *International Review of Financial Analysis*, 85. https://doi.org/10.1016/j.irfa.2022.102435

Waupsh, J. (2016). *Bankruption: How Community Banking Can Survive Fintech*. Wiley.

Weber, Y., Shenkar, O., & Raveh, A. (1996). National and corporate cultural fit in mergers/acquisitions: An exploratory study. *Management Science*, 42(8), 1215–1227. https://www.jstor.org/stable/2634453

World Bank (2021). Global Fintech enabling regulations database.

World Bank (2022). Global patterns of Fintech activity and enabling factors.

World Economic Forum (2017). How collaboration in the fintech industry can unlock digital growth.

Yathiraju, N., & Dash, B (2023). Big Data and Metaverse Revolutionizing the Futuristic Fintech Industry. *International Journal of Computer Science and Information Technology* 15(1), 1–13. https://doi.org/10.5121/ijcsit.2023.15101

www.ingramcontent.com/pod-product-compliance
Lightning Source LLC
Chambersburg PA
CBHW081811200326
41597CB00023B/4230